CONFRONTING
IRAN

ALSO BY ALI M. ANSARI

Iran, Islam and Democracy: The Politics of Managing Change

Modern Iran Since 1921: The Pahlavis and After

CONFRONTING
IRAN

THE FAILURE OF
AMERICAN FOREIGN POLICY
AND THE NEXT GREAT CRISIS
IN THE MIDDLE EAST

ALI M. ANSARI

BASIC
BOOKS

A Member of the Perseus Books Group
New York

Copyright © 2006 by Ali M. Ansari

Hardcover published in 2006 by Basic Books,
A Member of the Perseus Books Group
Paperback published in 2007 by Basic Books

Books published by Basic Books are available at special discounts for bulk purchases in the United States by corporations, institutions, and other organizations. For more information, please contact the Special Markets Department at the Perseus Books Group, 2300 Chestnut St., Philadelphia, PA 19103, or e-mail special.markets@perseusbooks.com.

Text set in Adobe Garamond

A CIP catalog record for this book is available from the Library of Congress.
Hardcover ISBN-10: 0-465-00350-8
Hardcover ISBN-13: 978-0-465-00350-1
Paperback ISBN-10: 0-465-00351-6
Paperback ISBN-13: 978-0-465-00351-8

10 9 8 7 6 5 4 3 2 1

$16.95 /44/972

In Loving Memory of My Mother

CONTENTS

Persia has alternately advanced and receded in the estimation of British statesmen, occupying now a position of extravagant prominence, anon one of unmerited obscurity. At one time she has been the occasion or the recipient of a lavish and almost wanton prodigality; at another, she has been treated with penurious meanness. Public opinion in this country . . . with regard to Persian politics has been either in white heat, or has subsided into an inert stupor. We have made treaties with Persia, imposing upon ourselves the most solemn offensive and defensive obligations. When the occasion arose for redeeming them, we have shirked responsibility and have subsequently bought our release from the self inflicted tie . . . we have at once pampered and neglected the Persian people. Our Persian policy in each successive stage, whether of interest or apathy, has ever been characterised by the note of exaggeration.

GEORGE NATHANIEL CURZON

Persia and the Persian Question,
1892, vol. II, pp. 605–606

CHRONOLOGY

1901	Concession granted to William Knox D'Arcy for the exploitation of oil
1906–1909	Constitutional Revolution
1908	D'Arcy strikes oil, forms Anglo-Persian Oil Company (APOC); changed in 1935 to Anglo-Iranian Oil Company (AIOC)
1911	Morgan Shuster hired by the Constitutional government to organize and manage state finances
1914–1918	First World War
1919	Attempted imposition of the Anglo-Persian Agreement fails
1921	Coup d'etat overthrows government; rise of Reza Khan
1925	Qajar dynasty deposed by Parliament, which transfers royal titles to Reza Shah Pahlavi
1941	Allies occupy Iran (until 1946)
1946	Soviet Union refuses to withdraw from Iranian Azerbaijan, precipitating the start of the Cold War
1951	Dr. Mohammad Mosaddeq, leader of the National Front, becomes Prime Minister and nationalizes the Anglo-Iranian Oil Company
1953	Mosaddeq overthrown in coup orchestrated by the United States and Great Britain
1963	Mohammad Reza Shah launches his White Revolution
1964	Status of Forces Convention causes consternation among Iranian nationalists; Ayatollah Khomeini condemns it and is forced into exile
1971	Mohammad Reza Shah commemorates 2500 years of the Iranian monarchy
1973	Mohammad Reza Shah announces quadrupling of oil price
1978–1979	Islamic Revolution overthrows Pahlavi Dynasty, establishing the Islamic Republic
1979	Radical students occupy US Embassy (November 4), taking staff hostage for 444 days
1980	Saddam Hussein invades Iran (September)
1981	Hostages released immediately following the inauguration of President Reagan
1982	Iran retakes occupied territory and launches the invasion of Iraq
1986	Iran-Contra scandal comes to public attention
1987	USS Stark hit by Iraqi Exocet missile
1988	USS Vincennes shoots down Iran Air airbus over the Persian Gulf UN cease-fire resolution accepted by Iran, end of Iran-Iraq War
1989	Death of Ayatollah Khomeini

Ayatollah Khamenei becomes Supreme Leader

Ali Akbar Hashemi Rafsanjani becomes President

1991–1992   Attempts to broker deal with United States involving release of
hostages in the Lebanon

1993   President Clinton takes office in the United States

1995   Conoco contract vetoed; Clinton issues executive order banning
any commercial activity between American companies and Iran

1996   Ratification of Iran-Libya Sanctions Act (ILSA) imposing
secondary sanctions on any company investing more than $20
million in any year in the Iranian oil industry

1997   President Khatami elected to office; beginning of Reformist
ascendancy

Khatami delivers speech at the Organization of Islamic
Conference in Tehran, urging dialogue with Western
civilization

1998   Khatami urges that measures be taken to reduce the "wall of
mistrust" between Iran and the United States

Iran mobilizes troops to the Afghan border following the murder
of Iranian diplomats by the Taleban

1999   Student uprising in Tehran and throughout the country

2000   Reformists sweep the Parliamentary elections in a dramatic
landslide victory

Conservative backlash begins in earnest

2001   President Khatami achieves second landslide victory

Attack on the Twin Towers in New York (9/11)

Iran cooperates in war against Taleban in Afghanistan

2002   Iran labeled part of the axis of evil in President George W. Bush's
State of the Union address

Leaks reveal extent of Iran's nuclear program

2003   Iran concedes it has not notified IAEA of all its nuclear facilities

Invasion of Iraq

US reportedly rejects Iran's proposal for a Grand Bargain to settle
disputes

EU3 sign Tehran Agreement; Iran agrees to ratify and implement
Additional Protocol

Bam Earthquake kills 40,000

2004   Seventh Parliamentary elections; hard-line conservatives retake
Parliament in an election condemned in Iran as fraudulent; new
Parliament refuses to ratify Additional Protocol

Paris agreement reached between EU3 and Iran (November)

2005   Iranian offer to break deadlock rejected by EU (May)
            Election of Mahmoud Ahmadinejad completes hard-line takeover
                of the institutions of government
            EU offer to break deadlock rejected as national insult by Iranians
                (Aug.)
            EU notes that talks may restart as long as Iran continues to
                suspend uranium enrichment
2006   Iran announces it is restarting uranium enrichment
            EU announces formal end of diplomatic negotiations
            IAEA Board votes to report Iran to the UN Security Council

IRAN AND
THE IRANIAN QUESTION

If they want peace, nations should avoid the pinpricks which
precede cannon shots.

NAPOLEON BONAPARTE

IN THE EARLY 1990S, an Iranian journalist published a book titled *Iran: The Superpower of the Century?*[1] The book argued that because so many US presidents had fallen foul of their encounter with Iran, it was Iran and not the United States who could rightfully lay claim to being the Superpower of the Century. For all the obtuse theorizing, the book was an exercise in wit as much as wisdom, and the author's Iranian readership, aware of the turbulent nature of their country's history over the past hundred years, delighted in the characteristic impertinence of the proposition. Yet for all the apparent (if unintended) levity, the author was also broaching the serious point of the awkward and difficult nature of Iran-US relations—especially following the establishment of the Islamic Republic—and the inability of a succession of US administrations to understand or cope with the problem confronting them.

It is a sobering fact that every American president since the Islamic Revolution has been unable to deal successfully with the question of Iran. President Carter was the most visible casualty, losing the presidency in the shadow of the hostage crisis. His popular successor, President Reagan, was himself held hostage by the quagmire of the Iran-Contra scandal, as was his heir, President George H. W. Bush, whose political woes were multiplied by allegations of further covert dealings with Iran. The Democrats returned to power in 1993, and President Clinton could be forgiven for concluding that it would be better to be safe than sorry and avoid Iran altogether. Yet Iran refused to be ignored, and by the middle of his first term, Clinton was persuaded to take decisions that would draw him inexorably towards the Iranian question, a question that would come to the fore with the election of President Khatami in Iran in 1997. Contrary to expectations, Clinton found himself increasingly engaged with Iran, only to be disappointed by the end of his presidency with the lack of progress. With the inauguration of President George W. Bush, and the tragedy of 9/11, the policy of neglect has been shelved, although its replacement has yet to be formulated.

Remarkably, a generation after the Islamic Revolution, the United States still does not have a coherent policy towards the Islamic Republic of Iran. This is all the more striking considering Iran's importance in the political stability and economic prosperity of the global community. Despite appearances to the contrary, this importance is not dependent on its alleged nuclear ambitions or the reckless and provocative rhetoric of its new hard-line president, Mahmoud Ahmadinejad, but is a consequence of more fundamental geopolitical and historical realities. Iran possesses the second-largest reserves of oil in the world, larger than those of Iraq and second only to those of Saudi Arabia. Given the growing importance of the Persian Gulf in the world oil market, Iran's position will strengthen with time. More important that oil, however, is Iran's position as the country with the second largest natural gas reserves in the world. Although Iran's oil reserves are being rigorously exploited, her gas reserves remain largely untouched.

But Iran's potential does not stop there. Iran possesses extensive reserves of minerals and metals, including copper, gold, and uranium, as well as the demographics necessary for industrial growth, with a population esti-mated at seventy-five million. To these material advantages must be added a rich and cohesive cultural inheritance whose influence far exceeds the boundaries of the modern Iranian state. As Iranians joke, they are blessed with all the facilities to be the industrial engine of the region, except good governance. Iran's political woes are in part caused by this embarrassment of riches. The stakes for the future are therefore high. The British in the nineteenth century defined the Persian question in terms of imperial de-cline and the management of that decline. The Iranian question facing the United States in the twenty-first century is that of the birth of the modern Iranian state, its reemergence as a regional power, and its success-ful and managed integration into the international community.

Americans familiar with Iran are fully cognizant of her potential as an ally in the region. They recognize the value of an Iran reintegrated into the international system and playing a constructive role in regional af-fairs. A brief glance at a map of the Middle East and Central Asia pro-vides ample evidence of this reality, while the practical benefits of a constructive relationship, shorn of its more extreme ideological senti-ments, are evident to Americans currently operating in Iraq and Afghan-istan. In the past, Iran benefited from the many trade routes that crossed its territory. Now it finds itself sitting astride the two great energy empo-riums of the world: the Persian Gulf and the Caspian Sea. It is in many ways the linchpin state of the region. Even if Iran had no oil and gas of its own, this simple geopolitical reality would make it difficult to ignore.

Yet this is precisely what a succession of US administrations have sought to do. Iran was simply too difficult a political issue to deal with, engagement was unpredictable, and the domestic political cost was too high. For much of the 1990s, the Iranian question was deferred and con-tained, waiting for better times. In the post 9/11 world, this policy of ne-glect has been replaced by the rhetoric of haste. We have leapt from containment to confrontation, from apparent disinterest to an urgent need to do something. Iran is not simply a problem, it's *the* problem. It's not just a member of the Axis of Evil, but the founding member, the chief sponsor of state terrorism, or to use a more recent characterization, the central banker for terrorism. No rhetorical flourish, no level of hyperbole, seems excessive in the ritual condemnation of Iran. We stand on the threshold of a conflict that many accept but few understand. To the modern observer, it must seem remarkable that the United States and Iran were once friends and allies.

Yet herein lies the source of our problem—and its potential solution. The Iranian question at its core is about a relationship and its transformation. It cannot be understood outside the shared experiences that have characterized, shaped, and determined it. Although these experiences have been narrated and understood in different ways, they defined a continuing relationship that persists despite the absence of formal diplomatic or political relations since 1979. To understand the current predicament, therefore, one must understand the evolution of the relationship. The enmity that exists today cannot be understood outside the intimacy that preceded it—friendship precedes betrayal. As with any betrayal, the two parties possess different recollections, suffer from selective amnesia (when the facts are inconvenient), and propose alternate interpretations of their shared experiences.

It is generally accepted that all nations and states are rooted in a series of foundation myths that underpin their historical identity. These foundation myths are often contested and challenged by professional academics, but they remain robust in the popular imagination and are frequently reinforced through mass media and the periodic reissue of patriotic texts. A good example in the United States is the myth of the Founding Fathers and the American Revolution. In this book, it is argued that international relations, as well as individual nations, possess foundation myths, and these myths are no less potent than their domestic counterparts in determining attitudes and policies.

This is all the more so because in our globalized community and our mass media culture, foreign policy is no longer the preserve of the professionals. It is a domestic concern driven by domestic needs, and the popular imagination matters. The practice of foreign policy has become politicized to an extent that would have been inconceivable a generation ago. Previously, professional diplomats mediated the effects of developments overseas. Today, anyone with access to a television has the illusion of direct access, forgetting that the mass media itself determines what we see and how we see it. Whereas the professionals were trained to rationalize developments, the mass media delivers the news raw with the avowed intention of exciting emotion. Consequently, foreign-policy professionals spend almost as much time managing the media and its repercussions as they do managing foreign policy itself. As a result, foundation myths become compounded and extended rather than explained and scrutinized. A consensus develops that few choose to challenge, and opinion repeated often enough becomes fact. Consensus become common sense, and common sense structures our thoughts. It becomes difficult to escape the paradigm.

This book is an attempt to understand, deconstruct, and explain the evolution of this consensus, to show how it has developed and determined Iran's relationship with the United States. The book begins by placing America's encounter with Iran within the context of the decline of the imperial Iranian state in the nineteenth century and the emergence of nationalism. America's encounter began by invitation, with much anticipation for the future. Yet by 1953, the first of several events began the transformation of the relationship from mutual trust to mutual suspicion. This transformation coincided with the dramatic growth in political consciousness in Iran, ensuring that the negative identification of the United States accompanied the birth of modern politics in Iran.

Henceforth, Iran's relationship with the United States was characterized by a powerful myth of victimization, which was soon mirrored by the United States during the hostage crisis in 1979. This televised trauma transformed American perceptions of Iran, removed foreign policy from the control of professionals, and dictated that Iran was a domestic political concern. The political myth of victimization—among the more pernicious of myths in that it empowers through the removal of moral responsibility—was later compounded in the United States by the experience of Iran-Contra. Now Republicans could share in the Democratic tragedy, and Iran affected not only the popular imagination but also the elites of the Washington beltway.

Strikingly, in the aftermath of the Iranian Revolution, relations—be they covert, informal, or social—continued despite the breakdown in diplomatic relations. Moreover, these relationships were dialectical and reciprocal. In the twenty-five years since the Islamic Revolution in Iran, the United States has moved from being the harbinger of realpolitik and realism to a global power that has rediscovered its revolutionary roots and sense of imperial mission. America as an idea has returned with a vengeance. Iran, on the other hand, has sought, with varied success, to moderate its revolutionary image, to reflect on its past, and to portray itself as a status quo power eager to work with international institutions. In 1979, Iran was a revolutionary power with scant respect for international law or the international order and eager to export "freedom" around the globe. In 2001, the United States acquired that mantle and two years later completed that which Iran had sought unsuccessfully to achieve in eight years of bitter conflict. Political divergence was matched by a cultural convergence that both belied and compounded the sense of enmity between the two countries. It was familiarity that bred contempt.

For this contempt to be replaced by mutual trust, familiarity must in turn be replaced by knowledge. This knowledge must be founded on history and culture and an acute awareness of the perceptions of the other. Iranians and Americans must confront their ogres and deconstruct the myths that have shaped their turbulent relationship. The nuclear confrontation is merely a consequence of a far deeper political malaise that neither side has effectively questioned or challenged. Nothing is inevitable about the enmity that exists, founded as it was on the intimate friendship of the past. The walls of mistrust have been built over decades and need to be deconstructed, brick by brick. This is not an easy task, but it is an essential one.

Turkestan, Afghanistan, Transcaspia, Persia—to many these names breathe only a sense of utter remoteness or a memory of strange vicissitudes and of moribund romance. To me I confess, they are the pieces of a chessboard upon which is being played out a game for the dominion of the world.[2]

IMPERIAL HUBRIS

Only the pen of a Macaulay or the brush of a Verestchagin could adequately portray the rapidly shifting scenes attending the downfall of this ancient nation—scenes in which two powerful and presumably enlightened Christian countries played fast and loose with truth, honor, decency and law, one, at least, hesitating not even at the most barbarous cruelties to accomplish its political designs and to put Persia beyond hope of self-regeneration.

W. MORGAN SHUSTER[1]

IRAN-US RELATIONS IN THE SHADOW OF 1911

In 1911, the new Constitutional government of Iran invited American merchant banker Morgan Shuster to lead a team of economists and financial experts in reorganizing and rationalizing the country's anarchic finances. The Iranian government had first sought the assistance of the US government, but the Americans, reluctant to become embroiled in the great power rivalry that characterized Iranian politics, decided it would be more prudent to approve a private delegation. Shuster arrived to find central government in the Western sense nonexistent, its presence replaced by an international menagerie of consultants: "Imagine if you will, a fast-decaying government amid whose tottering ruins a heterogeneous collection of Belgian customs officers, Italian Gendarmes, German artillery sergeants, French savants, doctors, professors, and councillors of state, Austrian military instructors, English bank clerks, Turkish and Armenian courtiers, and last, but not least, a goodly sprinkling of Russian Cossack officers, tutors, and drill instructors all go through their daily task of giving the Imperial Persian Government a strong shove toward bankruptcy, with a sly side push in the direction of their own particular political or personal interests. In this pleasant diversion, the gentlemen and even the ladies of the foreign legations were somewhat peacefully engaged, when several unfortunate Americans landed on Persian soil with the truly extraordinary idea that they were to be employed under the orders of the Persian Government."[2]

Shuster encountered an empire struggling to survive. That it had retained nominal independence in the face of European expansion throughout the nineteenth century was in large part a testament to the political skills of its statesmen. Shuster's invitation was a consequence of a dramatic political upheaval led by a network of the country's progressive elite, including members of the *ulema* and the *bazaar,* with a view to imposing a Constitution on an autocratic and corrupt monarchy and instituting a government of laws. The Constitutional Revolution was a foundational moment in the history of modern Iran, a reference point to which all the country's political activists return. The struggle for the Constitution encapsulated Iran's determination to confront the challenge of Western modernity head-on and revolutionize its system of government. Yet the difficult and sometimes contradictory relationship with the West, which the Constitutional Revolution revealed, was simply the tip of an encounter that over the preceding century had witnessed the decline of the imperial Iranian state in the face of the Western imperial challenge. The experience of this particular Western encounter was traumatic for Iranian statesmen and affected the attitudes of future politicians towards their Western interlocutors.

IMPERIAL DECLINE:
IRAN AND THE WEST IN THE 19TH CENTURY

The narrative of political decline that forms such a large part of the national self-conception is only half the story. The Iran that the Europeans rediscovered in the seventeenth century was an imperial power that they considered opulent, politically stable, and culturally influential. The Safavid Dynasty, which ruled Iran between 1501–1736, was justifiably self-confident, and the European traders and diplomats that ventured to the Safavid court in Isfahan came as supplicants, not as conquerors. For much of the seventeenth century, despite the emerging weaknesses of the dynasty, the Safavid State prospered, and the growing presence of European merchants reflected that prosperity. This prevailing image of the Iranian state survived the political turmoil that followed the overthrow and collapse of the Safavid State in 1722 and the succession of dynasts who contested the Iranian state for the next seventy years.

Indeed, far from disappearing from the map, the Iranian state had a capacity to regenerate itself that struck Western observers. This renewal was most dramatic under Nader Shah (1736–1747), who launched a highly profitable invasion of India in 1739. His military successes and subsequent extension of imperial frontiers led awed Western observers to hail him as the new Alexander. For Iranians, it was proof that even at their lowest ebb, Iran's political fortunes could be transformed by a charismatic and energetic leader. But Nader Shah's conquests were not to last, and the empire again fell victim to rival dynastic claimants until 1796, when Agha Mohammad Khan Qajar had himself proclaimed Shah. Agha Mohammad Shah had spent the better part of his life reconquering the Iranian state from within, ruthlessly eliminating rival claimants and restoring the borders of the Safavid State. He was driven by an imperial vision and made it clear that he had no intention of being crowned king if he could not be counted among the greatest of Iranian monarchs.

It was an ambition no European observer could dismiss lightly, and on his death in 1797, the smooth succession of his nephew, Fath Ali Shah, confirmed that the Iranian empire was back on a stable footing. Indeed, as European ambassadors flocked to Iran during the Napoleonic Wars, they came as suitors seeking a reliable ally. Unfortunately, the nephew proved no match for the uncle. First Russia, then France and Britain, soon discovered that the military might of the Iranian state was no longer a match for modern European armies. The opening battle of the first Russo-Iranian war (1804–1813) was testament to this brutal reality. Henceforth, Iran would seek assistance from competing European powers, but the relationship was no longer one of equals. The series of treaties negotiated by Iran between 1807 and 1828, and the European diplomacy that accompanied them, were indicative of this change in relations and established a pattern of behavior, along with a distrust of Western treaties, that has haunted Iranian politicians to this day.

Iran had initially turned to Britain for military assistance, and there was certainly interest in Britain given the growth of British power in India. But these initial enquiries proved unprofitable because, by 1804, Britain and Russia had become allies in the wider European struggle against Napoleon. Consequently, the Shah turned a sympathetic ear to supplications from Napoleonic France. The Treaty of Finkenstein, signed in 1807, was a straightforward affair that clearly outlined each side's responsibilities. France agreed to train and supply the Iran's armed forces in her war against Russia (recognizing her sovereign rights over Georgia), while Iran agreed to declare war against Great Britain and offer safe passage for French troops to access India. General Gardane was dispatched to Iran to oversee the implementation of the treaty.

Much to the relief of the British, Napoleon soon defeated the Russians at Friedland, concluding his war with the Treaty of Tilsit. Finkenstein was forgotten and abandoned. Britain moved quickly to fill the vacuum left by France, negotiating the treaties of 1809 and 1812, amended to 1814. This collection of successive treaties, reflecting the changing dynamics of the political situation, established the perception of Anglo-Iranian relations for the better part of a century and a half.

In stark contrast to the Treaty of Finkenstein, these treaties were detailed, ambiguous, and replete with caveats, exposing a pedantic legal mind with which the Iranians were not familiar. Such treaties were better suited to the diplomatic salons of Europe than the court of the King of Kings, whose diplomatic apparatus was rudimentary. Essentially, the

British agreed to train and supply the Iranian Army and to support Iran against any European incursion on its territory. This support was to be in the form of an army from British India or an annual subsidy of 200,000 tomans (approximately $260,000). From the British perspective, it was clear that help would be provided only as long as Iran was not the aggressor. In return, Iran was to annul its treaty with France and promise not to interfere in India. A more revealing detail, however, was the arrangement regarding Afghanistan. In a clause that has astounded subsequent Iranian nationalists, the Shah agreed to attack Afghanistan if the latter invaded British India, while Britain simply agreed not to interfere should the Afghans attack Iran.[3] These agreements were to be complicated by the clarifications of 1814, which were basically a British attempt to further limit the conditions under which they would be obliged to assist Iran.

This late addition of further small print was a reaction to the Iranian defeat in the first Russo-Persian war and the Treaty of Golestan, signed in 1813 with Russia, which effectively recognized the cession of Iran's Caucausian territories to Russia. The treaty reflected victor's justice, and Iran regarded it as deeply humiliating in tone and language. Among its clauses was a Russian guarantee of the Qajar dynastic succession, with a suggestion that intervention would be possible if necessary to support it. This clause, which may have been regarded at the time as beneficial to the Qajar Dynasty in that it promoted stability, was disastrous for the country as a whole because it depended on the support of outsiders. Not to be outdone, the British also inserted a similar clause in their 1814 clarification, thereby establishing the legal framework for foreign intervention in the domestic politics of the country. It was a lesson that would not be lost on a generation of nationalists more than a century later.

Nonetheless, as humiliating as Golestan was to be, it was to pale by comparison with the subsequent Treaty of Turkmenchai in 1828. Both Russia and Iran had viewed the Treaty of Golestan as temporary: Russian imperialism was determined to seize more territories, while the Qajar State could not contemplate the permanent loss of the Caucasus. That said, more sober minds in Iran realized that they were not prepared to take on an army that had helped defeat Napoleon, and frustration grew at Britain's lack of interest in fulfilling what Iranians considered to be her treaty obligations: to support and train the Iranian military. Iran had been attacked, so Britain was obliged to assist. Britain, however, argued that a peace treaty had been signed; consequently, with no war to fight, there was no need to provide assistance.

Meanwhile, the Russians continued to be provocative and contemptuous of Qajar court etiquette. The arrival of one Russian embassy caused considerable agitation in Tehran, and radical *ulema* urged the declaration of a *jihad* against Russia. An unprepared Iran went to war against Russia in 1826, and further excused any need for the British to come to her assistance because she was effectively the belligerent. The unsurprising defeat was institutionalized in the Treaty of Turkmenchai of 1828. Any remaining doubts about the loss of Iran's great power status in 1813 were now devastatingly confirmed. In addition to the loss of further territories in the Caucasus, Iran was faced with a 20-million-ruble indemnity, a huge sum for the time, the imposition of commercial treaties that signified the start of the system of capitulations, a reiteration of the terms of Golestan with respect to the succession, and an agreement, loosely interpreted by the Russians, that all prisoners of war, whenever taken, would be repatriated. This included people who had settled and married in Iran and had no wish to return. The new Russian ambassador, Griboedov, in his zeal and barely disguised conceit to gather as many prisoners of war as he could find, inflamed the rage of the people of Tehran, who (not for the last time) assaulted the embassy, slaughtering all occupants but one. Tehran quickly sent an embassy to St. Petersburg to apologize but found the new Tsar, Nicholas, more ambivalent than expected, blaming the entire fiasco on the arrogance of his ambassador. Nonetheless, this was not a propitious start to Iran's integration into the European diplomatic and legal system.

These formative experiences were crucial in shaping Iranian attitudes to the West. It was increasingly apparent that Iran was being treated as an appendage of a wider diplomatic and political system. The Treaty of Finkenstein was not a bad treaty; it was clearly written and reciprocal in its construction. However, despite the best intentions, changing priorities in Europe witnessed the treaty's sudden and abrupt lapse. From the

Iranian perspective, this was an exercise in bad faith. Napoleon's war with Russia might be over, but Iran's was not. Consequently, they turned to the British. But the British, anxious to limit their liabilities, introduced the Iranians to the realities of Western legal negotiation, with its caveats and small print. The failure of the British to provide any assistance until after the signing of Turkmenchai—when they provided financial assistance with the indemnity—convinced many Iranian politicians that the British were duplicitous at best. The Russians, however, were the bullies. The Russian treaties were not reciprocal; they were signifiers of defeat and a reminder that although the Shah might be the Shadow of God upon Earth, his world was shrinking. All that remained of Iran's empire were the pretensions, and as the century wore on, these appeared to grow in direct proportion to the reality of political decline.[4]

For the better part of the next century, Iranian politicians and statesmen sought to reverse this decline. The most revered was Prime Minister Amir Kabir, who between 1848–1851 sought to restore order to the kingdom and majesty to the monarchy. Like many before him, he fell foul of court intrigues and the monarch's ineptitude. Amir Kabir was forced to take his own life, much to the discomfort of the European legations who had connived to have him removed. The brevity of his tenure meant that his achievements in a practical sense were slight. But the promise he held for the future salvation of the country meant that he soon became the subject of national lamentation. He is one of the few statesmen from this period to have had films made of him by both the Pahlavi and the Islamic Republic, although the fact that he was effectively murdered by an ungrateful monarch has made him more popular among the republicans. Along with the later Dr. Mohammad Mosaddeq, Amir Kabir inhabits a pantheon of tragic hero statesmen whose continued popularity with the political consciousness reflects less the reality of their achievements, great as they may appear in comparison with their successors, and more the hopes and aspirations of the people.

After Amir Kabir's demise, the prospects of reform looked bleak, in large part because the ruling monarch, Nasir Al Din Shah, proved woefully inadequate to the task. A brief attempt to secure control over Herat (in modern-day Afghanistan) resulted in another humiliating defeat, this time at the hands of the British, and the permanent loss of territory. In desperation, some argued that reform could be achieved only with the assistance of foreigners, whose involvement could be ensured through concessions offered by the Iranian government. Concessions amounted to the increasingly extravagant privatization of the country's assets, by which a foreign state or individual would pay for the rights to exploit a natural resource or industry. They would then return a certain percentage of their profits back to the state, although these payments were small in relation to the profits. While Russia was busy expanding its imperial holdings in Central Asia, Britain was considered the most likely and useful partner for the award of concessions, although even she was to be surprised by the scale of the offer.

In 1872, Baron Julius de Reuter, the British entrepreneur, secured one of the most extensive concessions ever awarded. According to Curzon, the concession "was found to contain the most complete and extraordinary surrender of the entire industrial resources of a kingdom into foreign hands that has probably ever been dreamed of, much less accomplished in history."[5] All this was achieved for the princely sum of £40,000 (about $70,000), which not only caused a bombshell in Europe but incited agitation among the political elite in Iran.

Like Turkmenchai, the Reuter's concession is another signpost on the road to decline and impotence, and like the treaty before it, it is regularly recited by modern nationalists as indicative of European aggrandizement. But mostly European pressure ensured that it was cancelled, much to Reuter's irritation as he struggled to secure compensation. He was unlikely to find allies among the British establishment, where even the Foreign Office was discomforted that a private citizen with a "foreign name" could acquire so much control over Iran's natural resources. In 1889, Reuter was compensated by no less significant a concession, this one for the foundation of the British Imperial Bank of Persia, with monopoly rights over bank note issue. This concession and a later concession in 1901 to William Knox-D'Arcy for the exploitation of oil formed the basis of British economic (and hence political) influence in Iran until the 1950s. The later Reuter concession was not without its problems, although in this case the pressure was to come from within. A potent mixture of nationalism and Islamic revivalism was energizing the political mood, and combined with the downturn in the economy and the immediate loss of income entailed in the granting of monopoly concession to foreigners, the atmosphere was proving increasing ripe for revolt.[6]

During this period, the association of a reactionary monarchy with exploitative foreign powers began to take shape in the popular mind. The Tobacco Revolt of 1892, a nationwide boycott that resulted in the cancellation of another concession, was soon followed in 1896 by the assassination of the Shah himself. Revolt finally transformed into revolution in 1905. Faced with the unified protests of the elite, principally in Tehran and Tabriz, a dying Shah was forced to concede the establishment of a Constitution limiting the monarch's powers (inasmuch as they existed in reality) and the founding of a National Consultative Assembly, with powers to hold the government accountable and to enact legislation. This was a vanguard movement—organized and led by the elite, and radical and progressive for its day—but with limited social effect outside major cities. People were disgruntled, but there was no widespread understanding of the notion of a Parliament (Majlis) that could enact laws. On the contrary, such a notion was considered blasphemous by some of the more traditionally minded members of the elite. But these critics of Constitutional government had been silenced by 1909, and further radicalized by experience, they urgently moved to reform the state in their own image. It was into this brave new world that Shuster had been invited.

AMERICANS IN IRAN: THE PRELUDE

The United States had enjoyed a formal commercial presence in Iran since 1856 with the signing of a treaty, but had not pursued any political involvement, in large part because Iran remained beyond America's immediate political field of vision. Moreover, the United States had no desire to become embroiled in the imperial politics of the Old World. The treaty was straightforward, reciprocal, and remarkably balanced, establishing diplomatic missions and noting that "All suits and disputes arising in Persia between Persian subjects and citizens of the United States shall be carried before the Persian tribunal to which such matters are usually referred at the place where a Consul or agent of the United States may reside, and shall be discussed and decided according to Equity, in the presence of an employee of the Consul or agent of the United States." Similar rights were afforded to Iranian merchants in the United States, while criminal cases were likewise to be tried by courts in each country in a manner compatible with that of most favored nation. Indeed, the only imbalance in the treaty lay in the preamble, where the President of the United States found himself in treaty with "his Majesty as exalted as the Planet Saturn . . . whose splendour and magnificence are equal to that of the Skies . . . the Monarch whose armies are as numerous as the Stars," a continuing litany of titles that did little to disguise the growing impotence of the Iranian crown. The Iranian Parliament, impressed by American achievements and convinced of her 'anti-imperial posture (the Americans had after all thrown out the British), decided that the United States offered the least politically sensitive and most competent option for the procurement of administrative and financial expertise.

As mentioned, the American government remained disinclined to send a formal delegation but was happy to sanction a private mission. Therefore, Shuster and his team arrived not as employees of the US government but as employees of the new Constitutional government. Shuster found a government that was effectively bankrupt and whose finances, in the conventional sense, were nonexistent. "I might say that the Persian finances were tangled—very tangled—had there been any to tangle. There were no Persian finances in any ordinary sense of the word."[7] The central treasury, insofar as it existed, was being plundered by a rotation of ministers whose chief functions were to oil the wheels of patronage and replenish the coffers through taxation, customs dues, and the occasional concession. There was no civil service. Appointments were made not through qualification and merit but through access to an extensive personal network of pecuniary corruption that was going to be difficult to reform. Shuster's well-intentioned plans became the subject of general mirth: "the jest of the diplomatic corps at Teheran [was] that the Americans would not remain in Persia three months; the wife of one distinguished foreign service minister said that a month would see them back on the road to Enzeli; and the idea that any serious attempt would be made to straighten out Persian financial affairs only called forth laughter."[8]

For all the laughter, Shuster soon discover that the network of vested interests also included the Europeans, in particular the rival Russian and British Empires, who were keen for the status quo to remain. Britain had played an important and constructive role in the success of the Constitutional Movement—Edward Browne had been an enthusiastic lobbyist in Britain—sympathetic as she was to the idea of Constitutional government. In 1907, however, the British and Russian government had decided to bury their differences and delineate mutually exclusive spheres of influence, into which the other would not interfere. As Shuster notes, Iran was neither consulted nor informed and, when finally alerted to the existence of the convention, were indignant at "having their country 'partitioned' overnight."[9] Shuster could barely disguise his contempt of what he considered to be further imperial aggrandizement.

In practical terms, the convention effectively gave Russia a free hand in the north of the country, assured that the British would not interfere. And whereas the British had been sympathetic to the Constitutional Revolution, Russia was decidedly against such a development. The 1905 Russian Revolution had been crushed (many Armenians had fled southward to Iran), and with the assassination of Prime Minister Stolypin, Tsar Nicholas II determined that the best course of action was a rapid return to strictly authoritarian rule. Shuster's arrival was not auspicious, and while the British were being uncooperative (ostensibly not to offend the Russians), the Russians were aggressively antithetical. Shuster's determination to create a treasury civil service along with a gendarmerie (police) to collect taxation revenue was viewed as deeply problematic because it posed an overt challenge to Russian commercial interests, and the Russians demanded Shuster's dismissal. The Majlis (Parliament) refused. Russian troops began to move in increasing numbers into select cities in northern Iran, in particular Tabriz, where they began a systematic and violent suppression of all 'revolutionary' activity. In Shuster's words:

"On New Year's day, which was the 10th of Muharram, a day of great mourning held sacred in the Persian religious calendar, the Russian Military Governor, who had hoisted Russian flags over government buildings at Tabriz, hung the Sikutu'l Islam, who was the chief priest of Tabriz, two other priests and five others, among them several high officials of the Provincial government. As one British journalist put it, the effect of this outrage on the Persians was that which would be produced on the English people by the hanging of the Archbishop of Canterbury on Good Friday. From this time on the Russians at Tabriz continued to hang or shoot any Persian whom they chose to consider guilty of the crime of being a 'Constitutionalist.' When the fighting there was first reported, a prominent official of the Foreign Office at St Petersburg, in an interview to the press, made the statement that Russia would take vengeance into her own hands until the 'revolutionary dregs' had been exterminated."[10]

Fearful of further Russian brutality and the possible partition of the country, the government closed the Parliament and Shuster was dismissed. His period of service had lasted less than a year. Shuster himself could hardly contain his bitterness over the injustice inflicted upon Iran: "The Persians were anxious to adopt wholesale the political, ethical and business codes of the most modern and progressive nations . . . The East has awakened. Persia unfortunately awoke too late. Her futile struggles towards the light were quickly suppressed by a power whose own strength lies in the path of darkness."

1953

Persian political affairs, fraught as they are with misfortune and misery for millions of innocent people, are conducted very much as a well staged drama—I have heard some critics say, as an opera bouffe. The reader will find the same old characters weaving in and out of the story, at one time wearing the make up of a Royalist minister, at another the garb of a popular patriot.

W. MORGAN SHUSTER

S HUSTER DEPARTED with considerable regret but also with the affection of the Iranians, who valued his impartial and objective efforts on their behalf. They had emerged from a century of interaction with the European powers distrustful of what the West had to offer and what it had come to symbolize. Diplomats, lawyers, commercial agents—the very tools of Western modernity itself—were viewed through the harsh experience of defeat and subjugation. The sense of humiliation was made all the worse because Iran considered herself an imperial power with a historical lineage worthy of the best of her protagonists. At the same time, this humiliation was being channeled into constructive means of regeneration by new ideas of Islamic modernism and nationalism. Some considered that the best route would be to work with the Russians, admiring their brute might. Others preferred the political sophistication of the British. But the Constitutional government decided to secure the services of a neutral third party, the United States—a country that was unblemished by the foreign manipulations of the past one hundred years and that could be trusted to be sympathetic to the Iranian cause as a consequence of her own historical experiences. This generally positive impression ensured that after the end of the Great War and the re-constitution of government, the call went again for US assistance in the reorganization of the country's finances. The preference was for Shuster to return, but his unavailability resulted in the dispatch of another economic adviser, once again in a private capacity, Arthur Chester Millspaugh.

Millspaugh arrived to a different Iran than that which had confronted his predecessor. The circus of European consultants and employees was diminished due to problems at home and the effect of the Great War in Europe. Another obvious difference was the absence of Russia—the new Soviet Union was now a friend to all oppressed peoples. Pockets of socialism were emerging in northern parts of Iran. Britain remained the dominant power, albeit shaken by her own experiences and losses in the recent war and less assured about her capacity to contain and manage her empire. Nevertheless, on paper, British dominance in the Middle East appeared stronger than ever.

Iran had suffered not only from the breakdown of the central government after 1912 but also because her territory had been used as a battleground by competing armies. By some estimates, economic dislocation and famine had resulted in the loss of twenty-five percent of the population. But Iran emerged from the war less battered than one might have imagined—a reflection perhaps that just because central government had collapsed, government as a whole had not disappeared. Iranian society enjoyed a resilience and an autonomous existence beyond the reach of any central authority. Indeed, ignoring the political realities of the day, the Iranian government managed to send an embassy to the Paris Peace Conference at Versailles, with a view toward seeking redress for various grievances and recognition of Iran's apparent international status. European delegates, particularly the British, were both taken by and irritated by the Iranian presence, which seemed to announce that Iran remained a legally independent sovereign state with every right to attend international diplomatic conferences, a testament to Iranian skill in the exercise of soft power. Suffice to say, the Iranian delegation was politely ignored.

Britain had other plans to consolidate her imperial gains and protect British India. Economic difficulties necessitated a more efficient management of her empire, and the British had concluded that a stable and sympathetic Iran would be the best solution to the problem of Russian (or Soviet) expansion southward. In other words, an Iran that could defend herself against the Soviets but be no threat to British interests would be the best option, minimizing the need for direct intervention and hence expenditure. One might have thought that Iran would have welcomed the prospect of British support to strengthen the country against Russian encroachments, given their experience of Russian imperialism and the lingering bitterness over the loss of the Caucasian territories. But this view did not factor in immediate presence of the British and the absence of the Russians. British intervention had resulted in the loss of Herat in 1857 and, more importantly, her economic presence in the form of the Anglo-Persian oil company and the British Imperial Bank was immediate and pervasive.

The new Soviet Union, on the other hand, was anxious to distance itself from the imperialistic outrages of the Tsarist government. In portraying itself as a champion of the poor and a defender of national liberation movements, the Soviets found a ready audience in Iran, among not only the embryonic Communist movements but also the increasingly nationalistic intelligentsia. The British Foreign Secretary, Lord Curzon, seemed curiously oblivious to the intensity of this feeling when he composed the Anglo-Persian Agreement in 1919, with a view to providing the Iranian government with the framework and support it needed to initiate a period of needed reform. Curzon was familiar with Iran, having written a detailed two-volume tome on his impression of the country in 1892 and having served as Viceroy of India, where dealings with Iran were routine. His familiarity with the country and his affection for the people persuaded him to put much personal effort into an agreement that would ultimately be viewed with contempt by Iranian nationalists. Curzon was a patrician politician to the core, and his paternalistic care for his Iranian ward was regarded as inappropriate.

Recent research indicates that the details of the agreement prompted little immediate outrage, but later Iranian nationalists denounced it as yet another attempt by the British to reduce Iran to the status of a protectorate.[1] Curzon appears to have taken the failure personally. The backup plan among British officials on the ground was to support any movement that might achieve stability on its own merits. As such, tacit British approval was provided to the coup launched by the journalist Seyyid Zia Tabatabai and his strongman, the commander of the Cossack brigade, Reza Khan (Russian officers having long departed).

It was this coup d'etat government that sought US assistance in 1922, and Arthur Millspaugh soon recognized the need to cooperate with the real power in the new regime, Reza Khan, who rapidly moved from Minister of War to Prime Minister, and finally, by parliamentary decree in 1926, to Shah. Much like the Constitutional government before it, the new Iranian government was highly nationalistic and self-confident, except now it could provide its own military muscle. In reorganizing finances, Millspaugh facilitated the expansion of the new Iranian army. Ultimately, like all viziers, the Shah tired of his overmighty subject and had him dismissed. The reason for his abrupt dismissal in 1927 was revealing, "Dr. Millspaugh had 99 good qualities and but one undesirable: that was his disregard for the dignity of government. This was a very grave thing. . . . The government preferred to be in difficulties and be independent, rather than be comfortable and be deprived of that independence."[2]

Millspaugh was to return a second time in 1942, once again in dramatically different circumstances. Reza Shah had abdicated, and the Allies were occupying Iran in the interests of supplying the Soviet Union with much needed logistics in the war against Nazi Germany. The independence of Iran was temporarily suspended as the armies of the Soviet Union, Great Britain, and the United States settled into occupation. Despite some resistance, the Imperial Iranian Armed Forces had collapsed with frustrating ease, and the entire operation had taken barely a week. Yet again the Iranians were confronted with the reality of occupation, and despite the protestations of the Allies that their actions reflected wartime necessity and were not intended to impinge upon Iranian sovereignty, the resources of the country were to be turned over to the necessities of the war effort irrespective of its effect on the local economy and population.

The ambivalence, and in some cases joy, with which many Iranians regarded the abdication of Reza Shah was soon overtaken by irritation with the Allies, more so because they seemed equally interested in resuscitating old rivalries as in fighting the Nazis. Russian imperialism had given way to the Soviet propagation of Communist ideology (although national liberation movements would suffice in the interim), and the Red Army wasted little time in educating the public.[3] More significant, however, was the distribution of transistor radios throughout their zone of occupation, so that the workers could better tune into Radio Moscow. Technology had ensured that illiteracy was no longer a bar to a thorough political education.[4]

The effect of such propaganda was not only to agitate against the social order in Iran but also to draw the necessary links with global capitalism. Although this propaganda would have originally settled on the British— not a difficult target—the focus of attention was shifting towards the United States. As a natural consequence of the change in the balance of power, the United States was inheriting the mantle of Britain, but in a more intensely ideological manner. The stereotypes, prejudices, and caricatures of historical experience and resentment were being compounded and reinforced by an ideological explanation. It was in effect a double dosage of political myth. The British and Americans retaliated with propaganda of their own, but whereas the atheism in communism might have made Iranian Muslims wary, the materialism of the United States was no less disturbing to not only devout Muslims, but also the vast majority of the poor and of course Iran's emerging Socialists and Communists (themselves a consequence of encroaching modernity). America's materialism was having unfortunate effects on Iranian society in less obvious ways as well. The introduction of American films, in particular those dealing with organized crime, were having an unhelpful impact:

"In 1943 the Minister of the Interior, a jurist and former prosecuting attorney, conducted an investigation which demonstrated that many cases of juvenile crime on record in Iran, and many of delinquency, had been inspired by American gangster films. It is perfectly true that these films end on a moral note, but this is a thin apology for the techniques taught and activities suggested to impressionable minds. Under the guise of 'crime doesn't pay,' audiences and regions in Iran for the first time were being introduced to the existence of an organized underworld."[5]

Nonetheless, as far as the political elite of the country were concerned, the Americans were not problematic; what ire that existed was reserved for the British and, to a slightly lesser extent, the Soviets. This antipathy towards the British was not dispelled by the Americans, whose view of British (and Russian) imperialism remained unsympathetic. As one British diplomat complained, "it is disturbing that we should now be even more unpopular than the Russians . . . After all, we are doing far more for the Persian people on [the] food question than anyone else including their own rulers. . . . We shall be grateful for any suggestions for other ways and means of showing the Persians (and incidentally the Americans) that we really wish to help them."[6]

When the war ended, both the American and British troops withdrew from their respective zones as agreed, whereas the Soviets remained behind in Azerbaijan in support of the local nationalists. For Iranians, the spectre of Turkmenchai was revived. The ensuing Azerbaijani crisis is generally regarded as the start of the Cold War because Stalin was eventually convinced to withdraw his troops following a stern ultimatum from President Truman. The Iranian recollection of events is somewhat different, reinforced by the fact that the only evidence of an ultimatum came years after the event in the full glare of the Cold War. America did not approve of the Soviet's support of a separatist movement that probably would have been encouraged to "reunite" with its compatriots in Soviet Azerbaijan. But it is unlikely that the Americans would have wanted to launch themselves into a conflict with the Soviet Union so soon after the end of hostilities.[7]

That this testing moment never emerged was largely due to the achievements of Iranian politicians, inured to the benefits of aggressive diplomacy. Prime Minister Ahmad Qavam's elastic politics had been viewed as a test case of how to handle overbearing foreign powers. For his countrymen and foreigners alike, he was the epitome of Persian cunning. Qavam was a traditional patrician politician with acknowledged sympathies towards Russia, inasmuch as he realized that Iran's vast northern neighbor had to be engaged. Recognizing Stalin's desire for an oil concession in the north to match that of the English in the south, Qavam traveled to Moscow to negotiate the withdrawal of the Red Army with the promise of an oil concession as compensation.

Securing the Red Army's withdrawal, Iranian troops quickly reoccupied Azerbaijan, a triumph the young Mohammad Reza Shah appropriated for himself. Qavam prepared to submit the concession to a newly elected Parliament for ratification, aware that ratification was an effective impossibility, given the intensely nationalist views of the deputies. At the same time, he could turn to Stalin and protest his innocence against the duplicity of the deputies who had failed to ratify the agreement. It was a diplomatic triumph for Qavam: he had outwitted Stalin, who had no stomach for another confrontation. However, he was soon to lose the premiership because even his own compatriots found him too clever for his own good.[8]

The outmaneuvering of the Soviets was an empowering moment, and the deputies quickly turned their attention to a more emotive concession in the south: that of the Anglo-Iranian Oil Company (AIOC). The AIOC and the British Imperial Bank of Persia were the twin pillars on which British influence in Iran had been constructed in the twentieth century. They were essentially private companies, although Churchill's insistence that the British government buy a golden (veto) share in the strategic asset that was Anglo-Persian oil ensured that Iranians understood AIOC to be an extension of the British government. The direct connection envisaged by many Iranians did not exist; Foreign Office officials were often just as exasperated with the activities and behavior of their business-minded compatriots as were the Iranians. This was especially true of the British Imperial Bank of Persia, and its demise was partly assisted by the American decision in 1944 to transfer all their military accounts to the new National Bank of Iran (*Bank Melli*) because of the better service they felt they received. The governor of the National Bank, Abolhasan Ebtehaj (a former employee of the Imperial Bank), curtailed es of the Imperial Bank to such an extent that by 1949, when its concession ran out, the only business it retained was that of the AIOC.

Many professional Iranians considered the AIOC to be an affront to national dignity because of the colonial manner in which it operated in Abadan—including the importation of Indian labor—and because of its increasingly blatant exploitation of Iranian resources. It was widely known, for example, that AIOC paid more in taxes to the British Exchequer than it did in royalties to the Iranian government, and while supplementary agreements had been negotiated to ameliorate this imbalance, the sense of grievance ran deep. The increasingly profound sense of injustice was a result of renewed Iranian self-confidence and political energy, which was partly derived from historical experience and more immediately from the effect of the Allied occupation. In short, Iranian society was changing and becoming more politically articulate, but few in Britain seemed to notice or care. After all, AIOC was there by international treaty.

Into this labyrinthine political situation wandered the Americans. Despite the shift in attitude among some of the more radicalized political literate, the general perception of the United States remained positive. In 1950, President Truman had launched a Point 4 technical assistance program for Iran. Although Iranians complained that the level of aid was too low, Iran was amongst the highest beneficiaries in comparative terms. For example, in 1952, the United States allocated $23,450,000 in the form of technical (developmental) assistance to Iran, which compared favorably with sums allocated to other countries in the region according to the country director, William Warne.

In the same vein as Shuster and Millspaugh before them, Warne and his team continued to address the inadequacies in the Iranian economic administration, oblivious to the political storm brewing around them. In this case perhaps, the emphasis was more on technical matters, and the frame of reference had changed as the United States increasingly took on the role previously occupied by Britain. However, as far as the politics of Iran were concerned, the United States was a secondary target and, in popular terms, viewed with some affection. As Warne notes, "As we approached the first village a large crowd of men and boys came up the mountain to meet us. Village elders and Kadkhodas were drawn up at the end of the line . . . A heifer was sacrificed. The villagers welcomed and cheered us. I was pleased to hear one great shout, 'Zendeh-bad Dowlat Americaei'—'Long live the government of the United States.' Point 4 was known even here."[9]

For Warne, Iran was not on the verge of a revolution. Rather, its people were anxious for a better life, and this was what Point 4 was all about. Warne's assessment of the demands of the rural peasantry, as opposed to their politically active cousins in the cities, was probably correct. Although this impression of a simple and grateful peasantry—a picture that had also affected the Shah—remained a partial, if reassuring, view. In the cities, agitation was growing, and if these people remained a fraction of the overall population of the country, they were a political vital part. Warne was clearly aware of the anti-Americanism emanating from the left-wing Iranian press, but he seemed to consider it more a nuisance than a threat: "The advocates of 'Yankee Go Home' were a puny minority."[10] Yet within three years of the start of Point 4, America's political fortunes in Iran would be transformed.

OIL NATIONALIZATION, THE COUP, AND
ITS CONSEQUENCES

For most politically active Iranians, the history of Iran-US relations began in 1953 with the coup orchestrated by the CIA for the overthrow of the democratically elected Prime Minister, Dr. Mohammad Mosaddeq. The coup revealed America's influence and malevolent ambitions in Iran. The immense sense of betrayal that was felt—and cultivated for later generations—cannot be understood outside the context of a relationship that had been thought to be positive and benign. Nor can it be fully comprehended outside the parameters of Iran's relations in the nineteenth century with the Europeans, particularly Great Britain, whose mantle had been inherited by the United States. The effect of American influence in Iran after 1953 was likewise amplified by developments in political life, including the growth in education and technology and the realities of the

Cold War, which provided the US-Soviet contest with a totality and intensity that had been missing from the "Great Game" that characterized Anglo-Russian rivalry. American actions in Iran may pale into insignificance when compared to the Russian atrocities in Tabriz recounted with horror by Shuster, but what mattered was the changing environment. In 1892, the existence of the telegraph had enabled the opponents to stage an effective statewide boycott of the tobacco concession with an ease that would have been inconceivable twenty years earlier. Now radio and television ensured a wide dissemination of even the most trivial of incidents, and the audience was growing and receptive.

Warne's dismissive attitude of the growing anti-Americanism in the early 1950s was justified, insofar as the United States had little at stake in Iran. He could afford to be complacent because domestic politics in Iran were managed by the British, whose experience justified a certain proprietary attitude towards the country. British complacence, however, carried significant risks, especially considering that the target of nationalist anger, the Anglo-Iranian Oil Company, was Britain's largest overseas asset. Furthermore, having just emerged from an exhaustive and financially ruinous war, Britain could not afford to lose this asset and the access it provided to cheap oil.

Ironically, Britain's postwar Labour government could finance its impressive array of welfare programs only by maintaining the status quo regarding its overseas and colonial assets. Iranian Socialists had been impressed by the range of policies and the broad nationalization of industries that were being promoted in Britain. Furthermore, those who had hitherto encountered Britain only through the British Embassy in Tehran were favorably impressed and surprised upon visiting Britain. Khalil Maliki, the noted ideologue of the Left, was struck by the attitude of ordinary Britons when he visited Britain in 1946:

"I have come to know their qualities and their love of freedom and democracy in a way I could never before. It is my belief that if British policy in Persia were interpreted according to the will of the people of this country and if the democratic and human tendencies of the average Briton were to be the active agents of British policy in Persia then many of the present difficulties of my dear country would be resolved."[11]

It seems reasonable that some Iranians felt that the agitation against the old order in Iran was a natural development that would receive a fair hearing in Britain. But Britain, in the form of the Company and to a lesser extent the Foreign Office, was not listening.[12] Negotiations over the oil concession were not going well and calls for nationalization of the industry were growing. But the Prime Minister, General Razmara, was determined to reach a settlement, fearing that confrontation would be counterproductive. Razmara's moderation, caught between the demands of the Company and the nationalists in Parliament, delivered nothing but his own assassination. What was more striking, however, was the reaction to his death, which was at best dismissive and at worst triumphalist.

Even this stark warning was dismissed by the British, who were contemptuous of Iranian nationalism even though the involvement of the *ulema*, particularly Ayatollah Kashani, was giving the struggle a sacred quality that intensified emotions. This renewed synthesis between Shia Islam and Iranian identity and the exploitation of religious nationalism was highly effective in mobilizing the urban masses. It also ensured a radicalization of opinion into non-negotiable absolutes and proved fertile ground for the crystallization of myths.

Into this ground entered the oratorically brilliant Dr. Mohammad Mosaddeq. Mosaddeq was a patrician politician of the old school whose formative years were defined by the Constitutional Revolution and the rise of Reza Shah. A Swiss trained lawyer, Mosaddeq believed in the Constitution and the principle that the monarch must reign and not rule. He had publicly argued that Reza Khan should not be elevated to the throne—because then the country would be deprived of his executive abilities. Not having impressed the new king with his argument, Mosaddeq "retired" from public life, to reemerge only following Reza Shah's abdication and the Allied occupation. He gradually moved up the political ladder with a careful balance of theatrics and rhetoric calculated to reduce the most cynical of his countrymen to tears. Those beyond his reach remained skeptical, and early British reports labeled him a "demagogue and a windbag," a characterization that the British were unwilling to reevaluate.[13] As one historian noted, "Mosaddeq . . . was regularly described by the British Ambassador of the time in his despatches to London as a 'lunatic' and characterised as being 'cunning and slippery,' with short and bandy legs' and 'a slight reek of opium.'"[14] His ability to connect to the Iranian public, however, was undeniable.

Faced with a growing crisis over oil nationalization and the reluctance of other politicians to step into Razmara's shoes, the Shah casually offered the premiership to Mosaddeq. Much to everyone's surprise, Mosaddeq accepted, on the vital condition that the Majlis ratify the oil nationalization bill, which it did on April 28, 1951. The British had been caught off guard, and the British Embassy belatedly notified London that they were now faced with a serious problem. As one diplomat succinctly put it, "Dr. Musaddiq [sic] is personally popular and has succeeded in making himself a symbol of the Persian conception of nationalism," achieving this by doing "something which is always dear to Persian hearts: he has flouted the authority of a great power and a great foreign interest and he has gone a long way towards damaging the prestige of the first and the prosperity of the second."[15]

The British protested the illegality of the nationalization, although the procedure was no different than the nationalizations that had taken place in Britain. Mosaddeq was anxious to retain the British employees, and he had offered compensation while making it clear that Iran was a sovereign state entitled to make its own laws. These legal details made little headway with his supporters, whose appreciation of international law was not the impartial, objective set of rules and regulations understood by the British. For the vast majority of Iranian nationalists, international law had been written by Europeans for Europeans, and history suggested that the Europeans were just as likely to neglect the law when it suited them. Iranian Marxists defined this debate in clearer terms: international law was simply one ideological weapon in the bourgeois arsenal of oppression. This view was endorsed also by the religious classes, who were unmoved by the appeal to international law. Ayatollah Kashani, for instance, had been involved in the Shia uprising against the British in Iraq in 1922 and had a dim view of the British adherence to laws.

Despite all this pressure, Mosaddeq and the National Front leadership were determined to beat the British at their own game, and British contempt gave them an enormous advantage. Having declared the nationalization illegal, Britain proceeded to institute a boycott by suing anyone who attempted buying Iranian oil. The British believed that economic hardship would force Dr. Mosaddeq's hand and perhaps ensure his removal. Mosaddeq retorted by characterizing the dispute in terms of an historic struggle, rather than an intricate and somewhat legal confrontation. Iran, he argued, was the vanguard of a movement that would liberate the East. Thus argued Mosaddeq, "Sometimes great opportunities arise for nations which, if exploited intelligently, will change the course of history to their advantage and will end centuries of privation, misery, and despair."[16] Later, when sanctions and international pressure began to mount, he argued that, "No nation has succeeded in shaking off [a] foreign yoke without struggle, as can be testified by ancient and modern histories of nations and freedom movements. . . . Our movement served as [an] inspiration to national risings of other peoples, and today peoples of north and south Africa anxiously await our success."[17]

By thus embellishing the struggle, Mosaddeq made the pain bearable, and the view that Britain was all-powerful and therefore a worthy opponent was not difficult to cultivate. As one British diplomat noted in 1950, "My numerous denials that we were all-powerful and ubiquitous in Persian politics were greeted with polite laughter."[18] In language reminiscent of that used by Ayatollah Khomeini some twenty-five years later, Mosaddeq warned Iranians that, "Anyone who aims to belittle the holy struggle of our nation by assessing the achievements of the Iranian movement in economic terms and by comparing the independence of our country with a few million pounds has undoubtedly perpetrated a blunder."[19]

Having failed to resolve the dispute at the International Court of Justice in The Hague, the British changed its tack and decided to appeal to the United Nations, the symbol of the new world order. This was a mistake because it provided Dr. Mosaddeq with an international stage and a direct line to the American public, who were captivated by the aged man from the East seeking to overthrow the British Empire.[20] As Warne recounted:

"The American public, by this time inured to visits of kings, prime ministers and presidents, nevertheless took note of Dr. Mossadegh's [sic] dramatics. A feinting [fainting] spell in a crowd of reporters at Idlewild Airport was only the beginning. Inept though it was, people remembered the nickname 'Old Mossy.' For reporters it neatly dodged the problem, yet satisfactorily resolved, of spelling the real name. The final consonant has no English equivalent and might be written 'gh' or 'q.'"[21]

He might have also added that the nickname precluded any need to pronounce the name correctly, an arduous task that afflicts reporters of the Middle East to this day. Mosaddeq did more than faint. He cultivated an image that he knew would appeal to the common man in the United States: that of the selfless and beleaguered patriot seeking to overthrow the shackles of empire, which by happy coincidence happened to the British Empire. He had a reason to be optimistic. Americans expressed a dim view of imperialism, and Mosaddeq himself had enjoyed a good relationship with the American ambassador, Grady. On one occasion, "the wife of the American ambassador in a burst of not unwonted enthusiasm congratulated the Prime Minister on the spirit which animated the Persian nation and expressed the hope that it would continue and increase."[22] Furthermore, the Americans found the British attitude to be heavy-handed and patronizing, and not always towards only the Iranians, "We tried . . . to get the blockheaded British to have their oil company make a fair deal with Iran. No they could not do that. They know all about how to handle it—we didn't according to them."[23]

Consequently, as journalists noted, Mosaddeq was not averse to extolling the spirit of '76.[24] But despite the public relations success, Mosaddeq left dissatisfied at the official response, which remained lukewarm. Popular attitudes to the British were one thing, but no US administration was going to abandon its staunchest wartime ally for Iran. On his return to Iran, however, Mosaddeq was determined to put on a brave face. Energetically responding to a question on the floor of the Majlis, Mosaddeq announced:

"Wherever we went in America and elsewhere, they told us you have liberated your country (hear hear!) . . . You said we are in such a state that the Americans may not help us and we must foreswear our aim and independence, that is to say, we must accept whatever they tell us. I shall never accept such a thing (hear hear!). I shall fight for the freedom and independence of my nation as long as I live (well said!). I am shamed of being told that backward nations should be helped (hear hear!). It is a disgrace for us to be told by a government, that it is giving money to a backward nation (hear, hear!) . . . In looking at the Valley of the Nile from my plane, and comparing it with Khuzestan, I came to the conclusion that if agriculture in Khuzestan could be developed we would have a much bigger revenue than that obtained from oil (hear hear!)."[25]

Rhetoric aside, there was no doubt that Mosaddeq had been rebuffed by the US, and by the following year he was growing disillusioned. In a press conference with visiting American editors, a weary Mosaddeq complained, "We are very grateful to the American people for their very valuable moral support . . . but we expected the American government to pay more consideration for the rightful demands of the Iranian people, being cognizant of the fact that the American people have acquired their liberty and independence through their continued national struggle."[26] Moreover, some of his supporters warned against any unhealthy naivety towards the Americans, "Everybody knows that Musaddiq [sic] and Kashani are not the enemies of Persia and that they are not traitors. But, as they were struggling against the cunning British, they should not have been so credulous politically and should not have let themselves be deceived about American assistance."[27]

The inability to prize the Americans away from their British cousins ensured that the dominant view of the Americans was defined by the Iranian Left. This perspective was reinforced in 1952, when Mosaddeq, convinced of British perfidy, broke diplomatic relations with Britain and closed down their consulates throughout the country. As he stated clearly in a speech to the Majlis "all the poverty, confusion and calamity that now have befallen upon us are the results of unjustified interferences by the former Oil Company and the British Government in our internal affairs, to support their illegitimate and selfish interests."[28] In the absence of the British, the United States took the full brunt of the anti-imperialist and anti-capitalist invective. Even the relatively unaffected Warne noticed the shift in temperature, "'Yankee Go Home' in Iran got under way in earnest at the time the British were expelled. Earlier, only an occasional sign had appeared on a wall. With the British gone a carefully nurtured distrust of foreigners was directed against the Americans, the largest foreign group left in the country."[29]

Much of this might not have stuck were it not for the shift taking place in political responsibilities. Mosaddeq, convinced that he could hold out for better terms, had rejected a compromise settlement encouraged by the Americans.[30] The British, reluctant to legitimize what they considered an illegal act, were similarly convinced that conceding to Mosaddeq's demands would result in a slew of similar actions throughout the empire and throw an exhausted British state on the defensive.[31] A firm stand now would save considerable and perhaps unsustainable exertions later. Certainly officials from the Anglo-Iranian Oil Company were emphatic that Britain should put up a fight, noting that the next asset vulnerable to seizure would be the Suez Canal. An initial exercise in gunboat diplomacy, with the conspicuous dispatch of paratroopers to Cyprus, was treated with skepticism from the US administration, which felt that the days of imperial diplomacy of this nature were over. The British therefore decided that Mosaddeq was the problem and needed to be removed to allow a more reasonable interlocutor to come to the fore, and the oil boycott was intended to prepare the ground for such an eventuality.

Mosaddeq and his followers were more resilient than anticipated, so measures were then drawn up and adopted by the incoming Conservative administration under Winston Churchill to encourage a speedier demise of Mosaddeq's government in the form of a coup d'etat. The plan was based on the simple principle that the Shah had the constitutional authority to dismiss a government and appoint a new prime minister. The plan depended on creating an environment that would accentuate Mosaddeq's unpopularity while convincing a procrastinating and indecisive Shah that he should issue the *firman* (decree). As noted by Sam Falle, the British official responsible for the plan in the British embassy, "we must use all our influence, particularly with the Americans, to stir the Shah into at least expressing an opinion to the Majlis and Senate. . . . It can be pointed out that a continuation of the present situation is dangerous for the dynasty."[32]

These plans were cut short by the sudden termination of diplomatic relations. Britain no longer had the staff on the ground to commit to a coup attempt. The key now was to convince the Americans that they should shoulder the responsibility, and the way to do this was to exploit their anti-Communist sentiment or paranoia. This Cold War strategy was not difficult to cultivate given the Korean War and the atmosphere surrounding the McCarthy congressional hearings in the United States. Moreover, the election of Dwight D. Eisenhower as president in 1952 made the prospects of practical cooperation much more possible.

Iran's domestic political battles were being recast in a global agenda that few Iranians would have appreciated. Iran's oil nationalization crisis was situated in a framework with different priorities to those of the central protagonist. At the core of this new agenda were two distinct but interrelated considerations: the protection of Western commercial assets around the world and the fear of communism. Ironically, this ideologically inspired paranoia had a certain circularity. Western anxiety increased the pressure on Mosaddeq, who in turn was forced to take on more drastic autocratic powers and become increasingly dependent on the Left, particularly the Tudeh party. This redefined argument may have had the desired effect of diminishing his popularity among key sectors of the population. However, his fear of a coup—the threat of which was an open secret and perhaps cultivated by Mosaddeq to keep supporters on board—radicalized his politics and convinced the Americans that a Communist takeover was imminent.[33] Mosaddeq even tried to confront the threat head-on. The *New York Herald Tribune* noted that, "Premier Musaddiq [sic] warned the Western world today that any right-wing coup against his government would only pave the way for certain Communist dictatorship."[34]

By 1953, the CIA and its counterpart in Britain, SIS (otherwise known as MI6), were busy constructing and coordinating a plan for the undermining of and eventual overthrow of Mosaddeq. Recent (though incomplete) documents revealed under the Freedom of Information Act in the United States indicate the plan's thoroughness. Every aspect of the coup, from the creation of a favorable environment to the operational details, was prepared almost a year before it was carried out. Much depended on the determination of the Shah to fulfil his role, and the amount of encouragement he required is striking. Ultimately, the CIA operative in charge, Kermit Roosevelt, had to personally deliver the *firman* dismissing Mosaddeq to the Shah for him to sign. Despite all the preparations, the first attempt to have the *firman* delivered ended in fiasco because the military column sent to deliver it was intercepted by military units loyal to the government. On receiving the *firman,* Mosaddeq proved uncharacteristically complacent, noting that he would respond in due course. As the Shah slipped away to Rome on a "holiday," the general impression was that the coup had failed. In a dramatic seizure of initiative, local operatives, without recourse to either Whitehall or Washington, decided to have another go. Mosaddeq was overthrown and the Shah hurriedly returned to settle old scores. According to Roosevelt, the first words of the Shah were, "I owe my throne to God, my people, my army—and to you." But Roosevelt reassured the Shah that he owed the Americans and the British "absolutely nothing. Brief thanks would be received gratefully, but there is no debt, no obligation. We did what we have done to help our common interest. The outcome is full repayment."[35]

THE MYTH OF 1953

The coup, which occurred on the 28th Mordad 1332 (August 19, 1953), was a watershed moment in the history of modern Iran. For most Iranians, not just the politically active, that date marks the beginning of US-Iran relations, and much that preceded it is ignored or forgotten. For most Americans, 1953 is at best a curiosity of the Cold War and at worst ancient history, whose relevance to the contemporary era is unclear. Since 2000, when then US Secretary of State Madeleine Albright publicly regretted US involvement in the coup, American awareness that such an event took place has been growing, although it is doubtful whether Americans will fully appreciate the impact of this deep scar on the Iranian political landscape. Nevertheless, the sentiments expressed forty-seven years after the event were appreciated—and stand out in marked contrast to the deafening silence from British officials.

It is impossible to underestimate the importance to the Iranian political consciousness of the oil nationalization crisis and the coup that followed. The anniversary of the passing of the oil nationalization bill remains a national holiday and is perhaps the closest thing to an Iranian independence day. An attempt in 1999 by the conservative Fifth Majlis to remove the holiday was greeted with uproar by the Iranian media and populace, and the holiday was immediately reinstated.[36] Similarly, the media (of all political hues) religiously observes the anniversary of the coup as a day of perfidy that ranks with Pearl Harbor. It is as if all the foreign machinations of the previous one hundred and fifty years are symbolized by this single event. The Constitutional Revolution may have provided the framework, but 1953 provided the popular definition, and this may have been a reflection of the growth in political consciousness that had begun to transform Iranian society. It is to Russia's good fortune that the Anglo-Americans were the villain at the moment when modern Iranian political discourse was crystallized. Although she may have not appreciated it, America was present at the birth of modern politics in Iran.

This unique timing has had enormous consequences for US-Iran relations. Despite the fact that the US is absent from the scene, it remains a persistent negative reality in the modern Iranian political culture. The sympathetic perception of the United States that characterized the relationship with Shuster has been erased. Moreover, all the ills accumulated over the previous century and a half have been transferred, somewhat unfairly, onto the United States. This was accentuated by American policy in Iran since 1953 and the intensity of its relationship with the monarchy. Furthermore, any event that achieves iconic status in the popular consciousness is often simplified to eliminate contradictions in the narrative and to ensure a clear and obvious moral, in this case the pernicious and perfidious role of foreign powers in Iran's history. This narrative was not difficult to construct given the extensive nature of the planning, the use of propaganda, both grey and black, and the ultimate success of the coup.[37] Nonetheless, all the participants were involved in myth-making to justify their positions, and it is these myths, rather than the complex reality of the events, that have continued to influence politics and relations.

From the Iranian perspective, three interpretations of the coup competed for the public imagination. The monarchist perspective, that Mosaddeq was increasingly unpopular and the Shah was reinstated through a massive show of popular support by a grateful and loyal people, was largely dismissed from the beginning. This view was discredited chiefly due to the Shah's relentless determination to pursue it, up to the ludicrous point of erasing Mosaddeq from the official record of events. There was some truth in the view that sections of the elite were becoming frustrated with Mosaddeq and more amenable to throwing in their lot with the Shah. But undermining this was the persistence of the belief, understood and recognized by the Shah, that the post-1953 regime was illegitimate because of foreign support. This was a stigma the Shah would find difficult to shake and whose protestations could only accentuate.

The dominant interpretation was provided by the secular nationalists, who argued that a secular and moderate democratic leader was overthrown because he had the integrity and courage to stand up to imperialism. Like Amir Kabir before him, Mosaddeq suffered the tragic fate of being misunderstood and cut down by an ungrateful monarch with the support of reactionary foreign powers. This view continues to dominate today, particularly in light of the democratic failures of the Reform Movement and growing public disillusionment with the notion of Islamic democracy. Mosaddeq is seen as an opportunity lost and an icon to be lamented.

This sugar-coated view is challenged not only by the Western protagonists of the coup, which is no surprise, but also to some extent by the religious classes. The secular nationalist interpretation conveniently gives the *ulema* no credit in the movement, even though Ayatollah Kashani was instrumental in securing the support of the *ulema* and their followers, a crucial aspect of the popular base.[38] So important was Kashani to the National Front that, according to the partially declassified official CIA history, the US at one stage believed him to be a possible contender to replace Mosaddeq.[39] Kashani's role was sullied in the eyes of many members of the National Front by his subsequent abandonment of Mosaddeq due to political differences, a development that was rightly seen as presaging Mosaddeq's downfall. Yet Kashani was not the only member of the National Front leadership to move away from Mosaddeq. A number of key Socialists were likewise disaffected with Mosaddeq's increasingly demagogic style of leadership, but they were not maligned in the same way as the *ulema*. This may be a reflection of the fact that many senior *ulema* chose to side with the institution of the monarchy, and therefore the coup.

Unsurprisingly, the religious narrative diminishes the role of the *ulema* in allowing a coup, and instead emphasizes their importance in sustaining the movement. Nomenclature is an important political barometer in Iran, and at the outset of the Islamic Revolution, the main thoroughfare in Tehran, Pahlavi street, was temporarily renamed Dr. Mosaddeq street. This change was tolerated for a while, until Ayatollah Khomeini pointed out that Mosaddeq would have been nothing without Kashani and insisted that the street being given the suitably religious name of *Vali Asr*. This name has stuck, although in the contest to define the myth of emancipation, a narrative that stretches from the Constitutional Revolution to the Islamic Revolution and beyond, the secular nationalists have been more successful.

At this stage, it is worth reflecting on the Anglo-American myths of the coup. It has already been noted that the coup was in part justified by providing a global frame of reference. By emphasizing the imperatives of the Cold War, the particularities of the Iranian case were justified in terms of the greater global good.[40] This perspective is still used today to explain if not justify an historical event that some in the West are uncomfortable with, and the strategy has been resuscitated to good effect in the "Global War on Terror." Another myth, again not without some veracity but possibly more damaging, was that Mosaddeq was not a democrat and that the United States and Britain were not involved in overthrowing an embryonic democracy. This argument has considerable merit, insofar as Mosaddeq was quintessentially a patrician politician whose concept of democracy was more limited than what might be acceptable today. It is also evidently true that he abused his powers under the Constitution (though his supporters would claim exceptional circumstances). Yet this argument can be pushed too far. For all Mosaddeq's flaws, he clearly shared much more in common with his Western protagonists than many subsequent leaders of Iran, and his understanding of law and politics was broadly Western in its construction. The charge that he was not democratic sits uneasily with the reality that the West subsequently supported a monarchical autocracy that made little pretense to being democratic. In the cold light of history, Mosaddeq's democratic credentials compare favorably with those of his successors.

But the West's decision to support an autocracy (albeit an enlightened one) reflects the reality that this antidemocratic justification for the coup ran much deeper than Mosaddeq himself. For some in the West, the problem was not that Mosaddeq was undemocratic; it was that the experience of Mosaddeq and the National Front proved that the Iranians could not cope with democracy. They lacked the dispassionate logic required for systemic, legally ordered democracy, as evidenced by their inability to come to terms on the oil dispute. Elwell-Sutton's assessment of the oil crisis is refreshingly blunt in exposing this prejudice, "Really, it seemed hardly fair that dignified and correct Western statesmanship should be defeated by the antics of incomprehensible orientals."[41] This extraordinary statement exemplifies a particular British perspective, one that has not been entirely erased. The statement's significance lies in the fact that it reveals a dangerous extrapolation by which the madness of the individual is symbolic of the wider malaise of the nation, if not "orientals" as a whole. Mosaddeq, in coming to epitomize and personalize a weakness, was in effect merely representative of his people. As will be seen, this prejudice has been reinvented and embellished for our time, in slightly different language, and directed by Washington rather than London. Whereas the United States had found itself uncomfortably trying to mediate between two antagonists who characterized each other in the most colorful terms, after 1979 the role of mediator fell to the British.[42] That this was so reflected the growing intimacy of relations between Iran and the United States.

AMERICANS IN IRAN: THE CONSOLIDATION

Beginning in 1953, the United States supplanted Britain as the dominant foreign power in Iran. This process was neither smooth nor trouble-free, and the frictions that arose did not originate entirely with the Iranians. The British could barely disguise their irritation at having lost their monopoly over Iranian oil, and in the aftermath of the coup, some imperial condescension towards their colonial cousin reemerged. This was a view the Americans did little to diminish, moving in with enthusiasm to build, as one historian described it, their "client state." An important part of this client state was the development of the armed forces to sustain and protect the dynasty and ultimately to protect the free world against communism. As American military advisers and money began to pour in, much to the satisfaction of the Shah, the British looked on with astonishment. A Foreign Office official noted with incredulity in the margins of the military attaché's report that, "The Americans sent a military mission to Persia largely for political reasons. It is quite natural that the mission should maintain that the job which it was sent to do is worth doing, but they seem to me to be carrying professional optimism to [an] extraordinary length. . . . To judge from their past record, it is in fact inconceivable that the Shah or any Persian government would offer determined political resistance to a Russian attack."[43]

A report in the *Times* in 1961 made the following assessment of US assistance to Iran over the previous decade: "The figures are worth considering. Since 1952 or a little earlier American grants and loans in several forms to Iran have totalled about $1,135m . . . Of this about $631m has been for economic help and $504m for military assistance . . . All the military and well over half the economic assistance has been in grants, leaving only some $255m in loans whose repayment has scarcely begun."[44] The Shah insisted on this help, playing heavily on the US fear of communism and particularly on Iran's strategic role in being able to confront the Soviet threat. When even the Americans were finding the Shah too demanding, he would threaten to seek armaments from elsewhere, even Britain. The realization that Britain might consider selling the Shah naval vessels spurred the US administration into action. As a British diplomat noted, "The Americans wish to preserve US Navy's influence, and made this quite obvious to us. . . . It is natural that the Americans should be jealous if they suspect we are trying to supplant their influence over the Iranian navy."[45] All this resulted in considerable American investment in both the military and civilian sectors, with significant consequences.

As Elwell-Sutton was to write in the *Scotsman*:

"Financially, Persia is heavily and irrevocably indebted to the United States. Large American missions of officers and men advise the Armed Forces and the police. American advisers are attached to every ministry and American World bank officials watch carefully over the activities of the Plan Organisation. All the international agencies are at work, and semi-official concerns like the Near East Foundation add their quota. More than 100 American officials work in the huge new Point-Four building in Tehran. . . . Americans have reorganised the educational system. American cars, cosmetics and refrigerators fill the shops . . . Even the Seventh Day Adventists have opened a large church in a fashionable quarter of Tehran."[46]

The United States pandered to the Shah's worst excesses with respect to the armed forces and security. The Shah was playing the Cold War game well, emphasizing the need for a strong military so that Iran could assume her proper place at the vanguard of the free world's defences against an encroaching Soviet Union. In other words, he was playing to American's priorities and encouraging them in the belief that order and stability had to be achieved before other matters could be attended to. Others, including British diplomats, saw the matter differently and argued that a strong military was pointless in the absence of a stable and growing economy.[47] Abolhassan Ebtehaj, the brusque and determined head of the Seven Years Plan Organization, found himself arguing vehemently with the US military with respect to their priorities in Iran. According to one of Ebtehaj's colleagues, "Once Admiral Radford had finished talking about his purpose to look into military need and military requirements, Ebtehaj made a fist and raised it and banged on the table. . . and said, 'Admiral Radford, Iran needs development, not military expenditure.'"[48]

For most Iranians, the American presence was at best a folly, which exposed their naivety in contrast to British manipulation and Iranian guile, and at worst an exercise in blatant imperialism. According to a language student in Shiraz, the blatant exercise in American power and money was having a negative effect on popular perceptions:

"Almost no-one had a good word to say for the Americans presumably because their greater influence had won greater distrust. . . . Most literate people complained that they were supporting a corrupt and oppressive ruling class against the wishes of the nation as a whole. Landowners such as the Sheibanis seemed to dislike them (a) because they genuinely preferred British influence and the days of the South Persia Rifles (b) because the Americans wanted to change things and effect social and agricultural improvements which they considered of dubious utility. . . . Everyone thought the Americans were inexperienced and no match for Persian guile."[49]

These feelings were echoed by a perceptive British academic, Professor Ann Lambton. She noted that anti-Americanism was far in excess of anything felt against the British,[50] who at least bothered to learn Persian and were by and large respected if not liked. According to another report, "there seemed to be general unfriendliness towards the Americans. They were accused of throwing money about in Iran to little purpose and indeed of positively encouraging corruption. I was offered such comments as 'Oh well, no doubt the Americans will clear out one day, and the sooner the better,' and 'What a pity that the British do not possess, in addition to their brains and political sense, the money which is the Americans' only asset.'"[51] The Americans themselves were not oblivious to this sentiment and acknowledged early on that the popular perception was that they were "being had for suckers."[52] It may have been in recognition of this development that American officials decided to adopt a more robust attitude towards their Iranian interlocutors.

Having expended considerable time and money in overthrowing Mosaddeq, the US was determined to ensure that their political investment would not be squandered by the ineptitude of the Iranian leadership. Their manner did not go down well. In a conversation with British diplomats, Prime Minister Eqbal bitterly complained of the "tactless" and "impertinent" manner of foreigners, singling out the attitude of the American ambassador, who "lectures him in a heavy paternal manner and he resents it."[53] Such resentment went all the way up to the Shah, who noted with indignation that the Americans tended to circumvent him and go directly to the source when they wanted to know something about the political realities on the ground. The Shah also complained that the Americans were not sufficiently deferential to him.[54]

A frost was settling on the US relationship with the Shah. Having confronted his prevarication during the coup, the Americans were finding to their growing irritation that indecisiveness and procrastination were consistent character traits. As Lambton herself had noted, "There is nothing worse than a dictator who does not dictate."[55] This ineffectualness was compounded by the fact that he sought comparison with the great kings of Iran's past, a comparison that frequently invited derision. One American diplomat incurred imperial displeasure for having conceded in a moment of indiscretion that the Shah's image of himself was unwarranted.[56] Far more damning, however, was an earlier letter, which now appears to have been a Soviet forgery, from Secretary of State Dulles to US Ambassador Chapin, which reads in part, "You know, of course, that we have never cherished any illusions about the Iranian sovereign's qualifications as a statesman. The man tries to pose as the Cyrus of modern times. He has no grounds whatsoever for doing so. The Shah should long ago have reconciled himself to the idea that he is there to reign, not to rule. His talk about the need for some purely national policy as well as his nebulous hints regarding the possibility of his revising his present policy show that he is about as successful as a politician as a husband."[57]

Despite American protestations, the letter touched a raw nerve and was probably an accurate reflection of American views. At about the same time, the US was implicated in a scandal. In 1958, the Iranian security services, SAVAK (established with the help of the United States a year earlier), had uncovered a plot in the army that implicated the United States in an attempt to overthrow the Shah. General Qarani was intended to be the new strong man. The United States vigorously denied the charges and evidence remains scarce, but the coincidences were intriguing, especially the roles played by Ali Amini, then ambassador in Washington, and Hasan Arsanjani, the man who would later become Minister of Agriculture and spearhead the Land Reform Program.[58] Qarani, who received a light sentence, claimed that he had been a mole whose function was to uncover the plot. Whatever the truth, Qarani's lenient sentence convinced people that he had been working with the Americans, while the plot itself was not inconsistent with US frustrations with the Shah. As it happened, diplomatic relations were not severed and the United States remained secure in Iran.

But the changes America was encouraging were not fruitful. As Michael Leapman noted in *Spectator* magazine, "Iran is being Westernized in all the wrong places. Modern bottling plants for Pepsi, Coke, and Canada Dry have sprung up all over the place, while in the filthy poor quarters of the cities people still drink from the jubes—open watercourses that run down the sides of the streets, collecting all manners of rubbish. Teheran Airport is one of the finest in the Middle East, yet there is still no adequate road and rail system. A tall Hilton Hotel is being built, while hundreds of people sleep in the streets."[59] The British embassy, while more circumspect, was equally concerned about the consequence of rapid and uneven economic change, "A society, in effect, based quite recently upon the economy of camel and donkey is being propelled into the early jet age. . . . American assistance has equipped with American weapons and dressed in American uniforms an army of 200,000 men; peopled the administration with American advisers; sprinkled the country with American projects; and trained some thousands of young Iranians in American office procedures. All this is profoundly disturbing to traditional ways of life in Iran."[60]

Perhaps the most damning and prescient assessment came from an Iranian. Ebtehaj having lost his battle with the United States with regard to military expenditures and finding himself deprived of the Shah's support, retired to private life. Respected in academic circles, he was invited to deliver a lecture in the United States, during which he outlined the problems inherent in building a client state:

"Under the present bilateral approach, creditor governments are diverted from development projects by military and political considerations. . . . Even if a recipient government became convinced in all good faith of the fairness of certain bilateral programs offered by another country, it would soon be condemned in the public mind. Opposition leaders will charge the government with selling out to the imperialists, and the public will believe those charges. . . . Bilateral aid poisons the relationship between nations, frustrates the donor, and causes revulsion in the recipient. Donor nations are obliged to channel aid through the receiving country's officials whether they be qualified, honest, efficient, or otherwise. Where the recipient government is corrupt, the donor government appears, in the judgement of the public, to support corruption. . . . The bilateral approach cannot bring about reform. Furthermore, government-to-government aid delays internal pressure toward reform by providing considerable material resources to corrupt regimes and by unwittingly fostering the fear that development aid will be stopped if the old regime is overthrown. Under bilateral programs, the lending government cannot impose a creditor's normal discipline for fear of jeopardizing the entire fabric of international relations. I can think of no better summary of all the disadvantages and weaknesses of the bilateral system than the modern history of my own country. Not so very many years ago in Iran, the United States was loved and respected as no other country, and without having given a penny of aid. Now, after more than $1 billion of loans and grants, America is neither loved nor respected; she is distrusted by most people and hated by many."[61] Ebtehaj was thrown into prison for his efforts and was released only following concerted protests from friends and allies both within and particularly outside the country.

Meanwhile, the Shah faced another challenge. The Eisenhower presidency had given way to the Democratic administration of Kennedy, and the new president was determined to be proactive in Iran. The setback inflicted by the embarrassment of the Qarani affair was temporary and did not alter Iran's political vulnerability and the Shah's obstinacy and wariness of change. As Andrew Roth noted in the *Spectator*, "He [the Shah] often grew impatient when American diplomats urged him to modernize at a pace faster than his careful crawl. 'I can start a revolution for you,' he apparently told an American diplomat, 'but you won't like the end result."[62]

Spurred on by the Iraqi Revolution of 1958 and the coup against Menderes in Turkey in 1960, the United States impressed upon the Shah that the country's social structure required a fundamental change if his dynasty was to survive and his country not succumb to communism.[63] Social scientists had concluded that the necessary change involved land reform: the old feudal structures would be replaced by a system of freehold, in which individual farmers would cultivate their own land and reap the benefits of their labors. Land reform would alter the economic structure of the country, and farmers would remain loyal to the regime that had granted them such liberty. This White Revolution, as it was soon called, was essentially an exercise in *Bonapartism,* in which feudal tenants were replaced by small landowners with a vested interest in maintaining and defending the land, cultivating both economic regeneration and nationalism. "The Government's American advisers (the United States Operations Mission) appear to be working on the assumption that anyone who owns his own land becomes *ipso facto* hard working, thrifty and enterprising in the Middle Western tradition; and they have succeeded in communicating something of their conviction to the Shah."[64]

Unfortunately, while the Americans focused on the economic benefits of this "revolution" in land tenure, the Shah was more interested in the potential political rewards. His priorities were the disenfranchisement of the aristocracy and the centralization of power in his own hands.[65] What resulted was a less than satisfactory outcome for which the Americans were again held responsible.

"Almost all critics of the [land reform] bill are curiously united in blaming the Americans for imposing it. Some argue that it has been thrust upon the Shah and the Government by the Americans, regardless of special conditions in Iran of which they have no experience, out of a misconceived notion that the existing system of land tenure is 'feudal' or reactionary. Others are persuaded that the Shah is promoting the bill in an inept endeavour to ingratiate himself to ill-informed American public opinion as a 'progressive' monarch. Some even believe that the Americans are dictating legislation in this sense in order to break the political power of the landowners, traditionally the friends of the British in Iran, regardless of the natural order of Iranian society."[66]

The political nature of the reform was a view that even the Americans grew to appreciate. One adviser sent to monitor the land reform program held, "In conversation, generally I have said that we believe some form of agricultural revolution as regards techniques is necessary for Iran but that a technical revolution is quite different from re-distribution of land, which is a matter of politics and so largely outside our sphere."[67] The US ambassador's assessment was more candid:

"Firstly, land reform is not merely 'reform.' It is a revolution aimed at the destruction of the political and to a great extent the economic, power of the traditionally most influential class of the country and the replacement of this class with the previously disenfranchised peasantry. . . . Secondly, there is an incredible dearth of managerial competence and economic knowledge in the government, from the Shah on down. As the difficulties here are fundamentally political and managerial, there are very real limits to what we can do to help overcome them. Were we to intervene directly it would lead us into the midst of Persian politics and personal interests. If we give advice in these areas and our advice is accepted, we run a high risk of being held responsible for such failures as may result from our inability to control subsequent events. Revolutions can't be controlled by foreigners."[68]

Few in Iran believed or appreciated the American position. The immediate consequence of land reform—energetically pursued by the new Minister of Agriculture Hasan Arsanjani and Prime Minister Ali Amini, both widely regarded as American nominees[69]—was the alienation of both the landed aristocracy and the *ulema.* Both groups had been essential in facilitating the coup against Mosaddeq in 1953 and were vital to the domestic sustenance of the institution of the monarchy. In attacking them, the Shah was alienating the pillars of his regime with a view to replacing them with a grateful enfranchised peasantry. He grew more dependent on the United States, while America, increasingly divorced from alternatives in Iran, grew more dependent on him.

The senior *ulema,* often landowners in their own right, regarded the land reform bill as contrary to the Shia faith. The landowners, offended by the dubious legality of the bill, considered it an arbitrary measure ranking with the actions of the most despotic of Iranian monarchs. For some, it was not so much the principle of land reform as the manner in which it was being carried out, which was disastrous for the country. As one landowner informed his British interlocutors, "whilst he was not opposed to land reform in principle, he was bitterly opposed to the present compulsory sale. . . . The object of [his] visit was to ask whether the British Embassy would not now intervene with the government to stop the Ministry's illegal proceedings, which were promoting communism and provoking disaster. The Americans, in their inexperience and ineptitude were doing dangerous damage."[70]

The White Revolution was not as bloodless as the Shah would have liked. In 1963, conservative agitation, encouraged by the *ulema* and supported by a disgruntled and disenfranchised aristocracy, erupted into street violence in a number of cities. The catalyst for these riots was the arrest of Ruhollah Khomeini, a hitherto unremarkable religious jurist. With the death of Grand Ayatollah Borujerdi in 1961, a vacuum was created in the political leadership of the Shia hierarchy. Traditionally, the reigning monarch would indicate his preference for a successor from a number of leading clerics. This time, the Shah decided that divide and rule was a better policy. This policy left the field open for those with a sense of initiative. The *ulema* had earlier voiced its protests against land reform, and Ayatollah Borujerdi had issued a *fatwa* declaring it to be against the principles of Islam. Now with the prospective addition of a number of other reforms, including the political emancipation of women, the *ulema* were even more concerned. In 1962, Khomeini and other senior clergy protested the reforms in terms that were remarkably conciliatory, urging the Shah to adhere to Islam so that the clergy may "pray for His Majesty."[71]

Khomeini's objections did not have the desired effect, so he stepped up the protest a year later, following the suspiciously successful referendum on the White Revolution, in which ninety-nine percent of the people voted in favor of the reforms. This time his rhetoric resulted in house arrest, which provided the spark for riots in Qom and Tehran. These were crushed, thus staining the White Revolution with blood. Although the casualties were modest, they provided the first martyrs for a revolutionary movement that was to increasingly define itself in religious terms, against a monarch who likewise considered himself divinely mandated to rule. More importantly, it catapulted Ayatollah Khomeini into the top tier of the clerical leadership by casting him as a political leader. This role was confirmed a year later when the United States decided to seek ratification of an immunities bill, which would guarantee legal immunity for all US government personnel in Iran.[72]

The bill was similar to that granted to US personnel in other countries in which US had a significant presence.[73] To anyone with an understanding of Iranian history, however, its implementation would be anything but smooth, especially since its application in the Iranian case seemed unusually extensive.[74] For many Iranian nationalists, the bill would engender comparisons with the system of capitulations under the Qajars, by which foreigners were granted legal privileges while in Iran. It was a system that Reza Shah had dismantled and his son now appeared to condone. The State Department was aware of the sensitivities involved and urged the Iranians to not publicize the bill but instead ease it through both houses of the Parliament by arrangement with the Iranian Foreign Ministry. Prime Minister Ali Mansur, however, was anxious that the process be legally correct, and therefore insisted that it be legally ratified.[75] The Shah, encouraged by his referendum and the successful suppression of the riots, posed no objection. Others, including members of the US State Department, were less certain, noting the possibility of objections in the Majlis.[76] These were of particular concern because, despite the insistence on transparency, Mansur seemed anxious to minimize debate.

A telegram sent to Washington a day before the debate in the Majlis noted that, "Because Govt has until recently kept tight censorship on all information and discussion of the status bill, and since bill was pushed through Senate under urgency procedure without any discussion . . . many rumours are circulating at present and there is some talk that [the] bill involves 'capitulations.' Some of these misconceptions are inevitable and innocent and will be cleared up as soon as govt provides the necessary public explanations. Some however, are clearly malicious and involve latent opposition toward Govt and nationalist agitation with anti-Americanism. We are in close touch with Majlis majority and minority elements and are struck by present defensiveness of members of Foreign Affairs committee which recently passed the status bill. They tell us they are presently assailed by colleagues in the Majlis and other contacts."[77] Despite the attempt by some Iranian officials to play down the significance of the bill, former Minister of Agriculture Arsanjani was characteristically blunt, telling the Shah that the ratification of any capitulations would result in him losing his throne.[78]

The passage of the bill was bungled, with sixty-one otherwise pliant (and preselected) deputies voting against the bill, as opposed to the seventy-four who voted in favor. There was clear discomfort among the deputies that the bill implied a colonial relationship with the United States, and a number of deputies voiced their concerns with respect to the bill's applicability:

"I just cannot understand why does the Prime Minister insist that this bill has to be approved just in the way it is. . . . You should know it for certain that the common people of this country hold higher respect for the Majlis than for the Senate. No such discussions took place there. They were then sorry that they approved such an important bill with all that hurry. . . . The people disapprove [of] what the Senators have done. . . . This bill is applicable to all the personnel of the advisory missions. . . . There are many on these advisory missions and most of them are sergeants. Now, it is all of these sergeants that the people complain. . . . They say that if they go out with their wives and an American sergeant happens to pinch one of their wives there will be no place for us to file our complaint and follow up the matter. That is how people get mad. You read in the papers yesterday that an American sergeant killed three people running over them in his car. I had a similar case during my office in the Justice Department and you want to approve such a Bill. How can you do it without a guilty conscience? . . . why cannot we make it limited. We can say that officers of the American advisory missions since those may commit such felonies less than their sergeants . . . they get drunk less and offend less . . . that is all right but let us not extend the privileges to their sergeants. That is dangerous. . . . If my child is overrun by an American sergeant and there is no court to take up the case, what am I to do? I will go and kill that American and that is going to be to the disadvantage of them as well."[79]

As the British ambassador Denis Wright noted, it was a public relations disaster that "brought to the surface the latent widespread criticism, in the press and among the public, of the grant of such privileges to foreigners—which is even talked of openly as a reversion to Capitulations.[80] This discomfort was compounded by the realization that the US government was offering Iran a $200 million loan, whose ratification on the same day as the immunities bill led many to conclude that the Shah had sold Iranian sovereignty to the United States.

It was an extraordinarily ill-timed sequence of events that did serious damage to the Shah's self-proclaimed image as an uncompromising patriot. "The debacle in the Majlis on October 13th over the American Forces Immunities Bill . . . continues to be a matter of discussion—and to the government a bitter memory. But in marked contrast to the bill approving a loan of $200m from American banks for the purchase of military equipment and material . . . which was not mentioned at all in the press beforehand but hit the headlines as a fait accompli the day after it was approved by the Majlis, most of the publicity about the immunities bill came before the event—and at least one local editor has suffered for what he wrote afterwards."[81] Even the Iranian Foreign Ministry was unwilling to apply the terms of the agreement, arguing that they had to await US ratification of the Convention, a condition that US diplomats countered was irrelevant. The legal wranglings before and after ratification were reminiscent of the disputes that had accompanied Anglo-Persian treaty negotiations in the nineteenth century and did not build trust.[82]

It was not long before Ayatollah Khomeini entered the fray. Mansur had been keen to mollify the religious leadership in an effort to alleviate tensions. Khomeini, recently released from house arrest, was in no mood for compromise. The moderate language of previous statements was replaced with anger at what the Shah appeared to be reintroducing. According to Wright, "Last year the targets of Khomeini's preaching were land reform and the emancipation of women. Although the general public had little sympathy with his attacks on such progressive measures, his eloquence sparked off serious riots at the Muharram mourning period. In the present instance his target was a measure widely held to be unpopular. . . . As was the case then, so also now the Shah could not afford to ignore the affront and challenge of Khomeini's open hostility, expressed in terms which, as you will see from the texts, go far beyond anything we have heard from him in recent years."[83] Khomeini, protesting that other countries had not suffered such indignity, attacked the immunities bill in terms that were not dissimilar to those used in the Majlis. But he did so in language that was calculated, much as Mosaddeq had done, to incite Iranian emotions. In speaking out in such uncompromising terms, Khomeini captured the national mood and positioned himself as a champion of a national agenda. Politically, it was a highly astute move.

"I cannot express the sorrow I feel in my heart. . . . Iran no longer has any festival to celebrate; they have turned our festival into mourning. . . . They have sold us, they have sold our independence; but still they light up the city and dance. . . . If I were in their place, I would forbid all these lights; I would give orders that black flags be raised over the bazaars and houses, that black awnings be hung! Our dignity has been trampled underfoot; the dignity of Iran has been destroyed. The dignity of the Iranian Army has been trampled underfoot! A law has been put before the Majlis according to which we are to accede to the Vienna Convention, and a provision has been added to it that all American military advisers, together with their families, technical and administrative officials, and servants—in short, anyone in any way connected to them—are to enjoy legal immunity with respect to any crime they may commit in Iran. If some American's servant, some American's cook, assassinates your *marja* in the middle of the bazaar, or runs over him, the Iranian police do not have the right to apprehend him! Iranian courts do not have the right to judge him! The dossier must be sent to America, so that our masters there can decide what is to be done! . . . They have reduced the Iranian people to a level lower than that of an American dog. If someone runs over a dog belonging to an American, he will be prosecuted. But if an American cook runs over the Shah, the head of state, no one will have the right to interfere with him. Why? Because they wanted a loan and America demanded this in return."[84]

Ayatollah Khomeini was sent into exile on November 4, 1964, a decision that the US embassy considered ill-timed and one that gave "more currency to nationalist propaganda over the Status Bill than anything else."[85] A year later, Ali Mansur was assassinated.

3

1979

There are about 24,000 Americans in Iran. . . . There are 11,000 who are working here, 7,000 in civilian pursuits, and their families. So when people talk lightly about 'hostages,' the hostages are created by the nature of the connection of our societies and not by any particular decision having to do with military affairs alone or even primarily. . . . [I want] our Iranian friends to understand that, not out of sentimentality, though we are always happy here, but out of a calculation of our own national and global interest— just as Iranian policy is based on its calculation of its national interests—there has developed a parallelism of views on many key problems that has made our cooperation a matter that is in the profound national interest of both countries. This is the conviction of our Administration. It is this conviction that has brought me here.

HENRY KISSINGER[1]

OR IRAN'S EMERGING PROFESSIONAL and political class, the coup of 1953 marked a watershed moment in the history of US-Iran relations. What had transpired before paled into insignificance if not irrelevance when compared to the overthrow of the National Front government by a political actor that many Iranians had expected to be sympathetic to their cause. The contributions of Shuster and Millspaugh, the missionaries, and the educational philanthropists were all submerged within the growing and all-consuming mythology of the coup, in which the "hidden hand" of the United States, and the CIA in particular, loomed large.

This sense of grievance and betrayal was confirmed by the developments of the White Revolution and the immunities bill, which revived memories of the capitulations and the national indignities of the nineteenth century. The protracted negotiations over the precise jurisdiction of the immunities bill and the means by which the United States and Iran sought to disguise obvious disagreements echoed the legal acrobatics of an earlier age. When the system did not operate to one's satisfaction, the solution was to circumvent it as inconspicuously as possible. This did not engender faith in the Western legal system. Nonetheless, it is important to remember that after 1965, with the expulsion of Ayatollah Khomeini, the assassination of Mansur, and a failed attempt on the life of the Shah behind them, the United States and Iran settled down to more than a decade of relative political stability and economic growth.

THE EMPEROR OF OIL

In the decade after 1963, even before the dramatic increase in Iranian oil revenues, economic growth was impressive, leading economists to suggest that Iran might be the next Japan and was on the verge of an economic breakthrough. Such encouraging economic figures, along with the associated complimentary commentary from abroad, transformed the Shah's character. Not only had his gamble paid off, but Western, and particularly American, support for him seemed to have been justified. By 1967, the Shah was brimming with so much self-confidence that he finally felt secure enough to organize an impressive if belated coronation. Earlier, a grateful Majlis had awarded him the additional honorific title of *Aryamehr*, "Light of the Aryans," an indication of his intense national orientation. Iran was, after all, named after the Aryan tribes (principally Medes and Persians) who had settled the land, and the term Iranian/Aryan had been used in the ancient period. The Shah's use of the title therefore indicated his sympathies for pre-Islamic Iran, but it was also a title with racist overtones in a Western world recovering from the tragedy of Nazism. Still, his pro-Western leanings and tolerance of Israel meant that His Imperial Majesty could be indulged in his affection for Cyrus the Great and the Achaemenids. Even the Israelis were willing to massage the imperial ego by sending him Biblical parchment referring to Cyrus the Great on the occasion of the birth of his son.[2]

A heady mix of economic growth and political repression ensured that 1965–1975 were the halcyon years of Mohammad Reza Shah's rule. Any cracks in the edifice were quickly disguised by the steady growth in oil income. Moreover, doubters could be reassured by the praise coming from abroad. In 1968, the US electorate had returned a Republican, the party of choice for the Shah, to the presidency in the person of Richard Nixon. The Shah and Nixon developed a close affinity, even a friendship. Under Nixon, US-Iran relations became US-Shah relations. The relationship was based on personalities rather than states, and as a consequence became all the more intimate, if demographically limited. President Nixon's toast to the Shah on a visit to Tehran in 1972 was emblematic of this growing mutual admiration society:

"Since ancient times, this country has been one that has been known for its splendid hospitality, and we, of course, tonight have had a good chance to see why that reputation has become worldwide. It is always a great privilege to visit here, but I feel especially privileged to be here in this period in which you are celebrating what you have referred to, the 2,500th year of your country's history. I think of the fact that the United States of America in just 4 years will be celebrating its 200th anniversary, and then I compare that 200 years with 25 centuries of history, and I realise that as we compare our two countries, we owe so much to you. As you have spoken so generously of what you may owe us, we owe so much to you, not only for 2,500 years, but for a history that goes back even 6,000 years."[3]

The personal ties between the Pahlavi elite and the political establishment in the United States grew exponentially throughout the following decade, a trend that encouraged a broader social connection between Iran and the United States, particularly in student exchanges. More than forty thousand Americans were in Iran by 1978, and approximately sixty thousand Iranian students were in the United States. Technology enhanced this connection. As James Bill notes, "In 1973 a total of 53,597 telephone calls were completed from the United States to Iran. This number increased to 122,477 in 1975, but by 1977 the number of calls had exploded to an astonishing 854,382. In these five years, the number of calls . . . increased by over 1600 per cent. . . . By 1978, Iran had become the fourth largest revenue producer in the world for AT&T Long Lines."[4]

At a time when the Iranian student population was growing and the general political consciousness was expanding, decision makers in the United States were withdrawing behind the certainties of the Pahlavi veil. This was all the more ironic because a new generation of Iranian activists, enthused by the myth of 1953, were having their political culture expanded by their contact with the West at a time when the West was undergoing doubt and uncertainty. This was the Vietnam generation in the US and the period of social unrest on campuses in Europe. Iranian students found a more dynamic and sympathetic political environment than they had anticipated, much as Khalil Maliki had discovered a generation earlier.

Western students were just as critical of their respective governments as the Iranians were, and it was easy to draw connections and learn from the antiestablishment movements in the West and their own struggle against the Shah. This was an international struggle, and Nixon's resignation after Watergate and the American withdrawal from Vietnam served to encourage idealized student radicals that change could be imposed. As a State Department report noted, "One issue which needs attention concerns Iranian students. There are upwards of 60,000 Iranians studying in the US and the number is sharply increasing each year. Many of these students are not qualified or properly motivated, with the result that they are ripe for agitation and engage in political activities—often violent—which irritate Americans and create stresses in US-Iran relations."[5]

One way to achieve a change in US opinions of Iran was to internationalize the Iranian struggle. Highlighting the injustices of 1953 and 1964 would have made little headway among activists in the West. What was needed was something more immediate and relevant. As fortune would have it, in the 1970s the Shah began to emerge as an international figure, so he did the work of the radicals for them. In 1971, following nearly a decade of steady growth and continued internal stability, the Shah decided to announce his arrival on the world stage with a lavish celebration of the twenty-five hundred years of the Iranian monarchy. Some Iranian academics protested that twenty-five hundred years was too short a span of history and neglected the pre-Achaemenid history of the Iranians, in particular the Medes. Indeed, in traditional (mythological) Iranian history, the timeline would have extended much further back (as Nixon himself sensitively noted). In starting the national clock from the Ancient Persian (Achaemenid) Empire, Mohammad Reza Shah was paradoxically paying lip service to a Western historiography.

More important for the Shah was the association such a celebration would provide between himself and Cyrus the Great. The focus on Cyrus, among other great kings of the past, as well as the attention given to Iran's military achievements, led many to conclude that this was less a celebration of national rejuvenation and more a coming of age for the Shah himself. Significantly, Nixon declined to attend the centerpiece of the celebrations at Persepolis, sending his vice president instead. But the panoply of world leaders that did attend was impressive, and attention was drawn to Iran and the Shah in particular. Not all this attention was welcome. Along with eulogies of the Shah's achievements in the Western press came the prying eyes of human rights groups and other nongovernmental organizations destined to be a thorn in the Shah's side.

Such scrutiny was all the more important because 1971 also marked the flexing of Iran's regional muscle. In 1968, Britain had announced that it would no longer be able to service its imperial obligations east of Suez after 1971, and would consequently withdraw its forces. The Shah was anxious to fill this gap, a move that was more important symbolically because it would signify the withdrawal of Great Britain after one hundred fifty years of dominance in the Persian Gulf and a reassertion of Iranian hegemony in the region. The emerging Arab states in the locality were not reassured by voluble reassertion of Persian imperialism to their north, and anxieties were heightened by the dispute that was to emerge over the sovereignty of the islands of Abu Musa, Greater Tumbs, and Lesser Tumbs. Iran claimed sovereignty over the three islands, which they regarded as compensation for their "voluntary relinquishment" of their rights over Bahrein. An uneasy compromise was reached through British mediation because the Shah refused to recognize the new United Arab Emirates (UAE) until Iran's rights were recognized.[6] The resultant fudge lingers to this day and is periodically raised by the UAE and the Gulf Cooperation Council whenever relations sour or pressure needs to be exerted. In 1971, however, the United States was encouraging Iran, and the Shah in particular, to take on the responsibility for Persian Gulf security.

It seems inconceivable, therefore, that the United States did not at the very least acquiesce to this exercise in imperial power at this stage. At the same time, the development was presented in terms of a regional power asserting her natural rights, an image the Shah encouraged and one that brought with it a new set of problems. Power attracted attention and, according to Western norms, was required to be accountable. The Shah was not prepared for this change. Many Iranians remained skeptical because of the political reality of monarchical autocracy. But they also criticized Iran's assumption of regional security, noting with disdain that the Shah had become the "Gendarme of the Gulf," America's policeman, a distinctly subservient role that contradicted imperial pretensions. Moreover, far from being independent, Iran appeared to be performing a function within a broader US global strategy, in a similar if more proactive fashion to the British buffer state it had been in the nineteenth century. Iranians had already looked askance when, in the 1950s, it was imprudently revealed that the Western powers had no intention of defending Iran against a Soviet invasion beyond the Zagros line, in other words, beyond the oil fields.[7] US sincerity in coming to Iran's defense continued to be doubted by many, including the Shah himself, who drew his own conclusions from the Indo-Pakistan war of 1971 and the separation of

Bangladesh from Pakistan. As the 1978 Inspection Report on Iran revealed, "Iran is the capstone of the buffer zone between the Soviet Union and the oil rich Arabian peninsula."[8]

Yet if scrutiny of the Shah's policies was to gradually increase after 1971, his involvement in another development transformed his international image from one that was essentially positive into one that drew concern from wide sections of Western, and particularly American, society. In 1973 the Yom Kippur War erupted between the Arab states and Israel, accompanied by an oil boycott intended to punish the West for its support of Israel. For the first time, the balance of power shifted from the consumers to the producers, and Western economies felt vulnerable. The price of oil went up, and dour warnings emerged that the good times were over. Iran, one of the largest producers in OPEC, remained aloof, and the Shah in a protestation of principle argued that it was unethical to use oil as a weapon. Yet within three months, the Shah, having carefully gauged the situation, decided that it was time to seize the initiative and orchestrate a more dramatic rise in the price of oil. In December 1973, at a press conference in Tehran, he announced his decision to quadruple oil prices. Western economies that had been adjusting to the unprecedented rise to around $3 a barrel now faced the reality of oil at nearer $11 a barrel. As the Shah noted:

"As far as the industrial world is concerned . . . the era of extraordinary progress and income—and an even more extraordinary income—based on cheap oil has ended. They should find new energy resources and gradually tighten their belts, and eventually all the children of wealthy families who have plenty to eat, who have cars and who act almost like terrorists, planting bombs here and there, or choosing other ways will have to reconsider these aspects of this developed industrialised world. They will have to work harder."[9]

The Shah took particular satisfaction in patronizing the British. When asked by a British journalist what he felt about the Western, and particularly British, socio-political system, the Shah mused, "I do not really oppose it, but I should state my opinion on it for you. If you continue this unruly and in-disciplined [*sic*] social system, your country will explode. . . . You will go bankrupt, you do not work enough, you try and receive more money than necessary for what little you do, and this situation cannot continue; it can possibly continue for a few months or for a year or two but not forever."[10]

What was different about this change was that it affected ordinary people who otherwise would not have paid much attention to Middle Eastern events or their potentates. This was no longer a matter for elites and diplomats. Oil and Middle Eastern politics became a domestic political issue that affected everyone and was subject to domestic political processes and electoral politics. A new equilibrium was being constructed in US-Iran relations. Until now, diplomats would have engaged with their Iranian counterparts in an environment that was distinct from their domestic political constraints. The only politics that impinged on their decision making was that of Iran and the Iranians, whom they could approach with a certain distance and objectivity, frequently berating their Iranian counterparts for their attachment to the irrational antics of their compatriots. This ability to conduct diplomacy in a professional cocoon was as much a reflection of the professional contempt of an educated elite for the masses as it was an exercise in Western condescension against members of the third world. Together, they represented a powerful combination. Now, however, this imbalance was being addressed. Aided by the dramatic growth in mass-media communication, ordinary people and domestic politics in the West were beginning to influence the way foreign policy could be carried out. The political elite might indulge the Shah his lectures on laziness in the West as an aspect of a complex changing relationship that was best tolerated. But ordinary workers, who could see their comfortable livelihoods threatened by this curious figure from the East, were less impressed.

Initial press reactions remained respectful. By 1974, the Shah was gracing the front cover of *Time* magazine as the "Emperor of Oil," and its readers were warned that, "The Shah's power is exploding and Americans would be wise to pay attention to his dreams."[11] The editorial added for good measure that, "Mohammad Reza Pahlavi has brought Iran to a threshold of grandeur that is at least analogous to what Cyrus the Great achieved for ancient Persia." For the business and political elites, the dramatic increase in oil revenue spelled opportunity. Iran had been planning for a threefold budget increase between its fourth and fifth five-year development plans. Having injected some $7 billion in oil revenue into the economy, Iran's Plan and Budget Organization was preparing for an investment program involving some $21 billion over the forthcoming five years. The Shah now presented them with a budget of $70 billion.[12]

An economy that was already straining at the seams now had to accommodate a massive injection of cash. Rejecting pleas from his planners that money be set aside and growth brought back under control and managed, the Shah insisted on an accelerated drive for growth, determined that Iran break through the frontier of his utopian Great Civilization within his lifetime. As he proclaimed in an interview with Al Ahram, "In ten years, Iran's population will be equal to that of France and Britain today. Iran's population, in other words, will not be less than 45 million, but I can see Iran twenty-five years from now and we hope to be better off than France and Britain. Iran will have an income that will probably be more than Britain's."[13]

There was money to spend, and the Shah intended to exercise his new-found commercial might by buying shares in Western companies, including Mercedes and Krupp in West Germany. These investments were to further bind the West to the Pahlavi elite and ensure that Iran enjoyed financial and consequently political leverage. One of the more significant purchases of this period was that of nuclear technology. Having already acquired a research reactor in 1959 (built in the late 1960s), the Shah was encouraged to expand his nuclear interests with an ambitious program for nuclear energy. During a visit to Britain in 1972, the Shah, in a private meeting following a dinner at Downing Street, found himself in discussion with Lord Rothschild, then head of Downing Street's Central Policy Review Unit and a close confidante of Prime Minister Edward Heath.

"I raised the question of nuclear power with the Shah. He said he was interested in keeping technologically abreast of the United States and Great Britain. I explained to him there was a possibility of his being *ahead* of these two countries in the Breeder Reactor field. The Shah was well informed about Iran's electricity generating programme and said he thought there was room for the type of reactor I had in mind. I asked him if he was sufficiently interested for me to arrange that an expert should visit Iran. He said yes, and indicated he would like to meet the expert. Sending an expert to Iran does not, I think, present any problems; but what does present a problem is the present absence, so far as I am aware, of any sales organisation to whom one could, from now onwards, entrust the negotiations. When entrusting to an organisation, one must not ignore the rather peculiar nature of the negotiations in Iran, of which I had a good deal of experience when setting up the agri-business project. Presumably the DTI will soon decide what sort of nuclear power station procurement organisation the United Kingdom is going to have. Until it does, we can make no progress other than sending an expert to Iran . . . Knowing the peculiar and furtive way in which negotiations are carried out by Iran, I am particularly anxious that there should be absolutely no leakage of information about this project, which is one of the reasons why this note is marked Secret and Personal."[14]

It was not long before the Americans also became involved in the sale of nuclear technology intended to provide Iran with a diversified electricity supply and release more oil for sale abroad. In 1974, the United States signed a ten-year agreement to supply Iran with enriched uranium, while in the same year Iran announced its intention to order five nuclear power plants from France. Canada likewise signed an agreement for nuclear cooperation while the British concentrated on providing training to Iranian nuclear scientists. Overall, Iran intended to "install some 28,000 MW of nuclear capacity."[15]

For all the intimacy of America's relationship with the Shah, the United States remained cautious about Iran's nuclear developments and anxious about the possibility of the Shah pursuing a military program. A number of ideas were floated at the time about how best to manage nuclear enrichment, with Henry Kissinger arguing for the establishment of international collaborative ventures to manage and oversee enrichment, thereby preventing any one (developing) country from having an independent facility. As Dr. Etemad, the Shah's chief nuclear scientist, recalled, the Iranians did not regard the proposal as remotely practical. From these early discussions, it was clear that problems were already being discovered in the nonproliferation system. At the same time,

Etemad conveys a frank discussion he finally held with the Shah about his nuclear ambitions. The Shah noted, much as his successors have done, that there was no place in Iran's security doctrine for nuclear weapons; that Iran's Armed Forces were by far superior to those of any potential regional enemies; and that the concept of a strategic deterrence against the Soviet Union was meaningless because Iran could never match the Soviet nuclear deterrent. The situation could always change, and it was clear that the Shah wanted to keep the option open. This approach arguably has not changed today, even though the military situation has changed.[16]

For the Shah, the priority remained the acquisition of advanced military equipment. Fortunately for him, the Nixon administration was amenable to his suggestion that the United States needed to support her friends, a Cold War motif that resonated with greater effect as the United States sought to extricate herself from Vietnam. Along with the policy that Iran should serve as the policing power in the region came an approval from President Nixon in 1972 that Iran should be able to buy any military hardware it liked short of nuclear weapons. This carte blanche satisfied the Shah's yearning for high-tech military aircraft, and America's military-industrial complex benefited from the investment and research this facilitated.[17] The intense competition by Americans companies to secure a share of this multibillion-dollar market not only encouraged widespread corruption but also boosted the conceit of the elite. When Grumman International conceded that it had agreed to pay a $28 million commission fee to General Hasan Toufanian, the General retorted, "This shows that the foreign countries want to loot us. We will not allow this and we will pull the extra money out of their throats."[18]

Meanwhile, a Senate report issued in 1976 questioned the validity and usefulness of such extensive arms sales, noting that, "Iran has purchased large quantities of some of the most sophisticated equipment in the US inventory including the F-14 Tomcat Fighter and the DD993 modified Spruance Class destroyer. The F-14 system is so complicated that the United States Navy is having major difficulty keeping it operational." It added, "Most informed observers feel that Iran will not be able to absorb and operate within the next five to ten years a large proportion of the sophisticated military systems purchased from the US unless increasing numbers of American personnel go to Iran in a support capacity. This support, alone, may not be sufficient to guarantee success for the Iranian program." The report noted that sales of military equipment had amounted to $10.4 billion between 1972–1976, making Iran the largest single purchaser of US arms, and added that the twenty-four thousand US citizens currently working in Iran could easily rise to between fifty and sixty thousand by 1980.[19]

AMERICANS IN IRAN: THE CLASH OF CIVILIZATIONS?

Anxiety over the increasing intensity of relations with the United States and the presence of American personnel was not limited to the US State Department. Iranians were similarly registering concern over the implications of an increased technical presence, although a report commissioned by the US Embassy in 1976, in which they interviewed twenty-six middle and upper-middle class Iranians, most of whom occupied prominent positions as opinion-makers. The report concluded that, "Concern over the increasing foreign presence seems to be growing slightly among perceptive Iranians, but there are no serious immediate problems." It noted that, "Lower class Iranians care little about the American presence but fear and dislike the Indians and Asians who have flocked to Iran in response the Persian economic boom."

Despite the overall sense of reassurance, the intellectual elite, who should have been well disposed to the Americans, were expressing a growing disdain for them. Moreover, American workers, not culturally attuned to Iran, amplified the impact of a community that was relatively slight in 1976. A number of respondents believed that the US presence was at least double the actual figure, and almost all argued that they could spot an American (as opposed to a European) from his or her appearance alone.

One interviewee observed that there were at least thirty thousand Americans in Iran and that he understood there would be some fifty thousand additional families arriving in the next three years. He added that he could, "always tell a foreigner, and particularly an American. He said this is particularly true when he sees an American from the rear. 'You can tell by the hair cut and can tell by the cut of his pants,' he said. He explained that an American's pants look loose and sloppy in the seat because they don't wear them high enough. He also said he and his friends find American apparel very unattractive, particularly the loud clothing many Americans effect, such as bright green shirts, red pants, white shoes, and red socks. He termed American attire 'grotesque.'"

The interviewee complained about the lack of country orientation among US employees and the ease with which many of them boasted about their large salaries. "Educated Iranians react negatively to this and feel that these clumsy and bumptious people with minimal professional standing can't possibly be worth what they are getting." The picture being painted, however politely (although the language became increasingly intemperate), was of a dysfunctional expatriate community, with unhappy families drawn to Iran for the purpose of making a "fast buck." Despite all this, it was apparently the driving that most energized the following interviewee:

"He launched into a very strong diatribe about American drivers. He said Iranians realise that they themselves break all the rules in the book when they get on the highways and streets of Tehran. 'But,' he said, 'this is our country.' He said many Americans, after they're here for a while, 'drive worse than we do. They go through stop lights, they cross dividing lines and their driving gives us a very strong feeling that they just consider us as peasants.' Many times, [he] said, 'my friends have pulled down the window and yelled, 'look, this is my country; you can't drive that way and cut me off that way.' . . . 'The basic feeling,' he said, 'is that this American son of a bitch is doing well and living well in my country and not bringing anything to the country and now he is driving all over me.' . . . Further on driving, he said that foreign women are terribly aggressive behind the wheel."

As if this weren't enough, "The presence of Americans in public places is a problem," specifically supermarkets. "'Supermarkets are hotbeds of antagonisms,' [he] noted. He said foreigners have caused prices to skyrocket in the supermarkets and that when Americans go through a supermarket they clean out everything 'like locusts.' When the Iranians get there to shop, there is nothing left. He pointed out that he is not absolutely sure this is true, 'but what is significant is that people believe it.'" Interestingly, he distinguished the Americans from the Europeans, whom he considered had a "very deep and abiding interest" in Iranian culture.

Another interviewee asked, "Why doesn't the company [Westing-house] choose a better type of person? The children all run wild." The bad behavior cited included ten- and eleven-year-olds smoking and drinking in public.

A university professor who had been educated in the United States noted that, "The younger generation feels the presence of the American military here," and that some left-wing students considered American television to be a means of "colonizing" the country. Quite a few seemed to believe that the majority of Americans were members of the CIA. When asked about American driving, he agreed that the Americans had started to pick up the bad driving habits of the Iranians, although Irani-ans were allowed to drive like this whereas foreigners were not. He added that there was a feeling that, "the Americans pick up our bad habits too fast and do not pick up our good habits." When asked what good habits Americans could pick up from Iranians, the professor paused and sug-gested, "Well, our over-politeness." He added that, "when tea is served in offices and other locations, the host expects the guest to accept the first cup but at the same time anticipates that the guest will ask the host to take the first cup. There is this *tarouf* business in any kind of personal in-terchange, [he] said, and in the tea situation the host expects a 'little dia-logue.' [He] also pointed out that a number of Iranians have mentioned to him the very unattractive habit which Americans have of putting their feet on tables. This is strictly prohibited in Iranian culture."

There was a recurring view that with the increase in foreigners, the quality was being diluted such that the majority had now come for work and had little conception that they were entering a different culture. Fric-tion invariably emerged in encounters with less educated workers who were traveling to Iran, be they American or indeed European, although the Americans seemed to have a louder footprint. A journalist in Tehran felt there were positive aspects to the American presence, particularly with the promotion of democratic values, but echoed others in warning against a dramatic increase in numbers, "When asked about he would feel about a tripling of the size of the American community, the journalist looked glum and said that we ought to be very, very careful about this . . . [noting] that Americans really are noticeable and aggressive people and that there could be serious problems." He explained that while Westerners tended to have the self-confidence to absorb foreigners, in Iran there was a greater anxiety for foreigners to understand and respect the culture.

Two other interviewees made the astute observation that most Iranians had expected that development would result in a diminishing US presence but found to their surprise that the acquisition of high-tech military equipment made them more dependent on a growing American presence. "Both men saw this development as a serious problem in Iran-US relations, because Iranians had generally expected their dependence on foreigners to decrease gradually over the years. If this did not in fact take place, it would lead to serious frustration and then to increased xenophobia focused particularly on the US."

Almost all, the respondents rejected the notion that Americans should live in separate compounds, arguing that a culturally sensitive integration was the best option for all concerned. They nonetheless raised the issue of higher rents, although a number emphasized that this reflected the limited supply of housing rather than American extravagance, which existed on account of their higher salaries. This perception of higher salaries also extended to Iranians educated in the United States, much to the irritation of their European educated compatriots. A majority of the interviewees were familiar with the West, and the United States in particular, and one US diplomat considered their views tempered by their familiarity and sympathy for the West, and wondered aloud whether the exercise was worthwhile. His own comment was "that most of this society remains highly traditional, rather deeply religious and somewhat xenophobic." This view was not borne out by a street cleaner who could not understand the fuss about foreigners and was more concerned about the better tips provided by Americans.

Similarly, a restaurant owner could barely generate the enthusiasm to talk about where foreigners lived only noting that, "He personally would not mind some more foreigners moving in, especially if they like to eat out." Some felt that few lower-class Iranians were bothered about foreigners because they rarely came into contact with them and that growing resentment was a middle-class problem. Moreover, a growing sense of national self-confidence meant that even professional Iranians most sympathetic to foreigners were becoming less tolerant of their idiosyncrasies. However, others maintained that the problem arose from perceptions among the lower and lower-middle classes—the absence of direct contact encouraged xenophobic tensions because there was no way to test a prejudice against the reality of engagement.

Dramatic changes in Iranian society, particularly the rise of political consciousness and intellectual vitality, were creating a heightened sense of cultural insularity and a rising mood of national self-confidence. As the Embassy summary astutely concluded, "Perhaps the most important observation is that in a period of increasing urban frustrations and rising foreign presence, it is more than ever necessary that we send culturally sensitive and mature Americans here."[20]

REVOLUTIONARY MYTHS

The events of 1953 were a foundational moment in the construction of US-Iranian relations and transferred Iranian suspicions from the historic Anglo-Russian axis towards the Americans. The events of 1979 crystallized this tradition. The revolution of 1979 bound Iran and the United States in an intimate ideological relationship, defined by a collective and shared traumatic experience. The political hysteria that characterized British reactions to Iran in 1951 and perplexed their American interlocutors would now affect the Americans in a more intense and socialized manner.

The cultural consequences of engagement were to prove all too reciprocal—it was not only bad driving habits that the Americans were to acquire—and the intensity of the relationship was a consequence not only of the growing intimacy of the relationship but, crucially, further developments in the mass media. The Islamic Revolution and the hostage crisis that followed were televised events reaching a mass audience. The American public, and the international community, were not shielded from these events by diplomats and elites. This was no longer a local difficulty in a distant land that could be contained or ignored (as the Tsar had done in 1829). This was a matter of immediate domestic importance made all the more real by the presence of ordinary Iranians and Americans in each other's countries.

This was a popular and democratic encounter, and the masses on both sides were unlikely to be swayed by the rationalizations of their professional elites. Moreover, neither side was willing to be influenced by the restraints of the international community. Iran was in the throes of a revolution that rejected the international order as an unjust means of oppression. Like the French Revolution, it sought to reorganize the international order in its own image, liberating the oppressed through an export of its revolutionary ideals.

The United States, startled by its characterization as the villain, struggled to contain the consequences of revolution, but its failure to constructively engage with revolutionary Iran resulted in its appropriation of the means and methods of its antagonist. This transformation—a paradoxical process of political divergence and cultural convergence—is fundamental to an understanding of US-Iran relations since 1979. Crucially it handed Iran the initiative by allowing Iranian politicians to define the methodology of engagement. If US policymakers have consequently found Iran incomprehensible, it is largely because they have had to operate in an environment defined by their opponents. At the same time, and with no little irony, America's gradual acquisition of a revolutionary sensibility from Iran has been matched by a divergent process in Iran, by which the turmoil of the revolution is being incrementally replaced by rationalization and order. For the harbingers of this trend within Iran, America's steady rediscovery of its revolutionary heritage and mission has proved similarly startling and incomprehensible.

The popular nature of America's encounter with Iran's revolution and the amplification provided by the presence of the mass media ensured the mutual entrenchment of the mythology of the revolution. For adherents to Iran's revolutionary ideology, the Islamic Revolution indicates a definitive break with the past, defined by the termination of relations with the United States. This termination is defined by the seizure of the US embassy in November 1979. And the seizure is interpreted in a context of more than one hundred fifty years of foreign interference in the country, particularly the involvement of the US in the overthrow of Mosaddeq in 1953. Although the seizure of the embassy was a defining moment, it remains part of a wider process and is not regarded as an important event in itself by Iranian revolutionaries. Thus in the popular revolutionary conception, the break in diplomatic relations between Iran and the United States is divorced from the reality of the hostage taking, and instead interpreted as a natural consequence of the fact that the United States could not relate to Iran's Islamic Revolution. There is therefore a structurally determined revolutionary logic within which the embassy seizure is situated but for which it bears no responsibility.

For the Americans, on the other hand, the embassy seizure was the defining moment and the cause of the collapse in relations. Such was the sense of humiliation of the 444-day hostage crisis, broadcast nightly on US television, that in the popular conception the hostage crisis marked a definitive break with the past, much as it did for the Iranian revolutionaries. What distinguished the two interpretations was that the Iranians regarded it as an act of closure, while the Americans marked it as the beginning of an era. The crisis was also seen as a personal betrayal mirroring what Iranian political activists felt in 1953. Moreover, the immediate shock of the revolution and the need to absolve anyone of responsibility were such that, much like the revolutionaries in Tehran, the events of 1978–1979 were seen as extraordinary and unpredictable—characteristics soon to be applied to Iranians as a whole. In this way, both the revolutionaries and their victims became wedded to the idea that the revolution was unique and unforeseen, a product of forces that could not be analyzed.[21]

The reality was different from the mythology. First, there was more continuity than the perception of change would have us believe, and the processes just outlined took time to take shape. America did not sever relations with the Islamic Republic until nearly a year after the overthrow of the Shah, seeking instead to carefully manage the transition. Moreover, America's encounter with revolutionary Iran was initially a Democratic experience, and it took the events of Iran-Contra to transform it into a bipartisan affair that ruptured the intimate relationship between the elites. Recently released documents give lie to the popular conviction that the revolution was unforeseen. Politicians, anxious to pursue a particular agenda and reassured by elite ties, may have been selective in their reading of the evidence, but diplomats reported evidence of problems. Although revolutions by their nature preclude definitive prediction, it is remarkable how accurate many political assessments were about the nature of Iranian society and the impact of the Shah's style of rule.

As early as 1961, a State Department assessment noted that, "Persians tend to follow blindly a man who has convinced them that he is on the side of right, without examining political issues critically. Since members of the urban middle class have deep aggressive drives against the traditional ruling classes and the Westerner, it is natural to associate a saintly leader with opposition to these two forces. All the ingredients are present for what we would call demagogic politics directed against them as scapegoats and as evil forces."[22] The imposition of Ali Amini as Prime Minister and the launch of the White Revolution was intended to preempt and prevent such a development. By the time of the Shah's coronation in 1967, the threat of political instability had evaporated and the Shah himself had discovered a new vigor in his leadership of the country. British ambassadors who had been resolutely skeptical of the Shah's ability to lead were gradually being won over. Sir Denis Wright, in his valedictory despatch, conceded that he may have been too harsh in his earlier assessment of the Shah's abilities, although he warned that he could not "help fearing that over-confidence may yet cause him to take some ill-considered and damaging step."[23]

Indeed, in the next few years, British assessments of the internal situation hinged on the Shah's ability to extricate himself from his self-imposed paradox of power by which his increasing self-reliance was preventing the emergence of a competent administrative and political class, which was in turn encouraging him to concentrate more power in his own hands. Moreover, the assessments, which were undoubtedly shared with the Americans,[24] recognized the growth of disenchantment among students, the Left, and the religious classes, whose leader was Ayatollah Khomeini. (The view that Khomeini was an irrelevancy by this stage, put forward by monarchists, is not sustained by the evidence provided by these assess-

ments, which also indicate that SAVAK was well aware of the problem.)
More interesting was the assessment of the middle and professional classes,
who were not considered to be averse to the possibility of change, especially if they could be personally insured against disaster by the existence
of a European bank account. As a British diplomat noted:

"The one characteristic which all the groups seem to possess is that
they are anti-Western, particularly anti-American and anti-British because these Governments are today the most obvious supporters of the
Shah's regime. They are anti-American also because of the Vietnam War
(which is widely covered in the Iranian press and television), for they see
Vietnam as the exemplary anti-colonialist struggle in the cause of national unity and identity. They look forward to the day when a similar
struggle, for social and political justice, and for an end to the Shah's dictatorship, starts in Iran."[25]

Although diplomats tended to err on the side of stability, the fear of
revolution and its potential consequences remained. As Ambassador
Ramsbotham argued:

"This is not to say that conditions in Iran will develop to a revolutionary situation in the next six years; there are probably enough checks and
balances to make for orderly change under the Monarchy, if the Shah can
meet the problem of the expanding intelligentsia with a flexible mind of
his own. Meanwhile the Shah is sitting on a safety valve of political and
social expression: he realises this, albeit grudgingly, but does not know
how to get off. His son might weigh too little to hold down the pressure
from below, particularly if the change of Monarchy came about by the violence of assassination with all its emotive force. All I would wish to say
at the present time is that the dangers could be more acute for the
Monarch in five or six years time than they are in the shorter term."

Commenting on this assessment, a Foreign Official noted: "The longer
he [the Shah] waits, the greater the head of revolutionary steam he is
holding down. Six years in modern terms may seem a long time; but we
should bear in mind that by 1978 we shall just about complete delivery
of the 800 Chieftains, plus whatever other sophisticated weapons the
Shah may order (including perhaps a gun and ammunition factory). All
this equipment *could* be in the hands of a revolutionary government."[26]

This assessment of the potential difficulties ahead proved remarkably prescient, all the more so because it predated some of the Shah's more flamboyant political gestures. These were to make him even more isolated from his people and impervious to constructive critiques. As one Foreign Office official concluded from a discussion in 1972 of whether the Shah should be warned of the dangers around him, "If . . . we thought that there was any real possibility of persuading the Imperial leopard to change his spots we should need to balance the present risks of trying to warn the Shah against the future risks of being caught up in an explosion against him. . . . However there is no real chance of our being able to persuade the Shah to act against his wishes. We can therefore only continue to hope that a combination of increasing material well being, and the all pervading scrutiny of the security forces, will be sufficient to keep the situation under control until the time comes for the Shah peacefully to yield power up to his successors (monarchical or otherwise)."[27]

Increasingly impervious to critique, the Shah was also highly sensitive to criticism. A large part of the reason why the British and the Americans desisted from proffering advice was the recognition that the Shah would regard this as interference in the domestic politics of Iran and contrary to the impression of independence he wanted to convey. Political necessity as well as blindness brought on by the excesses of commercial gain ensured that by the end of the 1970s, economic interests relegated political interests to a poor second place. This was reflected even in the composition of the embassies, where commercial secretaries and military attaches were privileged over political officers. It is remarkable, for instance, that of the fourteen hundred staff at the US embassy as of July 1978, some twelve hundred were in the Army Mission–Military Assistance Advisory group (ARMISH/MAAG).[28]

At the same time, the increasing centralization of power in the Shah's hands and his sensitivity to foreign interference meant that independent assessments of the political situation were difficult, and the Shah insisted that the only medium of communication should be the state security services, and more particularly himself. By December 1977, when the Shah welcomed Carter, the new Democratic US president, to celebrate the New Year with him in Tehran, the Shah was comfortable in his autocracy.

Carter's visit signified that his much heralded ethical foreign policy, in which human rights was to feature heavily, did not appear to extend to the Shah. On the contrary, Carter had concluded that despite the persistent evidence of abuses and torture (in which the United States was generally considered to be implicated),[29] the region held no good alternatives to the Shah. In short, the Republican legacy was to ensure that the Democrats had no option other than to back the Shah, an exercise in political integration that was as complete as it was unnerving.

Nonetheless, as early as 1975, the Shah had inaugurated a period of gradual liberalization, experimenting with free discussion and debate within the strict parameters of the *Rastakhiz* party. It was a florid affair, more symbol than substance, that convinced few and was then overtaken by the Shah's resolute determination to reshape Iran in his own idiosyncratic image. Most worrying for traditionalists was his sudden imposition of the Imperial Calendar by decree, whereby Iranians found themselves overnight in a year dated to the foundation of the ancient Persian Empire (2535). It confirmed the fears of growing megalomania attested to in earlier reports. Still, it was better to indulge the imperial ego than to confront it.

The Shah had been invited to Washington in November 1977 (where the tear gas used to disperse demonstrators had resulted in the indignity of the President and his Imperial guests wiping away tears in the full glare of television), and now Carter was returning the compliment by spending New Year's Eve in Tehran. It was into such an environment of political reaffirmation that President Carter made his now notorious toast: "Iran, under the great leadership of the Shah [was] an island of stability in one of the more troubled areas of the world." This, the President added, was a great tribute the Shah's leadership, and to "the respect, admiration, and love which your people give to you."[30]

DIVORCE

Unfortunately, the Shah was increasingly sensitive to the criticisms of those of his people who refused to give the love to which President Carter alluded. With Carter's effusive praise lingering in the Shah's ears, providing him with renewed confidence, he decided to deal with the turbulent priest who had been causing him periodic trouble since 1963. Ayatollah Khomeini had been dispatched into exile in 1964 following his outspoken criticism of the Status of Forces agreement, which he had argued was akin to the reestablishment of the system of capitulations, so despised by Iranian nationalists. His political coming of age can be seen to have been defined against the United States, reinforcing trends established by the 1953 coup.

Having spent a short time in Turkey, Khomeini relocated to Najaf in Iraq, where he established his own school and maintained close contact with the opposition in Iran. Decried by the Shah as a reactionary, Khomeini was likewise lambasted by his fellow Ayatollahs for being too progressive and deigning to teach such dubious subjects as philosophy, including courses on Western philosophy, if for nothing else but to critique it. One of his earliest works was a stringent Islamic critique of Darwin's theory of evolution, a target of theological scrutiny that would not be out of place in some parts of contemporary America. He was also not averse to using technology and argued against the notion that Islam was against scientific progress, emphasizing that Islam, properly understood, provided the ethical basis for scientific investigation.

These unorthodox views, which reflected the intellectual legacy of such eclectic Islamic modernists as the nineteenth-century Iranian thinker Jamal al Din al Afghani, made Khomeini popular with the disenchanted young. Indeed, Khomeini showed himself to be a superior political tactician. He was anxious to maintain a following among the student body and was well versed in the writings of dissident thinkers such as Ali Shariati, who had sought to revolutionize Shia thought and make it a tool of political action, and Jalal Ale Ahmad, the author of the widely read *Gharbzadegi* (*Westoxication*), which berated the Iranian public for "Aping a tribe of foreigners, with unfamiliar customs and culture which has no roots in our own cultural environment."[31]

As the Shah continued to centralize power in his own hands and closed off possible avenues for dissent, the obstreperous Khomeini became the focus of dissidents anxious for some direction and leadership, having been disappointed and dispirited by the political class at home. Khomeini's ability to appeal to both traditionalists and the progressive young was dismissed by the Shah, who found it inconceivable that such an apparent anachronism could have any appeal to idealistic youth. Diplomatic reports indicated that some Western observers were not convinced by the blanket label of "reactionary" afforded to Khomeini by Savak.[32] Nonetheless, the Shah decided in January 1978 that it was time to deal with Khomeini. As a riposte to Khomeini's latest critical sermon, the Shah sanctioned a scurrilous opinion piece in the Persian newspaper *Etelaat* in which the aging Ayatollah was characterized as a British stooge of dubious Indian parentage. These insinuations aside, much of the piece involved a dull reiteration of the imperial vision, which left few doubts as to the source. Taken in isolation, it was a pointless exercise.

It says much of the powder keg of late 1970s Iran that the piece ignited a torrent of indignation and anger among Ayatollah Khomeini's followers. Some had been preparing for a moment just as this, and observers noted that discipline among the "mob" remained tight, with little indiscriminate looting and the targeting of specific government buildings. Demonstrations and riots broke out in both Qom and Tabriz, which the government was ill-prepared to contain, sending in Chieftain tanks where riot control was needed. The American Consul in Tabriz noted that the riots were largely religiously motivated—with antimonarchical chants and attacks on women who were not sufficiently modest—but with no indication of anti-Western sentiment apart from a brief attempt by the crowd to attack some Western residences.[33] By early summer, however, anti-Americanism was becoming an essential part of the opposition strategy, with a view to scaring American workers away and undermining what was widely considered to be a central pillar of the monarchical regime. As the Consul in Isfahan noted:

"The city, and particularly the American Community, has been filled with rumors. . . . None of these rumors had any basis in fact, and those that were traceable always came from Iranian (unidentifiable) sources. It appeared that someone was deliberately attempting to panic the Americans with these rumors. Finally, the security officer of one company received a call he took to be from SAVAK informing him that two women had been pulled from their car, stripped naked and photographed, and instructing him to issue a security bulletin to his employees telling all women to stay indoors. He did this, without checking the story, and this official bulletin was enough to make several American families flee from Isfahan, and many more request immediate transfers from the area. One University source reported that a pamphlet passed among students had commended their success in frightening Americans, and urged them to continue to spread rumors, but this is not confirmed. . . . Finally, I have one report that the mullah at the Husseinabad Mosque, and at least four other mullahs, have begun inserting inflammatory anti-foreign and anti-American rhetoric into already anti-Shah sermons."[34]

Further riots developed in Isfahan and Shiraz, where the government response was so poor that some Iranians conjectured that the riots were deliberately fomented to allow the government to instigate a nationwide crackdown without eliciting criticism from human rights organizations abroad. The government's inability to cope with the gathering demonstrations increased anxiety among the majority of Iranians, who were at best antagonistic and at worst indifferent to the religious character of the protests. According to the Consul in Shiraz, "There is widespread puzzlement in the face of what appears to be government vacillation, between tolerance for dissenting views and oppression. No matter that ambivalence not infrequently characterises the critics themselves, they find it an enigma in their government."[35] Having cultivated the image of a dictator in full control of his country's destiny, the Shah's inability to fulfil his autocratic promise was perplexing domestic opponents and foreign allies alike.

The Emperor of Oil was running on empty, and although his opponents at home and abroad rejoiced, his allies were concerned. As early as April 1978, General Pakravan, a former deputy head of SAVAK, urged US diplomats to take a more proactive role in advising the Shah because it was clear that he refused to take council from Iranians. "The point of his entire discussion was his plea that I convey the need for the USG or respected American nongovernment leaders (he mentioned David Rockefeller) to actively pursue an advisory role with the Shah. . . . He said he was hoping I would convey his suggestion to the Ambassador because he felt that the US was in the best position to give statesmanlike advice to the Shah which would be well received."[36]

Throughout the summer, as the demonstrations gathered momentum and broadened their base in Iranian society, decisive leadership from the Shah was markedly absent, contrasting unfavorably in the public imagination with the stubborn resistance to any form of compromise exhibited by Khomeini. By November 1978, concern was giving way to urgency because troops had fired on crowds demonstrating in Tehran, and the Shah seemed to be losing control over the situation. Although the Shah had conceded to regular consultations with the British and American ambassadors, this had not resulted in bold or imaginative leadership. On the contrary, it confirmed the belief that he was becoming dangerously ineffective. "So far the Shah cannot see beyond half measures designed to defer hard decisions. . . . His reversion to the moods of depression and vacillation he displayed in the early 1950s makes it doubtful that he can move to salvage what remains of national unity, unless others intervene on his behalf."[37]

The report concluded that, "If the Shah does not make a dramatic move before the beginning of the month of Moharram on December 2, far more serious violence is a certainty," adding that the only possible solution would be the seizure of power by the military. The best-case scenario of the Shah continuing as a constitutional monarch was now recognized as impossible, and preparations were being made for an abdication—or the total collapse of the regime. There was still reluctance to acknowledge that a smooth transition of power could not be managed. Although diplomats admitted that a military crackdown would damage US prestige, they believed there was the possibility that a vestige of the enormous commercial and military investment in Iran could be salvaged (to say nothing of political and personal ties). Unfortunately, by the end of 1978, the level of the social revolt was so high that all options were unsavory, a prospect that another close, if discreet, ally was observing with deep apprehension. "Like the rest of us, Israelis have watched with awful fascination Iran's progression to the lower depths. They believe the friendly and staunchly pro-West regime of the Shah has crumbled beyond repair and await with foreboding its successor. Few doubt that the next government, whoever its leader . . . will terminate most, if not all, aspects of the carefully constructed and close Israeli-Iranian relationship."[38] The Israelis were critical of US policy towards the Shah, arguing that Washington should have moved more quickly to support him, and that the fall of Iran served as an illustration that, "Israel cannot in the final analysis depend on Washington."

The truth was that the author of the revolution was the Shah himself—not so much because of what he did but as a consequence of a fatal inaction and inability to lead at the critical juncture when leadership was most earnestly required. Earlier British assessments correctly judged the Shah's incapacity for decisive leadership, though most were convinced of the Shah's reinvention of himself as omnipotent and in control and consequently all the more struck by his inability to act. Some US officials were further taken aback by the Shah's apparent yearning for US encouragement, a position of responsibility they neither wanted nor considered suitable. One military assessment made after the fall of the Shah and the return of Khomeini asked the question that has yet to receive a definitive answer, "Why did the Shah withdraw from active leadership?"[39]

The dramatic collapse of the Pahlavi monarchy and the enormity of the social revolt that had coalesced under the leadership of Khomeini were matters of deep reflection for US officials who agonized over how America "lost" Iran. The answer to this question is not as mysterious or difficult as some analysts would have us believe. As the diplomatic assessments have indicated, there were clear, early signs that problems were likely. The British assessments, undoubtedly shared with the Americans, were relatively accurate in their prediction of when trouble might emerge. The key unknown was the behavior of the Shah himself, but history suggested that he was not the decisive leader he sought to present himself as. Furthermore, it is increasingly apparent that political and commercial expediency, epitomized by the intimacy of elite connections, clouded judgements, and ensured that more critical diplomatic assessments were marginalized.

The embarrassment of the fall of the Shah was not shared by everyone. Outside the elites, many ordinary Westerners rejoiced as much as the revolutionaries in Iran at the failure of imperialism. In some quarters, hopes ran high for a transition to secular democracy, a view promoted by many left-wing activists in Iran. Furthermore, divisions existed even among the elites. Republicans considered the failure to be a Democratic one, specifically due to the woolly liberalism of Carter. Democrats laid the blame squarely on the Nixon administration's blind support of the Shah. The myth of the revolution and the loss of Iran were part of the domestic political agenda from the beginning and served as an object of discussion between Western intellectuals. Iran was rarely understood on its own foreign policy merits.

The groups in the US who were blaming each other then turned to blame the most satisfactory opponent, the Iranians, who were said to have lost all sense of rational perspective. (The Shah, the one with the most responsibility, was still technically an ally.) The extension of this absurd analysis from the particular to the general, from specific revolutionaries to the entire population, had profound implications for policy making, inasmuch as there is no point in negotiating with an irrational interlocutor. These views, normally considered ideological but now often characterized as group think, reinforced prejudices that had been long in gestation—the cunning Persian who could not be trusted—and were reflected in the belief in some quarters that the Shah had been attempting to change this mentality but had now obviously failed.[40] The evidence existed, but conclusions are reached on what we choose to see. And often what we choose to see supports our preconceptions, even if they are misconceptions. Unwilling to reassess our mistakes or to assume responsibility, it is easy to ascribe blame to the "other," and the more incomprehensible the "other," the better.

Thus it was that at the foundation of the revolution, the Americans acquired the very belief in the irrational "other" that they had long accused the Iranians of holding. These views were reinforced by fleeing expatriates, in the first instance part of the Pahlavi elite, who likewise absolved themselves of guilt by confirming the medieval incomprehensibility of their compatriots and reaffirmed their distinctiveness by defining themselves as (civilized) Persians, in stark contrast to the (fanatical) Iranians who inhabited Iran.

We should not forget that in the West, the history of the Islamic revolution was written by the victims, and they had to justify failure. Likewise, the revolutionaries turned to Divine Providence to explain their success. At this moment, therefore, two distinct myths emerged, fuelled by the trauma of a shared experience and amplified by the existence of a hungry mass media eager to disseminate images of the world's first televised revolution. What was most striking at this stage was the extraordinary polarization of each perspective, such that neither side could countenance the other. This process of distinction, which took time to crystallize, was assisted and encouraged by the hostage crisis and the experience of the Iran-Iraq war. It was also facilitated by the determination of Iran's revolutionaries to look the part—the French Revolutionary *sans culottes* of their age—and by the emergence of a new leader, Ayatollah Khomeini. For an age increasingly defined by images, Khomeini looked the part. Although some initially conjectured that he would soon be regarded as a saint, as the brutality of the revolution took shape on our television screens and religious nationalism overtook secular liberalism and the Left, Khomeini easily filled the void vacated so ignominiously by the Shah. The Shah was now seen as a paper dictator, a humble precursor to the real thing: Khomeini was a medieval theocrat, irrationality personified.

TOWARDS THE HOSTAGE CRISIS

As Westerners struggled to come to terms with a new and unfamiliar lexicon, both visual and semantic (what is an Ayatollah exactly?), and conveniently pigeon-holed that which they did not understand, the reality unfolding was more complex and bewildering than many would have liked to accept. The revolutionary overthrow of an autocratic and centralized system is rarely smooth, frequently anarchic, and no less frantic for those who inhabit the maelstrom as for those who seek to make sense of it all from the outside. American diplomats, who sought to manage the change they were witnessing, were aware that they were not simply observers (as Shuster had comfortably been) but part of the unfolding drama and, in the eyes of many youthful revolutionaries, part of the problem.

Almost as soon as Khomeini had returned, activists sought to vent their displeasure at the foreign presence in Iran by occupying a number of embassies. One of the first, occupied on Valentine's Day 1979, was the US embassy. As a US official recounted:

"1120 receive call from Gast, Embassy under attack. I call Adm Habibollah and ask for help—also Khomeini police station. 11:45 Gast calls back, 'Embassy overrun, we've surrendered.' Yazdi and Khomeini forces arrive and talk guerillas into surrendering prisoners who are taken to Khomeini headquarters for questioning. Guerillas claim to be Marxist; Fedayen. Claim to be looking for SAVAK members and records at US embassy. All Embassy/Milpers returned to embassy in late afternoon."[41]

Meanwhile, in Tabriz, the consul explained that, "The Consulate has been placed under religious seal as a place not to be looted or burned, which is something I would love to see discussed in the Protocol Office. Frustrated looters and loiterers have been coming up to the main gate ever since, reading the proclamation and wandering away, presumably to return another day." Return they did, and the Consulate and its staff were subjected to looting and arrest in what proved a chaotic dry run for the events that would take place in November in Tehran. Finally, after much confusion and harassment:

"Within a surprisingly short time (perhaps two or three hours) a Dr Ragai'i arrived from the Committee Headquarters, explaining that he had been ordered by Tehran to investigate the situation. He took almost immediate action, changing the guard detachment and giving the new guards a long lecture about Khomeini's instructions viz-a-viz foreigners, diplomats, et al, and the consequences if anything were to happen to us. The result was a perceptible change in the atmosphere. Dr Ragai'i came back to the Consulate some hours later and explained that arrangements had been made for a plane to take us to Tehran the next day."[42]

Significantly, in both cases, the religious authorities as well as the Provisional Government were instrumental in ending the diplomatic confrontation, removing the activists, and releasing the diplomatic staff concerned, which in Tehran included Ambassador Sullivan along with seventy diplomatic staff and twenty US marines. The experience of Tabriz and that of the Moroccan embassy—the Shah was temporarily residing in Morocco—should have been a warning of dangers to come. Certainly the Shah's Western allies were wary of playing host. The United Kingdom's new Prime Minister, Margaret Thatcher, refused the Shah's request to visit, given the danger this might pose to British diplomatic staff.

Nevertheless, it would be erroneous to suggest that 1979 was a period of unremitting turmoil for foreign residents. The various forces that had brought about the downfall of the Shah were still jockeying for power, and the target at this stage remained Iranians, agents of the previous regime, and any rival for power. An embassy report issued in June 1979 noted that while the US presence had been dramatically reduced—from an estimated forty-five thousand to a few hundred businessmen—many foreign firms were returning to Iran to continue with contractual work where possible, and that although incidences of harassment of US employees and businessmen were increasing, "many US businessmen have continued their work or returned permanently or periodically without incident."[43] The prevailing mood was that the dust was beginning to settle, and that a pattern of government was being gradually restored. Even another partial occupation of the embassy compound in August had been resolved by the arrival of the Revolutionary Guard, who removed the individual involved.[44]

As early as June 1979, US diplomats in Tehran hoped that the transition could be effectively managed, but this could be achieved only by public recognition that the revolution was a reality that the United States accepted. In fact, US officials had rejected repeated requests by opponents of the revolutionary regime for US assistance in the destabilization of the revolution, recognizing that, "It would be contrary to US policy [to] interfere in Iran's internal affairs . . . in the aftermath of Vietnam and Watergate foreign adventures simply would not be tolerated by the American people."[45] In stark contrast to the popular image of the United States amongst ordinary Iranians, there was a diplomatic push for a more proactive US policy towards the new revolutionary establishment, and as the following recommendation indicates, a desire to find ways in which common ground could be forged and developed. According to a dispatch sent by the Charges D'Affaire of the US Embassy, Bruce Laingen:

"As this Embassy has recommended earlier, we believe we can and should find ways to speak publicly and positively more than we have to date about having accepted the change in Iran. There are two reasons for this; the one obviously to reduce PGOI [Provisional Government of Iran] suspicions about our purposes and the other to remind our own public (only superficially informed in the US press) about our long-term interests in Iran. This is not to say that we need to publicly embrace and endorse Khomeini. . . . What we need to say, in ways that we have not yet done, is that we believe we have long-term interests in Iran that continue and which we believe can be preserved in an Islamic Iran. . . . Specifically, we urge the Department to find ways publicly to say that we wish Iran well in putting its revolutionary objectives into forms and institutions that will command the support of all its people: that the US has no interest in or intention of imposing any regime, monarchy or otherwise, on Iran; that we have an abiding interest in Iran's integrity and independence; that American interests in access to Iranian oil are synonymous with Iranian interests in sustaining and financing its future industrial and agricultural development. We should find opportunities as well to welcome revolutionary Iran's emphasis on Islam and its spiritual contribution to society as something that Americans understand and respect, given the way in which American's also see things of the spirit as important to human endeavour."[46]

This was a remarkable recommendation and one that regrettably was not acted upon. As Laingen's missive indicates, the US position had been largely one of wait and see: observe, collate, and analyze but maintain a discrete presence, in the possible expectation that the revolutionary government would fall and the US would then have an opportunity, on the back of opposition forces, to act, and act decisively. Laingen's comments reveal a sense of frustration with this inactivity and a realization that the United States could not be a passive player in Iran but had to take the position that it accepted the transition. There was much room for disagreement with the new government, but there was also much scope for improvement, especially if the provisional government headed by the moderate Prime Minister Mehdi Bazargan could consolidate its position in the face of immense pressures from radicals on either side of the political spectrum. As such, getting the fundamental structure of the new policy in place was important.

Political pressures in Washington, however, were making such a stance difficult. The old elite was battling to avoid such a public recognition, reinforced as they were by a stream of Pahlavi exiles, and convinced of the temporary nature of current developments. Indeed, the pressure had been effective enough that President Carter, in contrast to the British, relented and allowed the Shah into the United States for medical treatment. This was the decent thing to do, but it was not the right thing to do. The US diplomatic staff sitting in Tehran were anxious about the implications of this move for them. For the majority of Iranians, caught up in revolutionary fervor, and particularly the young idealistic activists, their impression of America had been shaped not by the experiences of Vietnam and Watergate but by the experiences of 1953 and the coup against Dr. Mohammad Mosaddeq. The notion, therefore, that the US had a policy of nonintervention in Iran's domestic politics would have been viewed with ridicule and incredulity. Despite the pleas of diplomats on the ground, both sides were guilty of fighting an idealized foe, one defined by 1953 and the other by the Pahlavi elite. The latter were adamant that Khomeini could not last, and it was simply a matter of waiting things out.

With the Shah's arrival in the United States, the dynamics of the equation changed. Some activists, spurred by genuine concern and political opportunism, decided that a blow must be struck against the United States, increasingly characterized as the Great Satan, an effective semantic tool by which Khomeini Islamized Marxist rhetoric against global capitalism and materialism. (In Islamic thought, Satan is temptation personified, and the United States therefore personified the temptations of material culture, the excesses of which were among the great faults of Pahlavi Iran.) Some feared a recurrence of the events of 1953 and were certain that the United States would use all its power to restore the Shah to the throne. Others felt that a symbolic action against the United States would help national unity and terminate a colonial relationship. A new relationship would inaugurate a period of mutual respect because the West only understood force and strength. And only when strength was respected could we begin the discuss the details of international law. After all, where was international law in 1953? In other words, an unfavorable mode of relationship had to be replaced with one that was more balanced. And in the political euphoria characterizing the departure of the

Shah, there seemed no better time to institutionalize the new sense of empowerment. The Capitulations Law of 1964 was already rescinded, so now seemed an opportune moment to wipe off the shame of 1953.[47]

On November 4, 1979, the Charge D'Affaires, Bruce Laingen, was discussing security arrangements at the US embassy with officials at the Iranian Foreign Ministry when word came through that students had invaded and occupied the compound. Few juxtapositions could have seemed so surreal. US officials and the marines guarding the embassy had initially supposed that this was a rerun of the initial seizure on February 14, which a few urgent phone calls would resolve. The British Embassy had similarly been assaulted, but the occupiers had been swiftly removed. On this occasion, however, although the Provisional Government condemned the seizure, the revolutionary organs of power, in particular Ayatollah Khomeini, appeared less anxious to resolve the issue immediately. Moreover, the appearance of guns among the students made it clear to the embassy staff that this was no ordinary sit-in.

Laingen himself was detained in the Foreign Ministry, and the US diplomats settled down to await the negotiations towards a solution. A relatively short sit-in, however unpleasant, might be just the political therapy needed to cure the US-Iran relationship of the malaise that had infected it over the last two decades and provide the means for starting afresh.

The seizure of the embassy, however, was not a managed crisis but instead a reflection of a much deeper problem in Iran's revolutionary body politic. It reflected not only the plurality of Iranian politics but also its inherent fractiousness. The decision to seize the US embassy unified Iran's disparate factions around a suitably grand cause. It is now apparent that there was no master plan to take the US embassy, but that radical students, imbued with the spirit of '68 and encouraged by the legacy of Vietnam, believed that such an action would not only be historic but would satisfy their leader, Ayatollah Khomeini. According to those close to Khomeini, he had not directed the seizure and the students were by no means certain he would be pleased.

The assault, widely televised and publicized, captured the public mood. Differences were set aside as the United States, personified by the diplomatic staff, became the target of popular anger. The United States moved to freeze

Iranian assets and to impose an oil embargo, though curiously Carter did not formally sever diplomatic relations till the April of the following year.

For Khomeini and his supporters, faced with the prospect of a disintegrating polity and all the dangers of a coup or, worse, regional separatism, the value of the developing hostage crisis lay in its capacity to unify the public and focus minds. As such, its immediate value outweighed the long-term implications of what amounted to a blatant transgression of international law. Still, international law was never a priority among the revolutionaries, whose very philosophy decried the application of a system of rules that benefited the oppressor, a philosophy that was amply supported by historical experience. Khomeini echoed this sentiment when he justified the seizure by explaining that diplomatic immunity applied only to those who did not use such privilege for political gain and espionage. Such comments reflected popular Iranian perceptions of foreign embassies from Griboedov in 1829 to the British in 1951–1952 and beyond: that they existed primarily as staging posts for intervention and not as a means to further international understanding.

THE MYTH OF THE HOSTAGE CRISIS

What hope there might have been for a managed transition in relations between the United States and Iran were savagely cut short by the ensuing hostage crisis. The image of US diplomatic staff being led out of the embassy building blindfolded became an enduring motif of the revolution and a tragic emblem of US-Iran relations. It personalized the tragic brutality of the revolution for Americans. This transformation had taken barely a generation and was all the more unfortunate because the individuals onto which two decades of Iranian frustration were unceremoniously heaped were in large part Foreign Service specialists who had volunteered to oversee the transition and who were by and large sympathetic to the social and political demands of the Iranian people.

The seizure of the embassy could have served as a symbolic break with the past, and had it been terminated swiftly, a short hiatus in diplomatic relations could have laid the foundation for a different, more constructive, relationship. Sir Denis Wright, in his valedictory despatch, said as much about the rupture in Anglo-Iranian relations in 1952, which he described as a "blessing in disguise." But times had changed and technology with it. The revolution that confronted the United States was more severe in its domestic consequences and international ambitions, and the United States fulfilled a role both in unifying the fractious body politic and providing Iranians with an enemy worthy of themselves. A great revolution had to be defined against the greatest of powers.

The tragedy of the hostage crisis is that in terminating a type of relationship, it crystallized a particular impression and stopped the process of reengagement. There were to be no more attempts to connect with and understand the revolutionary process. And in targeting diplomats, revolutionary Iran not only alienated the international diplomatic corps but also eliminated the one branch of the US government that was likely to offer a sympathetic and constructive reading of events. With the formal break in diplomatic relations, the United States ceased to have any official presence on the ground in Iran. The complexity of revolution gave way to simplicity, and objective assessment gave way to emotionally charged myth. The sober rationality of the bureaucrat gave way to the emotional excitement of the politician. To paraphrase Tallyrand, it was worse than a crime; it was a mistake. Laingen's recommendations still await implementation.

The relationship that subsequently developed took shape in the absence of the other party. Perception, in the absence of regular reality checks, took on a life of its own, and the ensuing decade of war resulted in the hardening of attitudes. Paradoxically, both the United States and Iran were to become significant players in the domestic politics of the other, in spite of, or perhaps because of, this absence. For hardline revolutionaries, the seizure of the embassy became the second revolution, the moment when the Islamic character of the revolution was consolidated. For the United States, emerging from the uncertainties of the 70s, it was a grave humiliation. For the revolutionaries, it marked a termination, an achievement. For the United States, it marked the beginning of an obsession with Iran, made all the more intense by the intimacy of the previous twenty-five years and the mutual sense of betrayal.

When Sir Denis Wright was sent to reestablish relations in 1954, he remarked that Iran and Britain were like estranged lovers for which reconciliation had to be carefully navigated. In the case of Iran and the United States, emotions ran deeper and were more complex. This was not an estrangement but a particularly bitter divorce.

A very proper nationalist, the elder Mr. B first treated me to a long lecture on how the United States had caused all the trouble in Iran by its long support of the corrupt, thieving, and tyrannical shah. He was also unforgiving of America for overthrowing his uncle, Dr. Mossadeq. After a few hours and few drinks, Mr. B proceeded to another lecture, this time claiming that all the present trouble in Iran was caused by the United States' plotting the revolution which overthrew the Shah. At least under the Shah there had been personal security, he said, and America's lack of support for the Pahlavis had resulted in the present crisis. Realising that America would always be the scapegoat for Mr. B, I made no attempt to point out the paradox in his very Persian logic. Despite America's perfidy, the two elderly Bs are now determined that it is the only country in which they really want to live, and they are trying to convince their only son to come with them.[48]

THE UNITED STATES AND THE ISLAMIC REPUBLIC

*The resurfacing of Shahpur Bakhtiar in Paris and persistent rumours about various Iranian émigrés being actively involved in plots to overthrow the Islamic regime of Ayatollah Khomeini poses a temptation to see in these political exiles the solution to a situation in Iran the US finds distasteful. After all, Americans can identify with Bakhtiar when he speaks (fluently in a Western language) of individual freedom and liberty whereas they are disgusted and incomprehending when Ayatollah [*sic*] Khalkhali (immediately after dispatching another gaggle of Kurds to their fate) proudly describes himself as the Iranian Adolf Eichmann.*[1]

THE SEIZURE OF the US Embassy along with the fifty-two remaining American diplomats was a watershed moment in the history of US-Iran relations, particularly in the way in which the US public perceived Iran and the Iranians. Extending over an agonizing 444 days, the experience burned itself into the popular imagination and became part of the political landscape. Yellow ribbons adorned trees, while television broadcasts amplified the emotive intensity of this particularly personal tragedy. Americans were no longer observing a bloody revolution in a distant land, nor were its bureaucrats preparing for better times ahead. The crisis had come home. It was not possible to think in terms of the objective management of an international and distant crisis, however much the Carter administration sought to present a rational and calm approach. Demands for action and an end to the interminable list of humiliations increased. The failure of the hostage rescue mission, televised in all its horror, with Iran's hanging judge Hojjat-ol Eslam Khalkhali gloating over the burned and charred bodies of US service personnel in the Iranian desert, increased the anguish and desperation of the Carter administration while encouraging the radicals and empowering the revolution. There was nothing like success against the United States to convince the doubters that Khomeini was indeed a providential savior.

Having consolidated his Islamic Republic and having filled the vacuum vacated by the Shah, Ayatollah Khomeini now fulfilled the role of dangerous autocrat far better than his predecessor, especially because he could add religion to the mix. A writer would have struggled to invent such a perfect villain, so alien was the notion of a religious revolution to the largely secular elites of the West. As a Muslim, Khomeini lay beyond the pale of comprehension. Khomeini now became simply the Ayatollah, despite the fact that he was one of many, surrounded by mad *mullahs* and fanatical disciples.

From the Iranian perspective, the seizure of the embassy was not an irrational act. It was justified by decades of oppression and underpinned by the mythology of 1953, and it served a particular political function. The emotive content that may have motivated the action was soon dissipated, and many Iranians simply could not relate to the profound anger the hostage crisis had caused in the United States. More perversely, some even went so far as to question the American "irrationally" that had led them to break off diplomatic relations! For Ayatollah Khomeini, this student initiative ensured that the revolution again had a unity of purpose and allowed the suppression of internal opposition. The Provisional government, in the throes of negotiations with the United States in Algeria regarding economic contracts, was caught by surprise and resigned in protest, effectively handing the radicals the result they wanted. Those ideologically antagonistic to the United States—a position with which

Khomeini was sympathetic—found to their glee that all prospects of rapprochement were now shelved.

The seizure of the embassy was an effective move in tactical terms, but the strategic consequences were less clear. Far from dispatching the Americans, as Mosaddeq had done with the British in 1952, the hostages were *in situ,* in Iran, and a focus of everyone's attention. As the future President Abol Hasan Bani-Sadr complained to Khomeini, "having kicked the Americans out through the front door, we have let them return through the back door." Moreover, by venting their revolutionary frustration against diplomats, the Iranians were alienating the entire diplomatic corps and ensuring a less than sympathetic hearing in the State Department.

The Iranian perspective was that old scores had been settled and now we should all move on. The American public was never going to accept this view, nor the argument that Iranians were directing their ire against governments rather than people and were happy to continue relations with individual Americans and even enquire about visas. The Iranian perception was that governments bore little relation to the people, who were on the whole good and victims like themselves (think back to Maliki's enlightening encounter with working-class Britons). An indication of this view was that "oppressed" black members of the embassy (along with the women) were released early. Khomeini also approved the sending of a priest to celebrate Christmas at the embassy in December 1979. One of the more surreal moments of the hostage crisis occurred when a student guard was overcome with emotion during the service. But such cultural nuances were meaningless, if not altogether hypocritical, especially when the hospitality of the guards left much to be desired. The result in enforcing this political eye for an eye was that both the Iranians and Americans were going blind.

That said, a public can be manipulated, and a certain amount of reiteration and recollection is required for an event to become a memory, and a memory to become a myth. For all the national trauma, the hostage crisis was a Democratic problem rather than an American one. Republican strategists facing an election in 1980 could see an advantage in Carter's difficulties, and while this might be a national tragedy, it was one that Carter had facilitated through a series of political misjudgements. First among these was an apparent failure to sufficiently support the

Shah, an ally. Pressured by members of the Republican elite who had close ties with the Pahlavis, Carter had allowed the Shah in for medical treatment (thus precipitating the crisis in the first place), and the notion that Carter had been insufficiently supportive is not sustained by the evidence. It is true that the Shah felt more comfortable with Republican presidents, but his program of liberalization predated Carter's presidency. In addition, Carter's determination to make human rights a central pillar of his foreign policy had scarcely been applied to Iran.

No one could blame Carter for not wanting to shoulder the responsibility for repressing the revolution. The Shah was, after all, the King of Kings, the Light of the Aryans, and should have been able to handle tough decisions on his own. Nevertheless, Iranians distressed by the religious leanings of the revolution supported the idea that the Democrats, particularly Carter, were responsible. Some argued that the Americans had facilitated the revolution because the Shah had been too soft on the Left and an Islamic Iran would provide a better defense against Soviet expansion. Others wondered why the US had done so little to support the secular elite. The conspirators argued that the Americans had persuaded the Shah to leave the country, a view the Empress Farah apparently supported but one that ignored the fact that the Shah had needed little encouragement to vacate the throne in 1953.[2] What these views shared with those of the revolutionaries was the redirection of blame towards the Americans. The Shah was a hapless puppet, America pulled the strings, and America must be blamed. For the purposes of winning the election of 1980, however, the focus was narrowed to the Democrats—and Carter.

This process was made easier by the Iranians' determination to make Carter suffer. The struggle was defined in increasingly personal terms. Carter had responded to the crisis by severing relations and seizing Iranian assets in the United States. These moves, along with the attempt to rescue the hostages, were interpreted by the revolutionary government as unjustified pressure by a foreign government determined to bring down the revolution. The conviction that the Americans were interfering in the domestic politics of the country and were determined to restore the Shah justified the seizure of the embassy to such an extent that there was no appreciation of the political damage the hostage crisis did to Iran's strategic interests. Iran's seizure of the embassy was therefore interpreted as a pre-emptive self-defense against the interventions of foreigners to which US retaliation was unwarranted. Hence the curious juxtaposition of being both empowered by the act while remaining a victim of US policy. The US seemed impotent and unable to take the initiative. A third party was to come to the rescue of this peculiar political stalemate.

Over the spring and summer of 1980, relations between the fledgling Islamic Republic and Baathist Iraq deteriorated dramatically as the new Iranian ambassador to Baghdad took the undiplomatic position of en-couraging the Iraqi Shias to throw off the shackles of Saddam's rule. The diplomatic approach might be to protest the ambassador's interference in the domestic affairs of another country, reminding him of Iran's justifiable grievance against the United States. Alternatively, one might decide to expel the wayward ambassador. Saddam Hussein, however, had other plans and recognized an opportunity to alter the balance of power in the region.

In considering the start of the Iran-Iraq War in September 1980, rec-ollect that Iran was not simply a revolutionary power but a revolutionary power with an imperial pedigree. Anxieties that the Arab states, and Iraq in particular, might have about Iran's revolution (which Iraq might wel-come in strictly revolutionary terms) were underpinned by a fear of Iran's inherent cultural imperialism, which could easily translate into political hegemony. This fear was cultivated by the Shah, whose megalomania was widely acknowledged and now heightened by the added dimension of a religious struggle.

Saddam Hussein's anxieties were not unjustified, although his response was entirely opportunistic. Many alternatives to war were available, and his carefully planned decision to invade indicated a more deliberate pol-icy than his subsequent protestations implied. It is now generally ac-knowledged that the Iranian embassy hostage crisis was orchestrated by Iraqi intelligence. Members of an Arab Liberation Front, anxious for in-dependence for the oil-rich province of Khuzestan (which they insisted on calling Arabistan[3]), had been recruited by Iraqi intelligence with a view to providing Saddam Hussein with a well-publicized pretext for in-vasion. This invasion, Saddam conjectured, would reverse previous hu-miliations at the hands of the Shah, particularly the Algiers Agreement of

1975 (which had demarcated the international boundary of the Shatt al Arab waterway).

The invasion would also damage an already weakened Iranian state, thus bringing glory to the Iraqi Army and strengthening Iraq, and by extension himself, in the eyes of the Arab world. In military terms, the timing of the invasion made sense because the Iranians were preoccupied with considerable internal bloodletting, the Iranian Army was demoralized, and desertions were widespread. Moreover, Iran relished its new international reputation as a revolutionary power intent on bringing about a new order. Few countries would rush to Iran's assistance at the best of times, and now some looked forward to the prospect of humbling the pride of the Persians. One such country was the United States.

When Saddam Hussein launched his invasion in September 1980, the international community did not react in the way Iranians had anticipated. Rather than an outright condemnation of the invasion, the United Nations Security Council called for an immediate cease-fire and a withdrawal of forces to pre-war borders. According to the British ambassador at the United Nations, Sir Anthony Parsons, who had just left his post in Tehran, the continuing hostage crisis had not won Iran any friends among the world's diplomats.

Iran appeared to rise to the challenge, interpreting its isolation as evidence of the truth of its revolutionary convictions and emblematic of the reactionary nature of the international order. For the majority of Iranians, the onset of war dramatically changed priorities, as internecine struggles and political indifference gave way to a determined national will to resist.[4] A year earlier, the Soviets had been invited into Afghanistan. For those less enamored with the notion of a holy war, what was emerging was a vast national struggle, with the Iranian world under siege. For religious devotees, the assault of the superpowers was proof of the power of a revitalized Islam.

Few Iranians believed that Saddam Hussein would invade Iran on his own initiative, such was their contempt for their Arab neighbor. Iranians felt that an invasion would occur only at the behest of the United States. Although Saddam Hussein received encouragement from Iranian exiles convinced that a military attack would precipitate the collapse of the regime, the decision to invade was his alone. Only subsequently would the United States take the decision to realign and fulfil the prophecy of Iran's revolutionaries. In the meantime, after the failure of successive negotiations, the hostages were finally released moments after the new Republican President, Ronald Reagan, took the oath of office in January 1981. Iran was now locked in a bitter struggle that would shape the next generation of Iranian politicians, but Khomeini had secured his presidential scalp.

WAR, SCANDAL, AND TRAGEDY

The Algiers Accord of 1981, in which the United States agreed not to interfere in the internal affairs of Iran and released some $10 billion of frozen assets, formerly ended relationships between the US and Iran. A tribunal was also established in The Hague to mediate commercial disputes that had arisen. All in all, these developments were meant to effect closure. Yet few regarded this legal process as anything more than a temporary truce. Disagreement persisted over the extent of the assets held by the United States. In addition, the accord was never ratified in the United States, leading some to challenge its legal status. Others, particularly Carter's successors, were contemptuous of Carter's acceptance of the clause on noninterference.

Indeed, with the change in administration came a change in approach. No love was lost between the Republicans and the new Islamic Republic. The Republican elite enjoyed extensive and intimate contact with the now-exiled Pahlavi establishment. The immediate consequence was that Republicans were unwilling to give up on Iran as a nation and as a state, even if the current regime was distasteful. In the early 1980s, many Americans, some in influential political and military posts, felt that Iran was worth saving. The revolution was an anomaly, the Ayatollah was old, and the United States should prepare itself for a reunion. Depending on one's political leanings, the nature of this reunion could be anything from a reshaped relationship, acknowledging the changes that had taken place, to a belief that the Iranians had indulged in a national temper tantrum and would recognize the error of their ways and return to the American fold.

This latter view, which was so wide of the mark, owed more to sentimentality than objective assessment and reflected a Republican contempt for the outgoing administration, on whose shoulders it laid most of the blame for the "loss" of Iran. In a curious, even "orientalist" twist, Iranians were absolved of their responsibility in the revolution, which was the largely the fault of Carter's ineptitude. Apart from disempowering the Iranians (something they remained quite capable of doing themselves), it prevented a thorough and critical analysis of the previous four years, perhaps the most transformative and revealing in recent Iranian history. It was Carter and the Democrats who were responsible for losing Iran, and now a more robust foreign policy, realistic and with a clear idea of friend and foe, would reverse the mistakes of the preceding administration. Unfortunately, little about the Reagan administration's policy towards Iran was clear or coherent. There was a general idea of where America would like to be vis-a-vis Iran but myriad paths led to this ideal scenario. As a result, the US sent contradictory signals to both Iran and her European allies.

The United States publicly denounced the new regime, with whom it had no formal relations, and continued to impose sanctions. Some sanctions, like those of the Europeans, limited of the flow of arms to both Iran and Iraq (although in practice arms sale restrictions to Iraq were more flexible). The US actively engaged the Iranian opposition, especially the monarchist exiles and the son of the late Shah, who was then a resident in the US.

The United States also attacked the growth of Islamic fundamentalism in Iran, while supporting it in Afghanistan against the Soviets, and pronounced against terrorism. This stance bound the US closer to Israel, who, like the United States, had lost a valuable regional ally with the Islamic Revolution. The official ideology of the Islamic Revolution denied the right of existence to the state of Israel, and Iranian propaganda made much of the utopian notion that Baghdad was simply a step on the road to Jerusalem—reiterating the theme that the United States (and Israel) were the villains behind Iraq's invasion.

Like the United States, Israel had an ambivalent attitude towards Iran, having based much of its regional strategy on the assumption of an Iranian (non-Arab) alliance and now playing host to many Iranian Jewish refugees. These exiles, like those who fled to the United States, had little affection for the regime but considerable sympathy for the country. Similarly, the hope was that one day Iran would admit to the error of its ways, recognize geopolitical realities, and return to the fold. One of Israel's first actions on the commencement of the Iran-Iraq War was to strike the Iraqi nuclear facilities at Osirak, the success of which was quietly appreciated by the Iranians.

Israel's second great gambit was less effective in maintaining links. Her invasion of Lebanon in 1982 brought her in direct confrontation with the Shias in the south, a minority who had hitherto enjoyed an un-Islamic ambivalent relationship with the Israelis. The level of Iranian involvement with the Shias in southern Lebanon is disputed, but it would seem that an Iranian presence predated the revolution. Certainly the Shah sought to play a greater leadership role in the Muslim world in the late 1970s, and Shia communities were a target of this strategy. The Shah also viewed Lebanon as a good place to dispatch irritable junior clerics, who could rabble-rouse to their heart's content, away from Iran. How far this policy developed remains unclear, and it would be fair to say that a coherent Iranian strategy in the form of *Hizbollah* (Party of God) did not emerge until after the Israeli invasion in 1982.

Hizbollah was an effective Iranian proxy in the Middle East and, consequently, was to become a bone of contention between the Iranians and the Israelis. As the Israelis withdrew to their safety cordon in southern Lebanon, they became involved in a bitter and debilitating guerrilla war with Hizbollah, the blame for which they increasingly lay at Iran's door. This was a simplification of the issue. Iran was present at the conception and birth of Hizbollah. But as the organization developed and grew in confidence, it took less notice of Iran's directives, despite its cultural and ideological affinities. Like an increasingly distant cousin, Hizbollah tended to choose which orders it would follow from Tehran.

A number of Western analysts adopted the view that Tehran and Hizbollah had a direct relationship. Their position did not do justice to the complex plurality of the revolutionary state, which remained politically dynamic and decentralized as a result of the onset of war and Khomeini's brand of charismatic leadership. There was considerably more local initiative, which might later be supported by the authorities in Tehran, than analysts cared to concede. Because most of their experience had been of the Shah's centralized government, these analysts were unwilling to adapt to the new circumstances. Such views would later be compounded by the surfeit of Sovietologists who would migrate southward following the fall of the Soviet Union.

One crucial consequence of the severance of diplomatic relations was the steady decrease in Iran specialists. As a result, those interested in the Middle East opted for Arabic over Persian, while the experts who remained were often relieved to find themselves assigned to completely different regions. The steady decrease in specialists was compounded by the bureaucratic rationale of rotating staff, such that a foreign service official would rarely stay in one post for more than three years. This was founded on the belief (which continues) that staff must receive the broadest possible experience while avoiding the tendency to "go native."

The fear of staff becoming too sympathetic to their country reached absurd proportions with Iran. Some specialists, having invested considerable personal time and money in becoming acquainted with Iran, were repeatedly assigned to monitor countries so far removed from the Middle East, let alone Iran, that their expertise became pointless. This did not stop officials appointed to Arab countries (or indeed Israel) from going native, which frequently resulted in an even more intensely antithetical perspective on Iran. Rotation meant that, increasingly, staff appointed to deal with Iran viewed it at best as a step along the career ladder and at worst as three lost years, during which the gulf of misunderstanding grew wider. In the Israeli case, the situation was more acute, in that there was no possibility of any Israelis traveling to Iran. (Westerners always had the option of grilling returning businessmen, students, and journalists.)

The identification of Iran with Hizbollah and the obsessive preoccupation with the latter took form in 1983 following the suicide attack on the US Embassy and marine barracks in Beirut. These devastating attacks shattered US confidence in the region and led to the withdrawal of US peacekeeping forces from Lebanon. It marked the first foreign policy crisis of the Reagan administration. As with crises of this nature, it was easier politically to blame the "other," in this case Iran or groups associated with Iran. The attack has traditionally been ascribed to Hizbollah and by extension Iran, but the perpetrators have never been definitively identified and Hizbollah did not claim responsibility.[5]

Although this does not necessarily obviate responsibility, it does mean that the certainty with which blame was allocated is misplaced. It also highlighted an emerging trend in American foreign policy judgements: where ambiguity existed, the balance of consensus concluded that Iran must be in some way responsible. The development of such a conspiratorial mentality among American analysts paradoxically ensured that the absence of evidence effectively convicted Iran and ascribed guilt, in a manner that overturned traditional Western notions of jurisprudence. It is of course impossible to prove a negative. Hawks on both sides of the equation were convinced of the complicity of the "other" in whatever outrage had been perpetrated. The absence of specialists, as noted, accentuated such trends.

In the long term, the consequence of the attacks meant that Israel and the United States now shared an enemy. Empathy abounded, and the Israelis were not going to let this communicative opportunity pass them by. Hizbollah became the *leitmotif* and effective shorthand of Islamic terrorism, such that even the most disparate groups came under its rubric. At the same time, the term became synonymous with Iranian-backed terrorism, which was Shia, revolutionary, and destabilizing. This terrorism was increasingly characterized as fanatical (Islamist) suicide attacks against civilian targets, an impression that effectively collated a series of unrelated events into one emblematic myth.

The truth has always been more complex. The link between Sunni and Shia groups has never been straightforward, and Shias have rarely if ever launched suicide attacks against civilian targets. Moreover, far from being a tactic developed by religious groups, suicide attacks as a form of terrorism may have originated with the Tamil Tigers in Sri Lanka and were adopted by secular nationalist groups in Lebanon before their adoption by Hizbollah and others. The attempts to draw links between suicide attacks in Lebanon (and later Palestine) and the costly human-wave attacks that took place in the Iran-Iraq War are tenuous to say the least.

Although the cult of the martyr was cultivated to encourage self-sacrifice in the war, drawing a connection between such actions in war and suicide attacks against civilian targets is nonsense. Iranian acts of self-sacrifice, of which there were many in the war, share more in common with the actions of soldiers in the First World War or Soviet troops in the Second World War than they do with suicide bombers. The attempt to draw a link between such selfless suicide attacks and the suicide attacks against civilian targets in Israel or Europe requires an awkward logic that would dictate that the Japanese Kamikaze pilots of WWII are responsible for the attacks on 9/11.

The attacks on the US Embassy and the marine barracks in Lebanon would have been considered legitimate (noncivilian) targets as a result of what a later US government report described as mission creep, which resulted in US forces intervening on behalf of the Lebanese Army, generally regarded at the time as one of the many factions contesting control over Lebanon. The marines may not have been aware of the role of the *USS Virginia* and *John Rodgers* in shelling sites in Lebanon in support of the Lebanese Armed Forces, but this intervention made the marines a target. Similarly, the embassy was regarded less as a diplomatic establishment and more as a center for CIA intervention. Under these circumstances, the view of some US analysts that the attacks were tantamount to an act of war is odd. A stronger case can be made for the attack on the embassy, which remained a diplomatic establishment, whatever its function. The uncompromising views were undoubtedly influenced by the fact many CIA analysts lost friends in the attack.

Even if one is determined to lay the blame at Iran's door, the truth is that Iran was involved in a bitter struggle with Iraq, who at the time was enjoying a productive relationship with the United States.[6] Iraqi bombers did not distinguish between civilian and military targets in Iran. From the Iranian perspective, therefore, if we assume her guilt in these attacks, supporters of Iraq, especially those who provided material support, were legitimate targets of retaliation, and the notion that they had initiated the conflict would have been regarded as absurd.

Throughout the 1980s and beyond, the frequency with which states could point to a Hizbollah connection, either through a local or international branch, became a measure of their alliance with the United States. Much of this was unsubstantiated, but Arab states anxious to secure American support and funding knew the key words, much as the Shah knew that he had to emphasize the Soviet threat to avail himself of US military technology. There was little doubt that the Iranians were involved in sedition and the destabilization of a number of states along the Persian Gulf. Part of this was a natural consequence of revolutionary rhetoric and fervor, which had succeeded in galvanizing Shia minorities (and in some cases majorities) in these states, a continuation of Iran's traditional cultural imperialism. The other part was politically directed from Tehran.

Yet, as noted, critics easily forget that Iran was at war, and the vast majority of these countries were supporting Iraq materially as well as morally. That is not to criticize their support, but it is too easy when applying blame to forget that the decision to launch a war was Saddam Hussein's. He had not exhausted all other options before deciding to invade, and Iran considered all those who supported him as legitimate targets.[7] The Iranian view that the Iran-Iraq War was an imposed war was vindicated in 1990 when the UN conceded to pronounce that Iraq did bear responsibility for the start of the war.

AN UNHOLY ALLIANCE

Growing American support for Saddam Hussein throughout the war, consolidated in the now infamous visit of Donald Rumsfeld to Iraq in 1983 and the restoration of formal diplomatic relations in 1984, ensured that the United States would remain a target. It may be fairly argued that the United States was already in Iran's sights, but US actions, especially when it publicly proclaimed a neutrality (a position shared by most of the Europeans), reinforced the belief among Iranians that the United States was duplicitous and hypocritical. The United States provided assistance to Iraq in a number of ways, including access to economic resources, support in relevant international fora, and most significantly, real-time satellite imagery indicating Iranian troops movements, a privilege hitherto accorded only to the Israelis.[8] Most controversial was the blind eye turned to Iraq's developments of biological and chemical weapons, which it subsequently experimented on Iranian soldiers. More damning, however, was the practical assistance afforded by a number of European countries. Iran was justifiably aggrieved with the West's complicity in Saddam Hussein's use of what is now labeled a weapon of mass destruction. The sense of distrust this engendered towards the West was enormous and was brought to a pinnacle by the tragedy at Halabja, where the town's Kurdish citizens were wiped out by an Iraqi gas attack. Iranians were convinced that this could not have been carried out without Western connivance. In the immediate aftermath of the atrocity, the silence of the West was deafening. It was only after the Iraqi invasion of Kuwait that Halabja became an issue of international concern.

As Saddam Hussein turned from convenient ally to inconvenient tyrant, the occasional criticism of his use of biological weapons against Iranians was heard, and the volume increased precipitously as we headed towards the first Persian Gulf War. Although protests against the use of these weapons were expressed throughout the 1980s, these protests were muted and largely drowned out by the chorus of general support for Saddam Hussein. One Defense Department report issued in 1990 even sought to place the blame for Halabja on Iran.[9] It was not the West's finest hour.

A curious consequence of this international realignment behind Iraq came with the onset of the Tanker War, and the subsequent re-flagging of tankers under American colors. After 1982 and the successful expulsion of Iraqi troops from Iranian territory, the leadership of the Islamic Republic took the fateful step of taking the war to Iraq—as a prelude, some may have hoped, of greater things. This action placed Iraq on the strategic defensive for the remainder of the war. As the pressure mounted and Saddam Hussein realized that his short war was descending into a protracted conflict, the war began to extend. One aspect of this was the determination to weaken Iranian resolve through the War of the Cities, in which the Iraqi Air Force and its missile capability were directed towards Iranian urban centers. The shortage of parts and the embargo on any weapons supplies from the United States meant that the superiority of the Iranian Air Force was not realized and Iranian cities were vulnerable to attack.

The other front to be opened was in the Persian Gulf. Both Iraq and Iran depended on a steady stream of oil revenue to finance the war effort. Iraq, largely as a result of the vulnerabilities of her limited coastline, had developed an extensive pipeline network for exporting her oil.

Iran, on the other hand, was almost entirely dependent on tanker shipments through the strategic Straits of Hormuz at the mouth of the Persian Gulf, a jugular Iraqi planners could not fail to miss. From the very beginning of the war, Iraqi planes attacked Iranian ships, along with foreign tankers that might be carrying Iranian crude, in an effort to starve the Iranian economy of funds. The Iranians retaliated and, by virtue of having a superior local fleet, were quickly able to dominate the shipping lanes, mining key areas in an effort to sabotage Iraqi oil exports and, in their absence, the oil exports of her Arab allies.

As these attacks mounted, the Kuwaitis sought foreign protection, intimating that in the absence of American enthusiasm they might re-flag their ships under Soviet colors. The anxieties this engendered delivered the desired result: the United States placed Kuwaiti ships under their protection and entered the Persian Gulf in force. By 1987, the United States had effectively entered the war on the Iraqi side and was now retaliating against Iranian attacks, real or imagined.

One of the ships sent to patrol the northern Gulf, the *USS Stark,* found itself the target of an Iraqi air-launched missile that resulted in the death of thirty-seven US sailors. President Reagan blamed this tragedy on the Iranians, whom he described as barbaric and the real villains.[10] These reckless statements reverberated around the Iranian community in Iran and among exiles, with the consequence that clarifications were immediately issued. Most Iranians could not understand how a plane and a missile system that were on loan or purchased from the French and fired by an Iraqi could be blamed on the Iranians, nor could they fully comprehend why the Americans had accepted the Iraqi explanation of their unfortunate mistake so easily. In public relations terms, it was a triumph for the Islamic Republic. Many Iranians with no affection for the revolution had to concede that the logic of Reagan's statement had escaped them, and that perhaps the Islamic Republic had a point when it argued that the United States was irrationally opposed to the revolution. Reagan's Freudian slip seemed to indicate a shift in American thinking. The Islamic Republic was no longer the problem; the people were barbaric—a dangerous generalization.

IRAN-CONTRA

It is perhaps no coincidence that the generalization and simplification of views occurred after the exposure of the great scandal of the Reagan presidency, the Iran-Contra affair. As noted, the Reagan administration took office eager to make amends for the perceived ineptitude of the Carter administration. Republican contempt was reciprocated by outgoing Democrats, who viewed with suspicion the convenient timing of the end of the hostage crisis. Rumors abounded that the Republican administration had concluded a secret deal with the Iranians to prevent the early release of the hostages. (Similar allegations had been made against the Nixon campaign team with respect to Vietnam in 1968.) These allegations, characterized as the October Surprise, were subsequently published, with interesting consequences for President George H. W. Bush's reelection campaign in 1992 and renewed attempts to broker a deal with Iran.

Allegations of interference in the negotiations by the Republican Party, and Bush in particular, are incorrect. However, senior Iranian sources argue that Republican supporters provided an estimated $20 million to key agents in the Islamic Republic to lobby for the delayed release of the hostages. The Iranian leadership had engaged in considerable debate as to when to release the hostages. At least one prominent negotiator later conceded that he would have preferred to have settled the matter with Carter.[11] Although there has been no suggestion of direct Republican Party involvement from the Iranian side, the conviction that political manipulation and interference did take place (albeit at an informal level) would have only further persuaded an already skeptical Revolutionary elite that American politics was eminently corruptible.

Whatever the veracity of these allegations, any new approach to Iran would have to be handled sensitively in the aftermath of the popular trauma of the hostage crisis. In addition, America's official neutrality towards the warring parties leant towards support for the Iraqis. Despite the absence of affection between the United States and the Islamic Revolution, there was a yearning for a reestablishment of a relationship and a belief that time would afford the necessary opportunity. This view was shared by the Israelis, who similarly lamented the loss of a strategic and immensely useful ally in an otherwise difficult region.

The opportunity revealed itself as the war progressed and the realist tendency in the Iranian regime recognized the need for a resupply of rapidly dwindling military stocks, most of which were Western (American) in origin. As noted, the Iranian Air Force had been badly hampered in its operational capability after 1982 as a consequence of a lack of spare parts, and it was generally known that Iranian technicians were stripping down one aircraft to ensure that another could fly. This problem was made more acute by the onset of the War of the Cities, Saddam Hussein's attempt to bring the Iranian population to its knees through a concerted aerial bombardment of its cities. Apart from the demographic changes this encouraged, as refugees moved to the countryside or to less strategic cities, the result mirrored that which occurred in European societies in World War Two: a consolidation of national spirit and resolve. The blitz mentality that emerged and the stoicism the bombardment encouraged had important social consequences for the Iranian sense of national cohesion. This total war, the first war of its kind that Iranians experienced in the modern age, had a different effect than that envisaged by Saddam and would shape politics in the next decade. By 1984, the Speaker of the Parliament and a key confidante of Ayatollah Khomeini, Hojjat-ol Islam Ali Akbar Hashemi Rafsanjani, made clear Iran's desire to replenish its military stocks.

Some resupply had been secured through third parties at vastly inflated prices, which resulted in commentators noting that superpowers and the West in general seemed intent on exploiting the war for financial gain and keeping the combatants sufficiently resupplied to continue fighting. By publicizing the threat posed by the Islamic Revolution, the Gulf Arab states were encouraged to exponentially augment their military capability. This capability would do little to combat the *ideological* threat posed by the revolution but would oil the wheels of the Western military-industrial complex, the momentum for which continues to this day. Rafsanjani's gambit, which could not have been pursued without official sanction from Ayatollah Khomeini, was to use the need for weapons to broker an engagement with the United States. An aspect of this exploratory relationship, which has yet to be fully investigated, was the intermediary role played by Israel. The record shows that the two sides who had publicly stated their mutual dislike appeared happy to engage in highly sensitive negotiations on an issue of critical political and military importance.

In light of the illegal means by which the Reagan administration pursued this policy, and the awkward decision to tie it to a desire to supply the Nicaraguan Contras and the release of hostages in Lebanon, the entire venture has been clouded by guilt and laden with a heavy veneer of cynicism. This has averted attention away from the significance of the developments for US-Iran relations and the genuine attempt to foster a relationship and renew ties.

No particular reason exists to doubt Reagan's subsequent justification that he had sought to reestablish ties with a strategic country, especially considering that many of the people involved were familiar with Iran and had served in the country before the revolution. The intent, as far as Iran was concerned, was nonetheless subsumed under the tide of a woefully misconstructed and poorly thought-out method that not only drew attention to the existence of a shadow government, a revelation that would have made the Watergate conspirators proud, but also made the Reagan administration, and the US government in general, appear hypocritical to its European allies.

The idea that the United States was effectively negotiating the exchange of weapons for hostages caused enormous embarrassment and irritation particularly in London, in part because the Thatcher government was kept in the dark but principally because it contradicted the stated (and highly voluble) policy against negotiations with terrorists. (The various Lebanese militias and Hizbollah in particular were defined as terrorists by the US government.) It encouraged and reaffirmed the cynicism with which European policy makers viewed American statements with respect to Iran and convinced many observers that US-Iran relations would be swiftly reestablished given the opportunity. This was an overly optimistic interpretation of events, but it was held by many skeptical Arab states in the region (increasingly aware that any US-Iran rapprochement was not in their interests) and by hard-line Iranians themselves.

Iran treated the debacle, including the much-feted visit of Robert McFarlane to Iran (complete with a cake and a Bible, an odd combination of gifts), as a curiosity. Indeed, revolutionary justice was not meted out against those who had sought to foster this policy. Ali Akbar Hashemi Rafsanjani was not punished for his involvement. Mehdi Hashemi (no relation) was executed for exposing the secret policy initiative and, as a result, embarrassing the Iranian government. In other words, he died for his vehement opposition to the policy, not for his support of it—a distinction rarely noted in the West. Iran interpreted the experience as an example of the continued desire of the United States to establish relations with the Islamic Republic. This awkward reading of events drew inspiration from Reagan's justification for the policy and convinced the hard-line establishment that Iran could establish relations whenever it chose to do so. The implications of this encounter for the official anti-Americanism of the Islamic Republic, in particular the salient fact that Khomeini by all accounts approved it, have been conveniently marginalized in the official record. However, far from justifying complacency, the political fallout from the Iran-Contra scandal served only to reinforce the growing gulf in US-Iran relations.

As the revelations emerged, a number of senior US officials found themselves indicted and imprisoned. Meanwhile, whenever the demands of domestic politics required, the Democrats reminded the Republicans of their imprudent foray into Iran. The scandal became more a reflection of a political struggle in America than an aspect of foreign policy, and the role of Iran was reduced once again to that of a villain, rather than a political actor with its own interests and ambitions. (The use of the term "Irangate" was a useful *aide-memoire* that served to reinforce the association with a previous Republican scandal.)

The Iranians became convinced that for all the rhetoric, the United

States was the ultimate realist in international relations, for whom commercial and geopolitical interests took priority. Moreover, they drew valuable parallels between their own support for Hizbollah and US support for the Contras. For the US political elite, the lessons included the curious conclusion that Iran had no moderates worth negotiating with, that the system as a whole was rotten, and that the people were duplicitous. Yet the individual considered responsible for leaking the secret talks was executed by the Iranian authorities, and no Iranian official was responsible for the decision to fund the Nicaraguan Contras, the development of the particular networks with Iranian expatriates (which were less than satisfactory), or the conviction of the American officials involved. The policy was a monumental failure, but to lay the blame entirely at Iran's door was more a reflection of domestic political expediency than genuine culpability.

THE *USS VINCENNES*

The pressures that mounted on the Reagan presidency, and the potential impact on his legacy, ensured that Iran became a taboo subject. Whenever possible, a suitable political distance was maintained. It was convenient to blame Iran when reality contradicted policy or an embarrassment loomed. Political disagreements could be set aside because blaming Iran was now a bipartisan affair to which all Americans could subscribe, Republican or Democrat, politician or bystander. Iran had transcended regular politics and become a myth, part of political folklore. This was quite an achievement—even Vietnam had not generated such a uniformity of dislike. This development was perhaps best exemplified by the next event that was to reinforce prejudice and mutual suspicion, albeit this time on the Iranian side.

By the late 1980s, the United States was playing an increasingly proactive role in its protection of shipping in the Persian Gulf. Iran was similarly concerned with the regular flow of oil out of the Persian Gulf, a critical lifeline for its own economy. Iraq sought to block these exports, and Iran retaliated. However, because Iraq enjoyed significant land-based pipeline routes, Iran's retaliation focused on the oil exports of Gulf littoral states that were financing the Iraqi state. Now that America was protecting these states, Iran and the United States found themselves in direct confrontation, even though their policies were essentially the same.

During the twilight years of the war, the United States Navy effectively opened up a second front against Iran, drawing Iran's limited naval resources away from any supporting role along the Shatt al Arab waterway. Instead, the Iranian Navy was reallocated to the defense of oil platforms, while the new Revolutionary Guard naval force set itself the task of harassing enemy shipping and, where possible, disrupting US attacks. This was a highly asymmetric struggle because the forces available to Iran were small, fast-attack boats, on which were mounted small rocket launchers and other hand-operated weapons. These boats and their crews faced the most sophisticated technology the US Navy could offer.

The David versus Goliath nature of this naval contest endeared itself to the Revolutionary Guardsmen, who regarded their determination in the face of such disparity to be emblematic of the revolutionary struggle. Far from being disheartened, the odds encouraged them. The lumbering yet powerful giant pitted against the myriad, agile, and dextrous opponent evoked the memory of struggles past and was a metaphor for the political contest taking place.

US naval power was expensive, both in hardware and training, and almost invincible when confronted in a straight fight. However, it was built to fight a different enemy than that which it now confronted, tended to be impatient to engage, and was easily provoked. These flaws were easily exploited, such that victories in battle were usually the consequence of crass decision-making and poor tactical judgement rather than the quality of the equipment or basic training.

As the *USS Vincennes* entered service in the Persian Gulf, it was generally acknowledged that its captain was eager for action and determined to make a name for himself. His ship was one of the most technologically sophisticated in the US Navy—and dangerously ill-suited to the theatre of war to which it had been dispatched, having been designed for a conflict with the Soviet Navy. Consequently, the captain was to find himself frustratingly impotent in the face of multiple, fast-attack boats, retaliation against any one of which was absurdly disproportionate.

The *USS Vincennes* could theoretically rely on overwhelming air cover if required. But this was withheld because the commander in Bahrain responsible for directing air cover from the local carrier was anxious that his colleague on the *Vincennes,* mired in a local firefight, might inadvertently target these supporting aircraft. At the critical juncture, therefore, air cover was absent.

The captain appeared to view the rules of engagement with contempt, an unnecessary constraint, because he pursued the attack boats when they withdrew into Iranian waters. In the process of swatting these numerous and undoubtedly irritating flies, the radar suddenly picked up what appeared to be an approaching aircraft. Having alerted the aircraft to their presence and warned them to no apparent avail, the crew of the *USS Vincennes* frantically dispatched a missile (the missile codes were incorrectly input twenty-seven times) to deal with the incoming threat. A Western documentary film crew were on the command deck to witness the scenes of elation as the blip vanished from the radar screen. But a short time later, after hearing a distress call, elation was followed by the stark realization that they had hit a civilian airliner.

This was not only a tragedy but a monumental embarrassment for the US government, and one that still has officials suffering from selective amnesia. It was several years before the full extent of the incompetence became apparent, supported by the statements of other naval officers in the area who were justifiably dismayed by the attitude and behavior of the captain of the *USS Vincennes.* While acknowledging and regretting the mistake, the initial report sought to absolve the *Vincennes* and its captain from any responsibility. The report argued that the airliner had not responded to warnings and had been descending towards the *Vincennes,* which, it was emphasized, was performing its duties in international waters. This last detail, along with many others, was incorrect.

The flight path of the Iran Air airbus from Shiraz to Dubai was well known, it was not descending but ascending, and it had not responded to the various warnings simply because of its inability to receive communications on a military wavelength. The pilot of the Iran Air airbus was therefore blissfully unaware that he was being warned by the *USS Vincennes* or that his plane was being viewed as a threat. On the contrary, other US ships had warned him—on the civilian wavelength—to alter his course to avoid an area of confrontation below his standard flight path. Having done all this, his plane was nonetheless struck by a surface-to-air missile, resulting in the loss of two hundred ninety lives.

The shock was palpable all round, particularly as pictures emerged of bodies floating in the shallow waters of the Persian Gulf. The precise details of the Iran Air flight path and the pilot's communications with the ground remain unknown because the black box was never recovered. The suspicion is that it was picked up by the *USS Vincennes,* which having entered Iranian waters was the ship closest to the debris. What remains shocking about this incident is not so much the criminal negligence that led to it but the whitewash that followed, in particular President Reagan's decision to award the Captain with a medal for distinguished service—this was in addition to the standard service medal the crew received. Even for Iranians with no particular affection for the Islamic Republic, this was a bizarre and offensive gesture. This event, along with those surrounding the *USS Stark,* convinced even the skeptics that the United States was the Great Satan. The US government later offered compensation—commensurate with the standard of living—while refusing to accept responsibility.[12]

RAFSANJANI AND THE REALIST ASCENDANCY

The one immediate effect of the tragic shooting down of the airbus was that Ayatollah Khomeini decided to accept the cease-fire resolution urged upon him by the United Nations, thereby bringing the eight-year war to an ignominious conclusion, a consequence that has led some US hawks to conclude that force works. Iran had not achieved her stated war aims, and many wondered aloud the point of the slaughter; estimates of the number of casualties ranged from five hundred thousand to one million.

The war had a profound effect on Iranian society, which emerged shaken, reflective, and determinedly anti-war. The war had always been considered imposed, and for all the rhetoric of revolutionary values, there was no distinctive ideology of militarism or glorification of war for its own sake. Heroic resistance and self-sacrifice were celebrated, but popular culture concentrated on the effects of war on society and the individual rather than glorying in any particular military achievement.

The cult of the martyr gained prominence, largely to acknowledge the many sacrifices that had been made, though the authorities of the Islamic Republic succeeded in demeaning its implicit sanctity by popularizing this traditionally select honor. For instance, it was possible to become a living martyr if you had been disabled and not killed, and even here, you were allocated a category according to the extent of your injuries. Such was the determination to be part of this illustrious group (and therefore gain access and privileges reserved for martyrs and their families), that some claims bordered on the absurd. The point is that the cult of the martyr is often less a reflection of the apparent suicidal fanaticism of Iranians and more an issue of semantics (in the West one would talk of veterans and heroes) and, in the worst cases, personal interest. At the same time, the sacrifices made by ordinary Iranians should not be dismissed.

Despite the futility of the war and the tremendous waste in both human lives and material resources, there were positive consequences for the long-term political development of the country. In the first place, Iran survived. This was no mean achievement for a state that had become accustomed to military defeat and territorial loss. The Islamic Republic, as its officials kept reminding its critics, may not have extended Iranian territory, but it did not lose any either. This was the first Iranian state not to lose territory in nearly two hundred years. That this was achieved in the face of superior odds, in terms of technology and economic resources, could not be easily discounted. More objective military analysts in the West conceded that the real question was why it took Iraq so long to bring Iran to the negotiating table. Not only did Iraq have access to far better resources (as would soon be revealed in the arms scandal following the Iraqi invasion of Kuwait), it was on the strategic defensive since 1982 and enjoyed the support of both superpowers, which in the American case meant active military support in the Persian Gulf and elsewhere.

Moreover, the Iranians had learned to adapt and fight on their own terms, using ingenuity that was at times stunning—particularly the enormous engineering attempt to drain marshes by constructing extensive canal networks—and compensating for the lack of spare parts by developing a logistical capacity of their own.[13] Far from starving Iran of military resources, the embargo had encouraged the development of an indigenous arms industry. The war taught Iranians the necessity of self-sufficiency and confirmed the ideology of the revolution, which regarded the West, and in this case foreign suppliers, as inherently untrustworthy. Companies that continued to work with Iran throughout the war were viewed with some favor, but on the whole a cynical realism with respect to the West was confirmed and reinforced.

Despite the prevalent view in the West that Iran had lost the war, the view in Iran was one of success, incomplete as it may have been. Some details, particularly the decision to take the war to Iraq in 1982, were the subject of considerable discussion. But on the whole, Iranians, as well as the state, had a sense of relief and accomplishment. Ordinary Iranians, who had surprised observers with their stoic determination, emerged from the experience of war with an acute sense of political realism, especially with respect to their own government. Gone were the unquestioning idealists of the revolution. The experience of war generated new critical thinking and a determination among many veterans to participate in the shaping of the Islamic Republic.

In many ways, the Islamic Republic that emerged from the war in 1988 was defined by its attempt to cope, often inadequately, with the process of demobilization—in both economic and ideological terms. Thrust from revolution to war, and characterized in its early stages by antagonism, conflict, and suspicion, Iranian society had little time to settle many of the outstanding issues about the revolution, let alone establish a firm institutional base. The Shah, followed by an extensive cadre of bureaucrats, were gone. Those who remained had been frequently marginalized in favor of revolutionary purists. The revolution had survived, and although the economy had stalled, Iran, unlike Iraq, was not significantly in debt and could begin the process of reconstruction with its finances in good shape.

Nonetheless, with the war over and attentions refocused on domestic issues, people were justifiably concerned that the old factionalism would emerge with a vengeance, especially with the imminent prospect of

Ayatollah Khomeini's death. The opposition waited for the internal chaos they predicted would follow the loss of the charismatic leader who had effectively managed and welded the disparate groups that had constituted the revolution. The fears and hopes of the various groups were misplaced. When Khomeini died in 1989, the outpouring of grief that accompanied his funeral convinced even the skeptics that the political system known as the Islamic Republic enjoyed a firm foundation. Even the new administration of George H. W. Bush in the United States briefly contemplated the prospect of initiating a dialogue, if only because the regime was popular and the United States ought to face the reality, however unsavory, confronting them.

Before this possibility could arise, however, Khomeini's heirs had to shape his legacy and institutionalize a system that had hitherto functioned as an extension of the late Imam's charismatic will. To understand and appreciate the system that was to emerge, we need to retrace the steps to the Revolution itself, which was the product of a number of anti-monarchical movements that came together to remove the Shah and ultimately abolish the monarchy. Broadly speaking, three groups coexisted at this time: the secular nationalists, who provided the initial leadership within Iran; the religious nationalists under the leadership of Khomeini, who brought with them the traditional masses; and the Left (both religious and secular), with a varied leadership but identified with the Mojahedeen-e Khalq Organization, who brought with them the urban middle and lower classes.

The secular groups and the Left tended to have Western-style educations; the religious nationalists were more familiar with traditional educations provided by the Shia seminaries. In this respect, these groups represented different traditions, and in the ensuing radicalization of the revolution after the overthrow of the Shah, those with a Western-style education were tarnished as insufficiently authentic, to the point where ultimately only the *ulema* claimed to be culturally unblemished. First, however, the secular nationalists were culled, following the seizure of the US embassy, after which the fight for control fell to the Left and the religious nationalists. This contest continued through the beginning of the war, taking on an increasingly brutal form as assassinations became the norm. Faced with the prospect of a radical left-wing revolution, the political and economic elites swung their support behind the religious nationalists, who at least were familiar and respected private property. Khomeini was able to reconcile these conflicting tendencies through the duration of the war. Although the Left were gradually eliminated as a distinct political force (the most radical elements fleeing abroad), many of their ideas came to influence the religious nationalists, and Khomeini himself tended to be sympathetic to a more egalitarian reading of Islam.

After Khomeini's death in 1989, the Islamic Republic was defined by the former speaker of the Parliament and new President Ali Akbar Hashemi Rafsanjani. Rafsanjani's ascendancy marked a shift in the political balance of power in the various parties, which partly reflected the reality that Khomeini could not be replaced, while also indicating Rafsanjani's own political determination to shape the fledgling Islamic Republic in his own image. Rafsanjani was a mullah, but he was also a shrewd politician and a merchant, with little time for Islamic austerity. For all his rhetorical training, Rafsanjani was to increasingly represent his mercantile over his clerical roots, and he sought to stabilize the Islamic Republic upon the pillar of mercantile capital.

History suggests that no Iranian state had survived without cultivating the loyalty of the traditional mercantile elite—the Shah had challenged their commercial interests and lost his throne as a result. Rafsanjani, however, sought to build his Islamic Republic on the shoulders of the mercantile elite. The state could not depend entirely on mercantile wealth, however, so an alliance of interests had to be forged with the Islamic authoritarians, for whom the republic was a poor second to the Islamic character of the state. These elements coalesced around the figure of the *vali-e faqih*, Khomeini's innovative contribution to Islamic political thought, which essentially established a constitutional position for the most senior of Grand Ayatollahs.

Khomeini's vision of the role of the *vali-e faqih* in everyday politics is a matter of bitter dispute to this day. According to one of the original drafters of the Constitution, Ayatollah Montazeri, supreme authority was intended to reside in the religious guardian—so that politicians would be reminded of the importance of spirituality and ethics—but the Supreme

Jurist was not intended to exercise power on a day-to-day basis.[14] On the contrary, the office holder was meant to arbitrate and guide, a role not too dissimilar from that of traditional monarchs, whose function was to manage the system and restore balance when necessary. Montazeri's interpretation may have some merit: the president of the Islamic Republic was (and remains) the constitutional head of state, and Khomeini himself, his charismatic authority permitting, avoided overt interference, preferring to set up committees to discuss issues.[15] In this way, Khomeini's *modus operandi* was the antithesis of that of the centralizing Shah, although in practice Khomeini's extensive charismatic authority, especially among his devoted followers, more than compensated for this tendency.

In 1989, Rafsanjani engineered a number of key constitutional amendments intended to smooth inconsistencies and streamline the process of government. Out went the position of prime minister, whose powers were now concentrated in the presidency—which had hitherto been a far more ceremonial figure, though by no means without power. In concentrating executive power in the hands of the presidency, Rafsanjani successfully eliminated a tier of government (and its accompanying bureaucracy) and thereby rationalized government. However, in achieving this, he inadvertently encouraged a growth in government around the *vali-e faqih*. Rather than pushing everything upstairs, Rafsanjani's reform opened the door to the possibility that the presidency would effectively become the premiership to the *vali-e faqih's* presidency. The other significant amendment to the constitution was the addition of the prefix *absolute* to the position of *velayat-e faqih*. This was a dangerous move, the problems of which were to take some time to emerge.[16]

There has been considerable debate about the precise ramifications of the term *absolute* and whether it applied to religious injunctions (to avoid disagreement among leading Ayatollahs) or had a political purpose. The authoritarians were determined to ensure that the prefix *absolute* applied to all matters, political and religious. In 1989, however, these problems lay in the future, because Rafsanjani's preference, and ostensibly that of Khomeini on his deathbed, was for the position to be occupied by the President of the Islamic Republic, Hojjat-ol Islam Ali Khamenei. Many of the rank-and-file *ulema* saw Khomeini's sudden elevation of Khamenei to the rank of Ayatollah as arbitrary and distinctly political. That the junior cleric could be successfully made *vali-e faqih* was testament to the inherent and immediate stability of the post-war Islamic Republic. Moreover, people tended to accept this change because Khamenei seemed to be a weak candidate who would have no choice but to let Rafsanjani steer policy. Khamenei's weakness made the constitutional changes palatable and few doubted that Rafsanjani had arranged for a younger man, who happened to be his close friend, so that he could better control him. In many ways, it was a classic Rafsanjani gambit, and even those who disliked him admired and respected his political nerve and audacity.

Not everyone was happy, and compromises had to be made. But the Rafsanjani settlement basically envisaged a state founded on the twin pillars of mercantilism and Islam. The Prophet of God, after all, was a merchant. Out went the austerity of the war years and in came a measure of material populism, tempered by regular and occasionally harsh religious admonishment. Part of the bargain with the Islamic authoritarians was a consistent dose of Islamic doctrine, epitomized by the insistence on Islamic dress code and frequent rhetoric against the United States, and its surrogate, Israel. (This relationship was occasionally reversed, with America as the unfortunate surrogate, by those who wanted to open the door of dialogue with the United States.)

The basic relationship worked as follows: the merchants and their associates would be allowed latitude to make money and integrate as far as possible into government. In return for financial support and commercial gain, the religious right would provide the veneer of religious sanction and authority. Obvious tensions existed in this relationship, especially among devotees for whom austerity and egalitarianism was a religious duty, but those in charge convinced themselves that it was better to become wealthy than to allow the country's wealth to fall into the hands of the corrupt secularists. By such curious justifications, therefore, corruption became a virtue. In the upper echelons of the establishment, corruption grew exponentially, in part because it became a means of governing and a mechanism for control.

If Saddam Hussein's Iraq was held together by the elite's complicity in murder, the Islamic Republic of Iran was held together through complicity in dubious financial ventures. The mercantile elites made money through trade, not investment. Profit depended on instability in the market, which should be opaque enough to allow a sufficient markup in the price of a given commodity. The law should ideally be flexible, and transparency was unhelpful. As any stock market dealer will tell you, the more instability and the fewer questions, the greater the opportunity to maximize your income in the shortest time. Insider trading adds to the profit margin, and in Iran, access and proximity to the levers of power provided people with the information they needed. And in a country regularly subjected to trade sanctions, smuggled goods could demand the highest price.

All this was invigorated by the steady flow of oil revenue, part of which was allocated in state subsidies and preferential exchange rates and then used to import goods that could then be sold at vastly inflated prices. The money thus earned was invested in property or swiftly dispatched abroad, because the political and economic instability that allowed people to make money also made the country an unsafe place to store money. The immediate fallout was that the Iranian rial remained weak; this situation was enormously beneficial to traders and other accumulators of capital because their hard currency income could be exchanged at generous black-market rates back into rials, which could then be spent liberally in Iran. A lot of economic activity occurred in the black market, so it was rarely registered in official figures. Observers who analyzed the state of the Iranian economy through official figures thought that the economy was on the verge of collapse, given the losses of the war years and the reduction in industrial capacity. Only those who went to Iran (and few Americans did immediately after the war) recognized that something was amiss with the statistics.

This analysis was one of the many examples of miscommunication between Iran and its Western critics (including exiled opponents), determined as they were to show the failure of the Islamic Republic. Iran was (and continues to be) a rich country generously endowed with natural resources that the elite exploited with a ruthless, competitive pragmatism. The problem was not the nature and extent of the resources but their management. The increasing dominance of the mercantile elite ensured the continuation of a system of government whose outlook was both traditional and short term. This attitude was to become a major obstacle in developing a modern economy and a culture of investment.

For the Europeans and the Japanese, not limited by politics, the Rafsanjani ascendancy proclaimed that Iran was open for business, and from 1989 onwards they renewed their acquaintance. At the time, an immense optimism was fuelled in part by the realization that there would be no competition from the United States. Yet if the naysayers had misread the durability of the Iranian economy, European businessmen also found themselves talking a different language. Trade was one thing they could all agree on, but as companies were invited to invest in the economy, attracted by the language of the free market, they discovered to their frustration that the culture of instability and managed crisis was ill suited to their needs. There was little transparency or accountability, and little evidence of the Iranians themselves investing in the economy. The absence of a private sector in any meaningful sense further reinforced the idea that the state must take control, thereby consolidating the autocratic function of the state and the need for political proximity. Getting ahead in the economy, especially in the absence of clear laws, meant gaining access to power and those who wielded it.

NATIONALISM AND REALISM

Domestic implications aside, the emergence of the mercantile elite and the infiltration of their attitudes into the organs of government influenced the way foreign policy was perceived and developed. The culture of instability that characterized mercantile relations began to permeate Iranian politics and foreign policy. In such a world view, crises were the rule, not the exception, and one sought to manage these crises as best one could. Negotiations took place to ensure a smooth management of a particular crisis and to gain advantage. The idea that both sides could benefit from negotiation, while theoretically possible, was regarded as unrealistic. These views reinforced a growing emphasis on realism in Iran's international relations, which reflected the fact that a number of Rafsanjani's

foreign policy analysts were academics and technocrats who had been educated in economic and international relations in the United States.

It was striking how many of Rafsanjani's cabinet and senior officials
had been educated in the United States, although having been there before the revolution, they remained dangerously unfamiliar with the important changes that had taken place as a result of the revolution. For the
Iranian foreign policy establishment in the immediate aftermath of the
war, the way back to America's heart was to locate her interests and pan-
der to them. These interests were defined in geopolitical and economic
terms, and the notion that culture, prejudice, and ideology might equally
affect American foreign policy was treated with ridicule.[17] In this respect
at least, Iran's international relations experts shared much in common
with those who had educated them. America's foreign policy elite could
not imagine that their policy was constructed outside the bounds of rational self-interest. Ideology was something that happened to the other
party, be it the Soviet Union or the Islamic Republic of Iran. Having defined itself against dogmatism, it was inconceivable that the United States
would succumb to the tyranny of ideology. This is one of the great myths
of the American Dream, itself a good and powerful political idea. Just as
the United States tended to define itself in simplistic terms, so too did it
afflict others with the political malaise known as generalization.

As far as Iran was concerned, the politics of generalization received an
accelerated boost by the onset of revolution, which argued, not unjustifi-
ably, that 1979 had marked an important break, when nationalism had
given way to Islamism and pragmatism to dogmatic ideology. This view,
which was reinforced by both the revolutionaries and their opponents (albeit with differing emphases), is held by many analysts to this day, especially because this simplification fits conveniently into the rubric of the
"clash of civilizations" thesis. The truth is always more complex. Setting
aside the fact that even pragmatism is determined and defined by the underlying culture and ideological world view of a particular state or individual, it is clear that Iranian foreign policy did not suddenly lurch into
an irrational, ideologically dictated orbit.

Ideology had existed before the revolution, and pragmatism would
continue after it. If that were not the case, Iran-Contra would not have

occurred. That is not to say that religion was unimportant, but as religious nationalists, these individuals tended to give increasing emphasis to the national part of the equation. Iranians antithetical to the regime have been loathe to concede this national legitimacy to the new elite, but this conception of nationalism, and its association with Shia Islam, was in many ways a return to the more authentic pre-Pahlavi conception of Iranian identity. That this was so was a reflection also of social changes and demands.

The revolution was launched by a number of different groups with various agendas, and the onset of war both facilitated and hindered the progress of Islamists in directing their particular agenda. Iranians may have been willing to tolerate Islamic austerity, and purify themselves of Pahlavi-inspired corruption, but as the war became prolonged, how much purification they would accept had its limits. Islamic ideology undoubtedly mobilized the masses, but this was increasingly defined in Iranian terms, a position that was generously aided by Saddam Hussein's rampant Arab chauvinism. As the war progressed, government propaganda swiftly recognized the value of a specifically nationalistic call to arms: the Islamic Revolution sanctified the nation, in a manner the Shah could have only dreamt about.

In highlighting the importance of realism, it is important to not become reductionist. Tensions continued to exist in the development of policy. The alliance of interests with the Islamic authoritarians was fraught with difficulty not least because of the problems of demobilization. The war had ended, but for many it was an inconclusive end, one that indicated a temporary truce rather than a settled and permanent peace. Iran may have reluctantly accepted the UN cease-fire resolution, but it bitterly resented the fact that the UN refused to recognize Iraq as the aggressor and the implications for potential reparations this entailed. The Islamic authoritarians determination to effectively continue the war by other means was to severely affect both domestic and foreign policy.

In the first few years of Rafsanjani's presidency, rogue elements in the intelligence and security forces settled old scores. A number of these operations occurred in Europe, principally Italy, Austria, France, and Germany, and included monarchists who had allegedly sided with Saddam Hussein during the war and members of the Mojahideen-e Khalq Organization (MKO), whose blood feud with the revolutionaries continued with vigor (for background, see page 198). In many ways, this feud was an extension of the intensely personal, even tribal, character of the political system—some in Iran defined it as mafia politics—where betrayal was dealt with harshly. It made for difficult international relations, but some in the Iranian establishment could see no difference between what they were doing and the targeted assassinations committed by the Israelis or Western intelligence services, except that they left a trail. This was true of the assassination of the Shah's last Prime Minister, Shahpour Bakhtiar, in Paris in 1991, the murder of the Kurdish leader Qasemlou in Vienna (who reportedly had been invited to attend a meeting with officials from Iran), and the most notorious case at the Mykonos restaurant in Berlin, where Iranian Kurdish dissidents were gunned down by masked assailants.

All these were attempts to eliminate potential political rivals and stabilize the regime. As others pointed out, such extrajudicial executions only reinforced the international view of Iran as a country of fanatics determined to exercise their power through terrorism. As if to leave no doubt that this impression was correct, Ayatollah Khomeini issued the now infamous *fatwa* against the British novelist Salman Rushdie, sentencing him to death for blaspheming against the Prophet Muhammad in his book the *Satanic Verses*.

THE RUSHDIE AFFAIR

The Rushdie affair is essentially an aspect of Anglo-Iranian relations and will not be dealt with at length here. But its origins and development are a good example of how Iranian foreign policy was forged and could itself be held hostage by a lack of strategic foresight. The Rushdie affair fueled and supported the views of those who regarded Iran to be in the grip of a radical ideology that exported terrorism. However, few people were agitated by the *Satanic Verses* in Iran and Khomeini appears to have issued his fatwa as a result of developments elsewhere, particularly South Asia, where a number of people had died in riots.

It was a full five months after the publication of the book and the ensuing disturbances throughout the Islamic world when Ayatollah Khomeini was encouraged to issue a formal judgement. Whether this judgement qualified as a fatwa in the traditional understanding of Shia doctrine is debatable, because it is unclear whether specific required procedures were followed. It is also unclear whether Khomeini read the book or was simply informed about it and its consequences and felt the need to make a political stand. Whatever the motive, his audience was the Islamic world, not the West, and the fatwa was Iran's effort to exercise its self-perceived role as leader of the Muslim world. There was a popular demand for an official response, and Khomeini replied with characteristic political immediacy, much like his reaction to the hostage crisis in 1979. The fact that he died soon afterwards absolved him of any responsibility to review his judgement and left his heirs with a peculiar problem.

The way all sides handled the crisis reflected the critical grip that ideology, in this case defined as principle, affected foreign policy and the way in which vocal interest groups, despite being in a minority, could seize the foreign policy agenda. Both sides had initially sought to downplay the political significance of the fatwa, confidently predicting that this local difficulty would soon be resolved. In the Iranian case, this required careful and not altogether credible semantic acrobatics. Officials first insisted it was a religious matter, with no relevance to politics—even though it was apparent that it had been issued with a particular political constituency in mind—and similarly insisting that there was no distinction between religion and politics in Iran. If some in Iran thought that the Rushdie affair might allow them to make this distinction in practice, they were to be disappointed by vocal hard-liners, who enthusiastically fueled the crisis, much to the delight of their counterparts in the West, who returned the compliment.

For the diplomats caught in the middle, this degeneration into principle ensured that the Rushdie affair was transformed from a matter for negotiation to one of political grandstanding and national pride. In the clash that followed, it was conveniently forgotten that Iran had awarded Rushdie a prize for one of his earlier books. And although amateur pundits sought to lecture Iran on the nuances of Islamic law, Iranians for their part lambasted perfidious Albion for its perennial assault on the Iranian senses. In other words, as usual, uncomfortable detail gave way to generalization, and reasoned debate gave way to myth, further exacerbating the gulf of mistrust.

As time wore on and relations between Iran and the West suffered, few Iranians seriously thought that Rushdie should be killed for what he had written. Neither did Iranians think that they should shoulder the responsibilities of the Islamic world. No doubt some took satisfaction in the fact that the Muslim world was exporting her values to the West for a change. The satisfaction gained was poor compensation for the difficulties caused, and the Rushdie affair cast a long shadow on Iran's foreign relations in the decade after the war. It remained a useful stick with which to beat the Islamic Republic, and the reluctance to deal with the crisis of the fatwa reflected the acute realization that to challenge the authority of Khomeini, particularly after his death, was to open a Pandora's Box of issues. The Rushdie affair would have to be another crisis to be managed, along with the various charges of terrorism—which many Iranians, isolated as they were for the better part of a decade from world opinion, found incomprehensible. With the war over, and with Rafsanjani and his realist technocrats at the helm, it was time for a new beginning.

THE FIRST PERSIAN GULF WAR AND ITS AFTERMATH

The world into which Iran's revolutionaries now reemerged was different from that of the 1970s. The Cold War was coming to an end and the US had a new Republican president, George H. W. Bush. Bush was a traditional conservative with realist sympathies, although he suffered from one Achilles' heel as far as Iran was concerned: his alleged involvement in secret negotiations with the Revolutionary government in the run-up to the 1980 presidential elections. There was little concrete evidence, but the allegation existed and it could be damaging.

Nonetheless, Bush was in a strong position to take a definitive and statesmanlike stand on the question of Iran. He was reaping the benefits of the end of the Cold War and announcing the dawn of a new world order, whose first expression was the successful expulsion of Iraq forces from Kuwait during the first Persian Gulf War of 1991. It was a perfect time to assess and rethink America's international challenges. Moreover, Saddam Hussein's invasion of Kuwait had made it clear that the real threat to Persian Gulf stability, complete with the spectre of weapons of mass destruction, was Iraq, not Iran. Iranians relished their vindication as the United Nations declared Iraq the aggressor, a symbolic yet highly important gesture. In a frantic bid to secure Iranian support in the forthcoming struggle, Saddam Hussein returned what vestiges of Iranian territory he had still clung onto. Iran's foreign minister was dispatched on a swift tour of the Gulf States to capitalize on this sudden stroke of good fortune, while the Minister of Oil gleefully announced that the price of oil had risen significantly. As if this were not enough, the Iraqi Air Force flew their planes into Iran for safekeeping, a responsibility Iran accepted as part of a long overdue reparations package.

More optimistic Foreign Ministry officials argued that finally the West and the United States would realize that Iran truly was an "island of stability" and that a new relationship could be forged. The fact that the Soviet Union was no longer a significant threat (and would soon no longer exist) was inconsequential because Iran remained an important state that could anchor and stabilize the emergent republics of central Asia and Trans-Caucasia. This made considerable sense, as it had in the decade before the revolution, and Americans would have been making the same case had the Shah been in power. Unfortunately, some Iranians did not appreciate that the status quo before the revolution, although rational, was not realistic. The first indication that this was so was the flurry of conjecture among some Western policy makers about the significance of Saddam's decision to send his air force to Iran.

Incredibly, despite Iran having just emerged from an eight-year struggle against Iraq, some fearfully pondered whether Iran would now enter the war on the Iraqi side. Perhaps the Iranians had suggested as much to make sure Saddam returned all remaining territory he held, but a political gambit for territorial advantage is one thing; entering a war in the defense of the one person most Iranians could be guaranteed to detest was another.

Further indications that the thaw was temporary came in the conduct of the war, when Arab states and the US became anxious about the possibilities that Iran might exploit Iraq weakness, especially in the south. This has been cited as one of the reasons the Coalition forces did not pursue the war all the way to Baghdad and seems to have been a factor in allowing Saddam Hussein to crush the Shia uprising, which had gathered momentum as an apparent response to President Bush's call to arms.

The brutal crushing of this rebellion left deep scars, and many Iraqi Shias fled to refuge in southern Iran, adding to Iran's expanding total of refugees (at this time there may have been more than two million Afghan refugees), but also providing Iran with a crucial lever for potential influence. Persian hospitality was to contrast favorably with the duplicity of the West, although at least where the Iraqi Kurds were concerned, there was determined action to relieve the pressure on them and provide them with protection against Saddam's retribution.

The effective demolition of Iraqi state power affected the regional balance of power, and Iran's Arab neighbors were anxious about the revolutionary Shia state benefiting too much in political and strategic terms from Saddam's folly. Despite official Iranian attempts to ameliorate any inferiority complex on behalf of the Arabs, unofficial comments left no one in doubt that imperial hubris was never far from the surface and that the Iranians considered the Gulf to be Persian. This suspicion of Iranian intentions in the region was reinforced and exaggerated by political expediency—local rulers understood that denunciation of Iranian perfidy was the best way to secure and maintain US support. This does not mean that the Iranians were not at fault, only that this was frequently exaggerated for political effect.

Iran's mismanagement of its regional relations was exemplified by the media storm following the rash decision by a local Iranian official on Abu Musa island. He turned back a delegation of two hundred teachers from the United Arab Emirates because their paperwork was incorrect. The international furor that erupted from this seemingly routine, if clumsy, decision caught many in Iran by surprise, especially because some in the Western media drew analogies between this apparent Iranian annexation of Abu Musa and the Iraqi invasion of Kuwait. This was absurd, not only because of the size of the islands involved (the Greater and Little Tumbs were also reiterated as an Arab grievance against the expansionist Persians), but also because of the historical fact that the islands were seized, with tacit Western consent in 1971, when the Shah was preparing to become the Gendarme of the Gulf.

Nonetheless, this latest crisis soon became defined as the issue of Persian territorial aggrandizement against the greater Arab motherland, fulfilling an agenda dear to Saddam Hussein's heart. For Iran, it was a salutary lesson in media management and the need to have a response to such allegations. As one Iranian official protested, the extent of the media coverage far exceeded the physical size of the islands, the smallest of which disappeared at high tide. Another complained that the Shah had given up Bahrein for three useless rocks that were now being used to beat Iran. Within the country, some advantage was be gained by whipping up nationalist indignation and presenting the Islamic Republic as the guarantor of national integrity. In other words, reckless and exaggerated assaults of this nature assisted the political establishment in developing further grounds for the political legitimacy of the Islamic Republic.[18]

This sense of unjust victimization was further reinforced when the United States began discussing post-war security arrangements in the region. The Iranians felt that they should be part of any security apparatus, but they were conspicuously excluded from any discussion. Instead, the US suggested that local states seek an alliance with Egypt and Syria, a security arrangement many Iranians considered to be directed towards them rather than Saddam Hussein. Despite the US excluding Iran from discussions, President Bush was amenable to the idea of a thaw in relations, and contacts were established with Rafsanjani's office. The prospective deal would revolve around the release of the US hostages in Lebanon, after which Bush would begin the process of normalizing relations, including the release of assets frozen in the United States since the revolution in 1979. Rafsanjani fulfilled his side of the bargain by bringing pressure to bear on the various groups in Lebanon (at a reported cost of some $2 million). Bush then asked that Rafsanjani formally condemn terrorism and soften the rhetoric emanating from Tehran. This Rafsanjani duly did at a Friday Prayer's sermon delivered on December 20, 1991, condemning both terrorism and anti-Western rhetoric.[19] But Bush procrastinated.

By 1992, hopes of a strategic rapprochement were fading and those in Iran who felt that some sort of *modus vivendi* could be reached with the United States were finding the odds stacked against them. Despite his high standing after the Gulf War, Bush was unwilling to risk valuable political capital in an election year by appearing to be soft on Iran. Reagan had suffered badly as a consequence of his involvement with Iran-Contra, and many questions were circulating about Bush's role not only in Iran-Contra but also in the hostage crisis, more than a decade previously. As the Democratic challenge of Bill Clinton became more serious, Bush unfortunately decided that it would be wiser to defer his response to Rafsanjani until after he had won the election.

CLINTON AND DUAL CONTAINMENT

The surprise election of Bill Clinton altered the political landscape in ways most Iranian analysts had not foreseen. It was generally acknowledged that the Democrats were unsympathetic to Iran, but the end of the Cold War and the shift in American international interests that followed were to alter the rules of the game. Not only were domestic US politics now weighted against Iran, but the international environment was ill suited to the realist interpretation of international relations that pervaded Iranian thinking. Rafsanjani had successfully managed to control most foreign excesses of the revolution by offering the determined zealots who remained the chance to pursue the revolution at home, if they avoided complications abroad. It was a compromise with dangerous implications for the development of domestic Iranian politics, but Rafsanjani was confident he could control the situation at home and reinforce his position by delivering abroad.

The charm offensive that had begun in earnest with the onset of the Gulf War continued with vigor and was directed towards expatriate Iranians, with shamelessly nationalistic overtures to return and participate in the rebuilding of the country. Foreign embassies were given a face lift.

Iranian diplomats were instructed to abandon their now famous adherence to revolutionary dress and to cultivate constructive links abroad, especially with expatriate communities, to which they were to extend all possible help with passports and travel.

In this sea change in attitude, quite a few Iranians were able to return and reclaim property seized during the revolution. The deal was economic rather than political, although much of the expatriate community, not having experienced the war, were content with the arrangement and saw no need to interest themselves in internal politics. Rafsanjani and his technocrats nonetheless recognized the political virtue of having these secular Iranians on their side. They could influence the rationalization and normalization of policy through voting and, crucially, perceptions abroad. The young were especially targeted and invited on tours of the country and reminded that their Iranian identity could not be taken from them. It was a clever strategy, and by and large it worked. Throughout the 1990s, among expatriate Iranians with little interest in politics, the image of the Islamic Republic began to soften, an achievement in part facilitated by the fact that the exiled opposition seemed to have little to offer.

This achievement was not matched by progress with foreign governments, especially European governments, who had decided to embark on a process of engagement that was alternatively constructive and critical. Despite the facelift, most Iranian diplomats were incapable of persuading their critics. They were woefully unprepared for the Western media—which needed to be regularly fed and nurtured—and seemed to have an aversion to learning foreign languages. Because the Iranian diplomatic corps were largely composed of political appointees with no training in diplomatic etiquette, they seemed at times oblivious to their stated task. Diplomatic immunity was frequently cited to cover up or excuse extraordinary breaches of standard behavior.

Many senior diplomats, retired by the revolution, lamented the stupidities of their successors, whose behavior exacerbated rather than ameliorated tensions. Indeed, the process of engagement was regularly reduced to the status of a discussion group, in part because there was no one meaningful to engage with on the Iranian side. This situation frequently resulted in Europeans lecturing or hectoring their Iranian interlocutors—a classic case of miscommunication—which only exacerbated matters as Iranians themselves complained that there was nothing reciprocal about the dialogue. When such frustrations combined with the assassination of dissidents, the activities of Iran's diplomatic corps only increased suspicions. A re-professionalization of the corps was urgently required. This was all the more important because most people abroad were inclined to see the Islamic Republic, and Iranians in general (distinguished from expatriate Persians), as synonymous with fanaticism and terrorism. Iranians, emerging from the Iran-Iraq War into the full glare of the Western day, were unprepared for this particular characterization, and some decided to define themselves in other ways. One Iranian student, who later went on to work in the Iranian president's office, commented that he could be assured of a more pleasant interaction and consequently a more productive day by describing himself as Isfahani rather than Iranian!

In the United States, the situation was worse. Expatriate Iranians who settled in Europe tended to be politically neutral or on the Left. Their distaste for the Islamic Revolution was followed closely by their dislike for the United States. Because the official Iranian attitude towards the United States overlapped considerably with the feelings of those on the Left, there was some potential common ground. In the United States, however, most politically active Iranians were monarchists with an intense dislike for the revolution and all that it stood for. For the Left, the Islamic Revolution may have lost its way. For the Right, despite the obvious similarities in political systems (they both lent towards autocracy, albeit different types), the Islamic Revolution was an abomination.

Moreover, the Islamic Republic had no diplomatic representation in the United States beyond its formal embassy at the UN in New York. Attempts were made to cultivate the Iranian diaspora, but political access and consequently the potential for political influence were limited.[20] One curious development was the strength and popularity of the Mojahedeen-e Khalq Organization (MKO), in part a result of their coherent organization but also a result of their effective exploitation of their name, which led many American donors to confuse them with the anti-Soviet Afghan Mojahedeen.

This problem was all the more serious because of changes occurring in the American foreign policy making establishment. Clinton had won the election on a domestic policy platform with a view to capitalizing on America's Cold War victory. Domestic politics were to take priority, and even European allies expressed concern that the United States might neglect important foreign policy issues and withdraw into self-imposed isolation. The debacle in Somalia, in which dead American servicemen had been dragged triumphantly through the streets by local militiamen, encouraged this development. It also highlighted the inadequacies and inexperience of the Clinton administration's foreign policy management.

As far as the Middle East was concerned, Clinton's first term was dominated by Israeli priorities, in a qualitative shift in US policy that had hitherto been unprecedented. Bush, and particularly his Secretary of State James Baker, were known for their unusually impartial approach to the Arab-Israeli conflict, epitomized by Baker's verbal reprimand to the Israeli government in a Congressional hearing. What delighted the hearts and elevated the hopes of the Arab Middle East was not appreciated in Tel Aviv, and the new Democratic administration sought to reinforce its position as the natural friend of Israel with a Middle East policy establishment that was dominated by those sympathetic to Israeli concerns. This was timely because the new peace process, initiated by Bush, had been launched, and Clinton was determined to make it a platform of his Middle East policy. The absence of a Soviet threat and the start of the peace process were to have two significant consequences for Iran.

Quite apart from changing geopolitical realities, a cadre of Sovietologists discovered that victory had made them redundant. Fortunately, they found new employment studying and commenting on the Middle East. Unfortunately for those in the Middle East, this switch was not accompanied by extensive retraining. The most obvious flaw was that these new experts in the Middle East approached their task with an admirable fluency in Russian. This was not considered a problem because the Middle East was similar to the old Soviet Union, and the states they encountered were adaptations of the traditional totalitarian model. Professional necessity (and the need for employment) ensured that inconvenient contradictions were ignored and the facts forced to fit theoretical preconceptions.

In broad terms, this meant that the analysis and understanding of Soviet communism was transferred wholesale to the Islamic state, along with analogies with Gorbachev and the inevitable collapse of a system that was ideologically dogmatic, incoherent, and aggressively expansionist.

The developing peace process resulted in an intellectual reorganization by which the traditional villains of the Israeli piece (that is, the neighboring Arabs) now had to be accommodated in a framework of respectability and potential collaboration. It was important to frame this new picture around certain commonalities, so it was suddenly discovered to everyone's satisfaction that Arabs and Jews were Semites and shared much in common. In terms of international relations, this was defined by core-periphery relations, in which Israel transferred its traditional enmity for its neighbors from the core to the periphery, in other words, to Iran. This ham-fisted attempt to provide theoretical legitimacy to political necessity was not altogether successful, although it did facilitate the development of the policy of dual containment.

Dual containment was the term given to a policy of neglect. It sought to legitimize inaction through the allocation of a recognizable brand name: a decision to perpetuate indecision. Iran, along with Iraq, was to be contained within a *cordon sanitaire*, within which Iran could do as it pleased as long as it did not bother anyone else. This political quarantine was to mirror, support, and sustain the intellectual quarantine, further exacerbating the gulf in misunderstanding and driving a growing wedge between European and American approaches to Iran. With no people on the ground and no apparent interest in Iran—it is at this stage that disinterest in Iran became a political virtue—America's accumulation of ignorance gathered pace and fed her contentment. It takes a peculiar type of bureaucratic rationality to turn indolence into a virtue. Every now and then, encouraged and reminded by various interest groups, the cordon would tighten, but initially there was a light touch. At this stage, the holy trinity of weapons of mass destruction (WMD), sponsorship of terrorism, and opposition to the Arab-Israeli peace process began to crystallize as benchmarks of American policy towards Iran. Each could be used to ensure that no progress in relations was possible.

The appointment of Warren Christopher as Secretary of State ensured that the possibility of political engagement with Iran was clearly off the agenda, because Christopher was a veteran of the tortuous negotiations that had finally resulted in the release of the US Embassy hostages. Not only did he find this particular interaction ungratifying, but his political career had been interrupted due to the Democrats being out of power for twelve years. Christopher's attitude towards Iran seemed to some observers to be more personal than political. As unprofessional as this may have been, it was no different than the personal animosity held by a number of senior revolutionaries in Iran towards the United States. It would be naive to assume that the hostage crisis was not going to affect people in an intensely personal manner.

At the same time, to let personal antipathy dictate the policies (or absence of policies) of a global power like the United States is indulgent. Some European powers regarded the barely disguised US obsession with Iran as idiosyncratic, at the very least. The fact that some regional powers saw considerable advantage in feeding this US obsession did not help. The Europeans had no intention of persuading the United States otherwise because this monumental political sulk ensured the continued absence of US companies in Iran. One continuing anomaly of the US position was that in seeking to quarantine Iran, the United States effectively isolated itself. It was a frustrating reality that few US corporations missed.

PIPELINE POLITICS

The pipeline politics that developed throughout the 1990s is a good example of the US obsession with Iran at work—and an excellent case study of how national interest is created and predicated on cultural outlook and historical world-view. With the break-up of the Soviet Union, a number of independent states emerged in the Caucasus and Central Asia, and anxiety arose about the reinvention of the Great Game, when Britain and Russia had competed for control of Central Asia and the wider region during the nineteenth century. Russia was keen to maintain what influence it retained, but despite her continued prominence, greater attention was focused on the activities of Iran and Turkey. The United States was anxious that Iran not expand her influence in the region, so great efforts were expended, some of dubious intellectual integrity, to show that the region was predominantly Turkic in cultural orientation and that naturally it was only right that Turkey should be allowed to extend her influence.

That most of the states, apart from Armenia and Georgia, were Turkic in orientation was beyond doubt. However, some scholars were brave enough to point out the historical reality that these states had existed within a distinctly Iranian milieu and that Iran consequently could lay some claim to cultural parentage. This was palpably true of Tajikistan and a number of the major cities in Central Asia, which were Persian speaking, and was reflected in popular cultural sympathies. For instance, ordinary citizens deemed Iranian television, with its female presenters modestly dressed in Islamic clothing, preferable to the rampant if glamorous secularism of the Turks.

If you were to seek US aid and backing, however, asserting your Persian cultural leanings was politically incorrect. Consequently, newly independent Soviet states who sought American favor did their best to downplay this cultural connection. What remained galling for Iranian observers was not so much the denial of any cultural association with Iran, but the appropriation of that culture and history, such that Tamerlane became Usbek, the Parthians became Turkmen, and the Persian New Year festival Now Ruz became a Turkic contribution. Having suffered the indignity of physical contraction, it seemed that Iran's cultural legacy was likewise being dismembered. In religious terms, new countries were largely Sunni, which was an important distinction with staunchly Shia Iran, although it is remarkable how quickly Iranians were to discard that which was inconvenient to their imperial aspirations. In fact, successive Iranian delegations discovered that their competition came not from the spread of Turkish language and culture, but from the desire of the locals to acquire English. The reciprocal impact of Central Asia on the continued secularization of Iranian politics has yet to be fully appreciated, though ironically, it was to be with Shia Azerbaijan that the greatest contradiction emerged.

The new republic of Azerbaijan, with its capital in Baku, was the focus of the emergent contest between US and Iranian interests in the newly independent republics. The reason for this was oil. Indeed, for most of the emerging states, oil and gas resources were their route to sustained independence. Azerbaijan, with access to the most readily retrievable oil reserves in the Caspian, was the immediate destination of Western corporations and, by extension, the West. A number of problems existed in gaining access to this oil. First was the outstanding issue of the legal status of the Caspian. The last treaty on the status of the Caspian had been signed between the Soviet Union and Iran in 1941, by which the Caspian was to be treated as a lake for the purposes of dividing its resources. This meant the neighboring states would share resources, principally caviar. This arrangement was not difficult to manage when only two states were involved. Now corporate entrepreneurs argued that the legal status was up for discussion because the Soviet Union no longer existed, a tendentious argument that ignored that the other state did exist. Furthermore, for all its revolutionary irrationality, Iran was capable of fielding effective lawyers at the international court to contest any unilateral abrogation of the Soviet-Iranian Treaty. (At the time, Iran was suing the United States for attacks on oil platforms during the Iran-Iraq War.)

This was all the more problematic because Russia likewise insisted on maintaining its rights over the Caspian. More serious, however, were the obvious problems of exploitation. Oil companies were cautious about investing in a region not known for its stability, with uncertain oil reserves, and with no obvious route to market. The first part was easily solved by stressing, and perhaps exaggerating, the available reserves. For a time, the extent of the reserves was said to compare favorably with that which existed in the Persian Gulf. Indeed the Caspian was sold as a safer alternative, away from that labyrinth of despair that included unfriendly countries such as Iraq and Iran. It was the economic salvation for the policy of dual containment. This was nonsense, and most serious oilmen knew it, but it served a public purpose of allowing the myth of the Caspian to continue unchallenged. Oil in the Persian Gulf was not only more abundant, it was far cheaper to extract and take to market. The only thing affecting supply was politics, not economics, and it was politics that would make the unattractive economics of the Caspian palatable to Western oil companies.

One geographic inconvenience that confronted US planners was the fact that Iran was also a Caspian power, a reality that excited Iranian foreign policy strategists as much as it disappointed those in the United States. Try as America did to ignore Iran, the geopolitical reality was going to make this difficult. Nonetheless, US policy makers were going to allow reality to get in the way. For the Iranians, the search for Caspian oil afforded them an opportunity removed by the demise of the Soviet Union. Any rational economic assessment of Caspian oil would conclude that Iran was important or even irreplaceable when it came to exporting the oil. Iran provided a ready market and the basic pipeline network that had been developed under the Shah. The Iranian vision was to construct further links that would ultimately enable oil to be pumped through to Turkey (and Europe) and South Asia. Alternatively, Iran offered the possibility of oil swaps, whereby oil would be sold to feed the Iranian markets in the north of Iran, while an equivalent amount would be sold from Iran's Persian Gulf reserves for the Azerbaijani government.

Iran's offer made considerable economic sense, and most oilmen recognized this, but it did not fit into the political vision of dual containment promoted by the United States. While the United States acknowledged the need to placate Russia by allowing a pipeline route through Russia to the Black Sea, its preferred option was the construction of a pipeline through Georgia and Turkey to Ceyhan on the Mediterranean. Some analysts pointed out that this route would take the pipeline through some of the more unstable parts of the Caucasus and Turkish Kurdistan. Any hesitation was set aside when careful lobbying was matched by the US declaration that it would financially underwrite this expensive option. Caspian oil supplies were of strategic importance, and of course it was crucial that Iran did not benefit.

This was unfortunate because Iran's overall role in the Caucasus had been constructive, and many technocrats viewed Iran's integration into the pipeline network as a vital means of normalizing the revolution and its international relations. What they had not appreciated was that normalization and acceptance were not on the American menu of options. In regional terms, the result of being frozen out was an increase in tensions.

Iranians were incensed by the Azerbaijani government's determination to accentuate all things Turkish, often to absurd extremes, and to distance themselves from Iran. This flew in the face of historical experience and provided Iranians with a stark reminder of the indignities of the Treaty of Turkmenchai. Iranians were particularly angered by vocal calls from Baku for reunification with southern (that is, Iranian) Azerbaijan, haunted as they were by the spectre of 1946.*

That this irritated Iranian sensibilities only seemed to enthuse certain parts of the American policy-making establishment, which curiously concluded that irritation equaled effectiveness. Nonetheless, this elementary approach to international statecraft continues to this day, with more intensity, and is a poor excuse for policy.

The immediate consequence for Azerbaijan was a vital loss of a strategic partner in its conflict with Armenia over the contested territory of Nagorno-Karabagh. Armenia had no such qualms about seeking Iranian assistance and made much of the Armenian connection to Iran, both in terms of the historical Armenian minority in Iran and by stressing their common Aryan roots. In many ways, Iran was their natural ally because the Armenians were not overly enthused by the possibility of a Turkish or Russian alliance. Iran, meanwhile, openly professed neutrality in the war, but leaned towards Armenia, with some reports that Iran went so far as to supply Armenia with weapons. Thus it was that the Islamic Republic of Iran supported Christian Armenia over Shia Azerbaijan, because the Azeris had offended Iranian *national* sensibilities.

Having been let down by the Bush administration and now faced with a Democrat administration that was showing itself to be deeply antithetical, Rafsanjani decided that the best strategy was to offer the United States an explicit material incentive. Rafsanjani was under considerable pressure in his second term. The political concessions he had made to the hard-line conservatives were coming back to haunt his presidency, especially because the economic miracle he had promised had failed to materialize. Money was coming into the economy, but the limited distribution

---

*It is worth noting that the appellation *Azerbaijan* was only adopted by the Caucasian republic after the First World War, and that this had resulted in a vigorous protest from the Iranian government, who noted, rightly as it turns out, that it would be later exploited to encourage separatist movements.

of wealth contradicted the Islamic precepts of the revolution, and his own extraordinary wealth made him vulnerable to arguments that he had materially polluted what had been a spiritual revolution. The elusive philosopher's stone remained the United States. Rafsanjani conjectured that if he could successfully reconcile America to the revolution, not only would the Islamic Republic be secure but the revolution would be complete. Others argued that the revolution was not so much complete as over and were reassured by the continued American reluctance to engage. The consistency of America's refusal allowed them to convince the skeptics that America *was* the Great Satan, the Global Arrogance, or whatever other epithet happened to be fashionable.

Rafsanjani was aware, however, that US companies were keen to do business. Some US companies were among the largest purchasers of Iranian oil (although they sold it to markets other than America), and other US companies, such as Microsoft and Coca Cola, were cautiously investigating opportunities through offices in Dubai and agents in Iran itself. Among the most enthusiastic supporters of access was the airline manufacturer Boeing, and President Clinton found himself under considerable pressure to allow the sale of new airliners to Iran Air. With all this evidence, it was natural to conclude that the engine of global capitalism would have a weak spot for profit, and that a lucrative contract would be the means by which relations could be tentatively established. This also suited Iran because Rafsanjani could argue that in signing an economic contract, political integrity had been kept intact, an exercise in smoke and mirrors that would nonetheless keep the hawks on all sides quiet, if not contented.

The decision to offer a significant ($1 billion) contract to the US oil company Conoco did not meet with the required reaction. Conoco found itself under enormous pressure, especially from the American-Israeli Public Affairs Committee (AIPAC), to relinquish the deal, while President Clinton moved quickly to impose an executive order restricting any such economic relations. The embargo, announced at a meeting of the World Jewish Congress, took many in Iran by surprise, not least Rafsanjani. Saudi Arabia, meanwhile, was encouraged to place a major order from Boeing (reportedly eighty planes), thus relieving the pressure in that quarter. Rafsanjani's gambit had met with unmitigated failure, but this was only the beginning. In the aisles Senator Alphonse D'Amato awaited.

ILSA AND THE FAILURE OF DETENTE

By the latter half of the 1990s, the realist strategy adopted by Rafsanjani and his acolytes had not only failed to dent the US position, it seemed to have hardened it. Clinton had moved to impose a wider range of sanctions on Iran through the executive order, thereby closing off one significant nonpolitical possibility for engagement. US companies may not have boasted of their links with Iran, but they pursued a strategy of indirect engagement largely through their European subsidiaries and particularly through an economic intermediary, Dubai. Faced with mutual political difficulties, businessmen from both sides relocated and networked through Dubai, which fast became the hub for the Iranian private sector.

Clinton's executive order put an end to any such exploratory economic ties, much to the satisfaction of America's competitors, who relished the prospect of an Iranian market free from American competition. American companies, on the other hand, were less than impressed with the free run afforded to their rivals by the continuation of the political obsession with Iran. Rafsanjani hoped that corporate pressure might yet modify this latest Democratic punch below the Iranian belt, while others considered it typical of Democratic animosity towards Iran. Such views were dangerously anachronistic.

D'Amato represented a new type of Republican politician who was more ideological and beholden to the Israeli lobby. The new Republicans had learned not only the bitter lessons of Iran-Contra but also the harsh lessons of President Bush's tough stance against Israel in the aftermath of the first Persian Gulf War. D'Amato, a senator from New York, was particularly attuned to this reality. Far from lobbying for a lifting of sanctions, D'Amato's proposed legislation turned Republican policy on its head by arguing for an extension of sanctions and their express use as a political tool against not only the target country (in this case Iran) but all third parties that might contravene US policy.

The Iran-Libya Sanctions Act (ILSA)—Libya was added later by Senator Kennedy—sought to impose secondary sanctions on any country that intended to invest in the Iranian oil and gas industry by depriving that country of access to American markets and finance. The choice was simple: you are either with us or against us. The European Union was not impressed with the imposition of this commercial fatwa. Nor were many other countries, in particular Canada, who railed against this imperial extension of American power and the sheer effrontery by which America sought to impose its political position. For the Americans, this was a matter of principle. For the Europeans, this was the irrational expression of an American obsession, which in the absence of the Soviet threat was beginning to dominate US foreign policy making.

D'Amato's legislation inaugurated a flurry of similar legislation, occasionally initiated at the state level, such that the State Department in Washington began to protest that legislators at all levels of government were determined to hijack US foreign policy. Clinton discovered to his chagrin that in the absence of a constructive policy, others would create one for him. The Iranians for their part looked on in curiosity at a United States determined not only to isolate itself but to engage in fratricidal infighting with its European allies over a country that had offered it a contract and a share of its oil industry. Pragmatists and moderates might have been perplexed; hard-liners in the regime were overjoyed.

Yet there was little to be satisfied about. The determination to contain Iran led to another policy initiative, which was to rebound on the United States, involving the extension of pipeline politics into the politics of Afghanistan. The United States had shown uncharacteristic idealism in pursuing the Baku-Ceyhan pipeline option instead of alternatives through Iran or Russia. But Iran, acquainted as they were with the vagaries of Afghan politics, believed that economic rationality would force America's hand regarding the exploitation of Central Asian oil and gas. Few took seriously the notion that the United States would support the construction of a pipeline through Afghanistan, noting sarcastically that the mountains were the least of the problems to be faced by any prospective pipeline builder. Security would be difficult to achieve at the best of times, and the times were not propitious. The Afghan Mujahideen—originally supported by the United States, through Pakistan, in their war against Soviet occupation—had now turned on each other in the absence of a common enemy. Afghan factionalism multiplied and attitudes polarized. They drew the interest of neighboring powers, which following the collapse of the Soviet Union meant Iran and Pakistan.

Iran had been contending against a brutal drug war on its eastern border for some time. This broad security operation merged with the overall strategy of maintaining a tribal frontier driven by the proceeds of smuggling. Iran suffered significant casualties in the war to curtail drug trafficking (even if some within the system were profiting from opium smuggling), with estimates by the late 1990s running at more than three thousand dead.

Iranian authorities could barely disguise their frustration at the wilful ignorance shown by Western countries, who condemned the flow of drugs from Afghanistan (and by implication Iran), while refusing to acknowledge Iran's efforts to curtail the smuggling. This was all the more galling because some of the sophisticated weapons used by the drug smugglers (particularly surface-to-air missiles) were obvious hangovers from the days of the resistance against the Soviets. The United States went so far as to block UN assistance to Iran in the war on drugs. For some Europeans watching these developments (as well as more impartial American observers), America's obstructionism was a clear example of ideological blindness. More was to follow.

In the contest for control of Afghanistan, Pakistan and Iran moved from tacit collaboration to implicit confrontation. The former allies were effectively fighting a proxy war in Afghanistan, and it is remarkable how the status of Pakistan decreased dramatically in Iranian eyes throughout the 1990s, to the point that by the presidency of Mohammad Khatami, Iran's diplomatic sympathies increasingly lay with India over Pakistan. This change in attitude was the result not only of developments in Afghanistan but more generally of the radicalization of Islamist politics.

In 1979, the Islamic Revolution sought to present itself as a pan-Islamic revolution that was relevant to Sunnis and Shias alike. Throughout the Iran-Iraq War, this view dissipated, particularly with respect to the Arab world. Ties to Pakistan lingered a little longer. But by the 1990s, developments in radical Sunnism, through a growing network of *madrasas* generously funded by the Saudis, among others, dramatically increased sectarian tensions, and attacks upon Shia communities in Pakistan increased. These developments were matched by the rationalization of the revolution in Iran and the emergence of realism in the Rafsanjani presidency, espousing a more national and economically orientated foreign policy. Growing sectarianism was therefore compounded by a return of nationalism.

The significance of these changes seems to have been lost on the Clinton administration, whose central focus remained the containment of Iran within an overall framework of minimizing foreign commitments. Consequently, as long as containment was not violated as a principle, the details could be left to allies. The sponsorship of Sunni radicalism was less important, and more amenable, because the agents of this development were traditional regional allies of the United States. The Taleban were one consequence of this delegation of political responsibility. While Iran railed at the perversion of Islam espoused by this new hard-line group, the West appeared more sanguine. A firm hand was exactly what the factionalism of Afghanistan needed, and in any case the zealotry exhibited would soon be tempered by the realities of government.

For the United States, the Taleban ascendancy represented the victory of their proxy over Iran, the further delimitation of Iranian regional ambitions, and crucially, the realization of their ambitions to extend a pipeline from Central Asia to South Asia. The Taleban would impose the security required, thereby facilitating the pipeline cordon around Iran. The cautious welcome the State Department afforded to the Taleban was treated with incredulity in Iran and derision by those who were aware of what the Taleban represented. It took a while for the consequences of this move to be understood by Iranian officials, but the message was ultimately clear. Radical Islam was *not* the problem.

KHATAMI AND THE REFORM MOVEMENT

Our age is one of [the] domination of Western civilization and culture. Understanding it is necessary. An effective understanding goes beyond the frills of that civilization and reaches the roots and foundations of its values and principles.

MOHAMMAD KHATAMI, DECEMBER 1997

THE FAILURE OF President Rafsanjani to broker a detente with the United States had interesting repercussions. In the United States, the tendency was simply to ignore and contain Iran. In Iran itself, rejection resulted in reflection and a review of the nature of the relationship. Many Iranian policy makers were perplexed by America's response to the offer of an oil contract and could not understand America's failure to act according to rational and reasonable norms.

Some considered that America's behavior exhibited their ideological enmity towards the Islamic Republic. Others went further and decried the latent racism that now seemed to determine an American enmity towards Iran and the Iranians.

America's initial welcome to the rise of the Taleban in Afghanistan confirmed the apparent double standard that permeated US policy towards the region. But the extremism of the Taleban removed any remaining ambiguity as to the political and ideological nature of the problem. Many Iranians, echoing Rafsanjani's exhaustion with the domestic struggle, responded with further procrastination, arguing that they had done all they could, that the Democrats were clearly beyond comprehension, and that the best thing was to wait for a Republican presidency—old views die hard in Iran. Others were acutely aware of the depth of the mistrust that had grown up between Iran and the United States and were determined to take a more proactive stance.

The origins of the Reform Movement, as it came to be defined during the presidency of Mohammad Khatami (1997–2005), can be found in the vigorous debates and discussions that emerged in Iran's universities following the end of the Iran-Iraq War in 1988. For the better part of eight years, political discussion had been put on hold while the war with Iraq took priority. At the same time, more conservative elements in the revolutionary elite took the opportunity of the war to impose austere social restrictions. For many Iranians, especially those on the Left and the younger generation, the Islamic Revolution had been fought to establish an Islamic Republic. This synthetic structure by which Islam would be married to a quintessentially Western concept, that of Republicanism, was a goal worth fighting for and pursuing. In other words, while the republic would be defined by Islamic values and traditions, it would remain a republic with all the traditional characteristics of the separation of powers, elections, and most importantly, the rule of law.

In many ways what the Reformists were seeking was a definitively modern state, in which the personal nature of power was diminished in favor of a legally regulated and transparent structure. For moderate Reformists, this could be achieved through the Constitution by reducing the powers of the Supreme Leader and his burgeoning household government. In the Constitution of the Islamic Republic, the Supreme Leader enjoyed no formal position within the state. The head of state was (and remains) the President, and while the Leader's powers were constitutionally defined, his position was more of a religious guardian with a transnational function. In many ways, the office of the Supreme Leader, as it was to grow in the aftermath of Khomeini's death, was the ideal mechanism by which an Iranian imperial reach could be realized. Ironically, however, a limited international reach—in particular the fact that Khamenei did not enjoy the religious credentials or charisma of his predecessor—meant that the Supreme Leader tended to matters at home, equally if not more than he did abroad. This domestic agenda was enhanced by Rafsanjani's amendments to the Constitution.

In the early 1990s, many who felt that the republican aspects of the Constitution had been neglected threw in their lot with Rafsanjani—in the hope that his populism would translate into something more meaningful—or were excluded from the political process. The Islamic Republic prided itself on elections and the popularity of the system. The myth of the revolution dictated that this had been a mass movement against a powerful dictatorship supported by the United States. Elections therefore continued to occur, but they were heavily managed and at times openly orchestrated. They were tolerated by those with more ambitious political aspirations because they held the promise of more political freedoms.

At the same time, in the aftermath of the war, the population was experiencing a general exhaustion and a desire to rebuild their lives (and the country as a whole), which resulted in economic matters taking priority over political issues. Rafsanjani's political settlement also involved a compromise with the Islamic authoritarians, for whom any talk of republic was blasphemous; Ayatollah Khomeini's tolerance of the republic was merely transitory and tactical. All this resulted in little practical political reform. In Rafsanjani's second administration, when he found his economic policies under attack from a staunchly conservative Parliament, the only developments of note were in marginal social areas. For example, the religious policing of courting couples was gradually reduced, and the state television and radio service took the bold step of playing instrumental versions of Western music.

Rafsanjani's contribution to the transformation of political life in Iran was more implicit than explicit. First, he sponsored and nurtured a cadre of ministers and technocrats who were practically minded, highly educated, and in some cases, very capable. Many of his ministers had been educated in the West, notably the United States. Many retained a deep affection for the United States as a country, if not for the government itself. Their attitude towards the United States tended to be not ideological. More importantly, their mere existence in the highest offices of the land was both significant and influential.

Second, Rafsanjani's lifestyle and those of his sons erred on the side of capitalism, and the unashamed acquisition of wealth and the consumerism that accompanied it was orientated towards the West. Nobody wanted to buy goods from the Far East (Japan excepted) if an alternative American product was offered, and shopkeepers would sarcastically offer customers the choice of buying from the Great Satan. To be sure, the rampant materialism overseen by Rafsanjani caused him immense political problems. But a clear contradiction existed between the official rhetoric and the reality of American goods flooding the country.

Finally, and probably of the greatest significance, was the tactical sponsorship of progressive intellectuals, who began to expand the debate on the role of religion in politics and Iran's relationship with the West. There were two principal reasons for this. The first was a widespread belief among the political and religious establishment that the Islamic Republic had nothing to fear from the truth. This in part explains the tremendous increase in historical research conducted in the aftermath of the war. The results of much of this research were not always palatable to the Islamic Republic. Many zealous researchers came away from the archives more confused than when they had entered, realizing for the first time that perhaps the Shah had not been so wicked. The immediate consequence was that the Shah was rehabilitated as an Iranian who was mislead and tragically manipulated by the wicked Americans, although this image was also to come into question. The second reason was the tactical and political advantages such sponsorship afforded Rafsanjani.

The rehabilitation of the Shah allowed Rafsanjani to co-opt technocratic elements of the old elite and resurrect old economic and foreign policies as entirely legitimate. The most obvious examples of this were in the reaction to the Abu Musa crisis of 1992, in which ministers rejected the notion that just because the Shah had seized the islands, it must have been wrong, and in the application of urban planning to Tehran after the war. The new mayor, Gholamhussein Karbaschi, made no secret of his debt to Nikpay, his royalist predecessor who had been executed by the revolutionary authorities. Another aspect of this process of imitation was in nuclear policy, with wholly unforeseen consequences when Iran's nuclear ambitions met resistance from the West.

Associations with the era of the Shah lent a curious sense of legitimacy to programs of development, allowed the reconciliation of the elite, and by extension opened up the forum of debate. One of the reasons the Shah had failed, it was argued, was because of his failure to politically liberalize and because his relationship with the United States was too dependent and too servile. A new relationship could perhaps be contemplated, although Rafsanjani and his acolytes had little idea how to approach this. Conservative hard-liners were appalled at such developments, but Rafsanjani found it useful to protect progressive thinkers as a stick by which he could occasionally beat his opponents.

Although some of these thinkers were appreciative of the protection, they recognized that Rafsanjani's motives were tactical and not the result of conviction. At the same time, such ideas and debates were not easy to control. For every moderate discussion supported by Rafsanjani, many other more radical discussions were taking place in the margins, especially within the boisterous and energetic university campuses. Iranian campuses were unusually large because Khomeini had encouraged Iranians to procreate (a policy reversed in the early 1990s). The number of students exceeded one hundred thousand during the Pahlavi monarchy, but mushroomed to more than a million by the 1990s. Those who failed to get into the main universities could attend (for a fee) the Islamic Open University, which was established by Rafsanjani.

Added to this combustible mix was the fact that many veterans who emerged from the war were anxious for a better deal from their government—a renegotiation of the social contract—and were less willing to be deferential and listen uncritically to the admonishments of their leaders. In addition, modern technology, particularly satellite television and the internet, provided people with diverse windows to the outside world and information that had hitherto been out of reach. And last but not least, the existence of an extensive Iranian diaspora provided personal contacts for many Iranians.

As noted, the official relationship between the Islamic Republic and the diaspora was always tense. On the one hand, the diaspora were regarded as dangerous reactionaries with little to offer the revolution. On the other, Rafsanjani sought their capital and expertise. Informally, they were invaluable in the transmission of information, especially about the realities of Western culture, and a personal window to the outside world. Soon, members of the new elite were likewise anxious to send their children to the West for education and livelihood. Iran's political isolation was compensated by myriad international social networks. All this contributed to a dynamic intellectual environment.[1]

The central focus of much of this debate was domestic: the role of religion within politics, the development of civil society and Islamic democracy. An important facet of this discussion was the international significance of Iran's Islamic Revolution and, by extension, Iran's relationship with the West. For all but the most conservative thinkers, the Islamic Revolution was an event firmly located in a Western historical frame of reference. This may seem odd for a revolution that was anti-Western in its inception, but it reflected Iranian intellectual sympathies and the fact that they defined themselves in relation to the West. There was an inescapable logic. A student, without apparent contradiction, could proclaim that the Islamic Revolution was the greatest intellectual movement since the Renaissance, a quintessentially European moment of little relevance to Islamic history. A senior Ayatollah could confidently enunciate that the Islamic Revolution was the third great revolution after the French and Russian ones! Indeed, some Reformists went considerably further in their analogies by comparing themselves to Protestants fighting Catholic absolutism.[2]

The Iranians were not interested in being part of the Third World; their aspirations lay elsewhere. It may be argued that, with time, the Islamic Revolution became Iranian, with all the implications that held for their cultural affinities and sympathies. In the debate between Iran and Islam, the balance was tipping towards Iran. By the mid 1990s, for all the lip service to the greater Islamic community, national ethos was shaping public opinion, with a dramatic upsurge in interest in all aspects of ancient Iran, including Zoroastrianism, the pre-Islamic faith. Society's move towards nationalism and secularism would begin at the philosophical level—cultures were not absolute and opposed but integrative and mutually dependent—and lead to a fundamental reexamination of Iran's relationship with the West and the United States in particular.

THE DIALOGUE OF CIVILIZATIONS

Seyyed Mohammad Khatami was a middle-ranking cleric with an unorthodox career. A keen supporter of the revolution in 1979, he nonetheless espoused views that were both idealistic and cosmopolitan. A Muslim firmly grounded and located in the Iranian tradition, he had seen no contradiction in fulfilling his military service under the Shah. On the contrary, he considered it a positive experience. Moreover, his training was in the philosophical tradition of Islam rather than the juridical, thereby precluding any possible elevation to the rank of Ayatollah (Khatami remained one rank lower at Hojjat-ol Islam). These philosophical interests both reflected and further fuelled his complex and integrative view of the world. Controversially, Khatami had also studied Western philosophy, which he seemed to have enjoyed, and spent time managing the Islamic Centre in Hamburg, which gave him first-hand experience of Western culture and an appreciation of the German language. His conception of the historical march of freedom, for example, had a strikingly familiar feel when he argued during a speech at the United Nations that, "one can discern the trajectory of history towards liberty. The history of humankind is the history of liberty."[3] In short, he recognized that for all its flaws, Western civilization had much to offer the world, noting that it was a "phenomenon . . . whose positive achievements are not few."[4]

Khatami represented the new Islamic Republican man, educated, worldly, and sophisticated; eager and perhaps confident enough to reach out to the wider world; modest though not puritanical; and certainly not a proponent of the school of revolutionary thought that argued that piety was reflected in poverty (or at least the appearance of it). Recognizing previous failures in communication between Iran and the international community, Khatami argued that, "the first rule of dialogue . . . is to know yourself and identity. The second rule is to know the civilization with which you want to maintain a dialogue."[5] In many ways, Khatami was a natural successor to Rafsanjani, in whose first administration he had served as Culture Minister before hard-liners in the Parliament pressured him to resign. But in other significant respects, Khatami represented a qualitative shift, and his victory in the presidential elections of 1997 took many people in Iran, and more especially beyond its borders, by surprise.

As far as the United States was concerned, Mohammad Khatami did not fit the blueprint, and the instinctive and safe response was to profess skepticism that Khatami's ideas on Islamic democracy and a dialogue with the international community were anything more than window-dressing. In taking this position, they were ably assisted by a curious amalgam of Iranian opposition groups as well as traditional, if sympathetic, observers of Iran and Islam in general, who balked at the idea that democracy might be desirable, let alone possible.

All these groups shared an ideological conviction, consolidated over many years, that made the Reformist movement in Iran and Khatami's leadership of it deeply uncomfortable. Rather than radically reassess these convictions, they chose the comforting reassurance of denial, which was both politically expedient and effortless. Khatami, however, was not going to be so easy to dismiss. Well versed in Western philosophy and acquainted with the language of communication, Khatami recognized that interest, simplistically defined, was not the issue. The essence of the problem was to define that interest and draw attention to its coincidence where it existed.

In suggesting this coincidence, one had to then show a commonality of purpose, perhaps initially through small transactions, whereby trust—the core of the problem—could be gradually and methodically rebuilt. To use the language of international relations, Khatami essentially discarded vulgar realism and introduced a measure of constructivism into Iran's foreign policy strategy. The culture of mistrust had to be deconstructed and replaced by a more suitable edifice. This was not an approach that enamored him to his conservative critics in Iran, the more hard-line of which were firmly wedded to a confrontational distrust of the West.[6] Nor did it immediately relate to the foreign policy establishments in Europe and the United States, to whom Khatami seemed an interesting if quaint intellectual. Diplomatic caution dictated a wait-and-see policy, although it soon became apparent that this was another excuse for inaction and intellectual unpreparedness. The latter was on full view following Khatami's decision to give an exclusive interview to CNN, where he would elucidate on Iran-US relations.

In the interview, Khatami not only categorically rejected terrorism but also expressed regret for the embassy takeover in 1979. He added that the burning of US flags was not something he endorsed or encouraged but that such actions should be seen in the context of broader US-Iran relations, in which Iran had been repeatedly humiliated by the United States. In particular, he drew attention to the fact that "there is a bulky wall of mistrust between us and American administrations, a mistrust rooted in improper behavior by the American governments. As an example of this type of behavior, I should refer to admitted involvement of the American government in the 1953 coup d'etat which toppled Mosaddeq's national government, immediately followed by a $45 million loan to strengthen the coup government. I should also refer to the capitulation law imposed by the American government on Iran."[7]

Anti-US slogans, he emphasized, were not intended to insult the US people or undermine the US government, but reflected a desire by Iranians to "to terminate a mode of relationship between Iran and America."[8] In seeking to terminate and replace this particular "mode of relationship," Khatami had another strategy in mind: "In his [de Tocqueville's] view, the significance of this [American] civilization is the fact that liberty found religion as a cradle for its growth, and religion found the protection of liberty as its Divine calling. Therefore in America, liberty and faith never clashed, and as we see, even today most Americans are religious peoples. There is less war against religion in America. Therefore, the approach to religion, which was the foundation of Anglo-American civilization, relies on the principle that religion and liberty are consistent and compatible.

. . . We feel that what we seek is what the founders of American civilization were also pursuing four centuries ago. This is why we sense an intellectual affinity with the essence of American civilization."[9]

This was a remarkable statement to make, but it was largely lost on his American audience, and commentators focused on his various expressions of regret or on those parts of the interview that could—at a stretch—be interpreted as unhelpful. Senator John McCain, who was invited to provide a post-interview assessment, concentrated on criticizing Khatami for his anti-Israeli comments. Khatami had in fact not dwelt on the issue of Israel but had pointed out that one of the reasons for distrust was the perception in Iran that US foreign policy towards the Middle East was made in Tel Aviv.

The American response, incoherent as it may have been, largely dealt with political consequences rather than philosophical roots. Thus the emphasis was on particularities as they related to American grievances—the hostage crisis, flag burning, attitudes towards Israel—along with some grudging recognition that America may not have conducted herself well in the past (for example, the events of 1953). But there was little appreciation of the fundamental message Khatami delivered, which related to the profundity of the ideological problem and the need to redefine this with an emphasis on the commonalities between the two countries.

Khatami was arguing that far from being inherently antithetical to each other, Iran and the United States shared a common interest in religion. He particularly sought to identify Iran with a specifically American notion of religious democracy. As a political strategy, it was similar to that adopted by the Israelis in their relationship with the United States, a coincidence of interests so intimate it was philosophically grounded. However, this philosophical leap of the imagination was beyond most American interlocutors, and there was no supporting network on the ground in the United States to disseminate and promote it. Even those who, after reflection, understood what he was doing rejected the notion of commonality. Instead, they highlighted the differences and stressed that the United States was a secular country that remained antithetical to the totalitarian theocracy in Iran. (The United States may be a secular state, but it cannot be described as a secular society.) Yet Khatami was not saying that Iran had achieved a religious democracy; he was arguing that Iran was seeking this eventuality, and that in effect it looked to the United States as a model. This was a remarkable and bold attempt to breach the cultural divide, and it caused consternation among hard-liners in Iran, who were appalled at this attempt at a rapprochement.

Khatami and his allies thus faced opposition from critics both at home and abroad, making the strategy enormously difficult to navigate. When the United States subsequently announced that it would be happy in principle to open formal talks, Khatami suddenly appeared less than forthcoming. This was partly because the offer of talks by the United States was invariably prefaced by a long list of grievances for any proposed agenda—a list that may have mollified US hard-liners but antagonized their counterparts in Iran—and partly because the offer of formal talks was regarded by many in Iran as moving with indecent haste. Khatami also recognized that one had to bridge the cultural divide and prepare the terrain before direct political talks could be fruitfully initiated, and that this terrain could best be shaped primarily at the social level. Hence the enthusiasm for academic, economic, and most publicly, sporting links—the most prominent being the soccer encounter at the 1998 World Cup in Paris.

Iranians as a whole admired the straightforward manner of Americans—and contrasted it favorably with the ambiguous position often taken by Europeans. In this, they perhaps related and understood the American attitude towards what would later be defined as Old Europe, although this perception is ironic given the general Western perception of Iranian ambiguity. Nevertheless, there was a sense, certainly among Reformists in Iran, that for all America's frankness, Americans had an unfortunate tendency to rush things when what was required was a delicate diplomatic courtship. As one Iranian diplomat commented, it sometimes seemed as if the Americans were determined to consummate the date on the first night!

The Europeans, and the British in particular, were seen as more empathic and politically aware of the realities of Iran. Iranian Reformists often hailed the ambiguous but mutually satisfactory settlement of the Rushdie affair in 1998 as an exemplary case of British diplomacy. Over the next five years, British diplomacy was to move with considerable skill towards reestablishing Britain's political and cultural influence. This achievement was a testament to the skills of the individuals involved but may be seen as double-edged.

The Europeans had diplomats on the ground. The Americans had not had anyone in Iran since 1980. The Iranians had only an embassy at the UN, which was restricted in its access to the wider United States. That is not to say that European countries realized this obvious advantage. Western diplomats were not necessarily aware of the significance of the intellectual debate taking place. Even those who did make the effort to understand and were astounded at the intellectual vibrancy of the movement had enormous difficulty convincing their colleagues of the significance of what was transpiring and the need to engage with these developments. One British diplomat serving in Tehran, for instance, could barely disguise his frustration at the lack of interest among his Arabist colleagues who, inured to years of political staleness, found the reports from Iran to be inconceivable. Such attitudes were replicated in London, and in many ways this reflected not only the cumbersome structures of European bureaucracies, which move and absorb change slowly, but the nearly two decades of diplomatic isolation and disinterest. Iran was not a career-making move for many diplomats, and the British had a generational gap in Persianists, which by the mid 1990s was proving costly to all concerned, not least Iran.

For all the unwillingness or structural inability to respond, the intellectual ferment was real. Almost all subjects previously considered taboo were up for discussion in a national press that was unprecedented in its vigor and comparable to the Western press in its reach. In Khatami's first year, more than two hundred new newspapers and magazines were granted licenses, increasing the total by some 25 percent (mirroring the ninety-five licenses granted to political parties and organizations). The daily circulation of the top Reformist newspapers regularly reached one hundred fifty thousand, which together totalled more than one million newspapers per day.

More importantly, these papers dared to print that which had hitherto been forbidden. This is something rarely appreciated in the West, largely because most of the material was in Persian, and the English-speaking world tends to ignore anything not in English. Khatami's interview with CNN was a highly effective foray into this world, using the best medium of its day, but it was not supported by a network of proponents and lobbyists. Once he was off the air, interest and awareness dissipated rapidly. But in Iran, in addition to discussions on secularism, the role of religion, and democracy, there were vibrant discussions on the relationship with the United States, Britain, and surprisingly Israel.[10]

Israel had always been decried in the official media as the Zionist entity, in a rigorous if dogmatic attempt to deny it legitimacy. Anti-Israeli rhetoric had become a staple of conservative ideology and was an area that Reformists and the more centrist technocrats around Rafsanjani had left to their opponents. Along with headscarves, it was an iconic reminder that Iran was in the throes of an *Islamic* Revolution: it was politically cost free, much like Iran-bashing was in the United States, and it kept the conservatives occupied. Moreover, the notion that Israel dealt with the Palestinians unjustly could easily be accepted by many Iranians, even if they happened to be apolitical.

Others argued that ignoring the reality of Israel was ludicrous and that the debate had to change, especially because the Palestinians themselves had come to recognize the two-state solution. It was ridiculous, they argued, for Iran to be more Palestinian than the Palestinians, or as one Iranian politician noted, "more Catholic than the Pope," a phrase that scandalized the conservative opposition. They protested that the Palestinian Authority had misread their public and it was Hamas and other more militant groups who understood the Palestinian pulse. If this was so, argued Reformists, why did the Palestinian Authority enjoy formal diplomatic status in Tehran? If they were illegitimate representatives of their people, close them down and invite Hamas to open a diplomatic office! Reformists enthusiastically took advantage of the internal contradictions and inconsistencies of conservative dogma. It may be justifiably argued, as foreign critics were apt to do, that little practical change in Iranian policy occurred, but it is difficult to overestimate the scale of the taboo that had been broken.[11]

DEBATING IRAN-US RELATIONS

With respect to the United States, there was considerable more room for maneuvering. For the Iranian state, as the aspiring defender of Islamic interests, Israel's legitimate existence was a profoundly ideological issue. No one but fringe hard-liners doubted America's right to exist.

The issue with the United States was, in a curious parallel, a matter of behavior rather than legitimacy. Ayatollah Khomeini had, after all, decreed that the Islamic Republic could have relations with all countries, save Israel, on the basis of mutual respect. This meant that relations with the United States remained a possibility if not yet a probability. Reformists never tired of reminding skeptics that even the enmity of the founding father of the Islamic Republic did not preclude a change in relations some time in the future. Just look, for instance, at Iran's growing relations with Saudi Arabia, a state Khomeini had decried over and above that of Saddam Hussein's Iraq. And despite an eight-year war and the absence of a firm peace treaty, it was still possible to have some sort of relationship with Iraq. Here in fact was the perfect example of a relationship in which tensions persisted and yet dialogue was possible.

Reformists were simply arguing for a dialogue in which Iran's interests and aspirations could be aired and myths dispelled. Iran and the US may well be enemies forever, but at least let this be based on facts as opposed to false impressions. Moreover, clear areas of mutual interest existed in which dialogue and discussion would be useful. Examples frequently mentioned were the negotiations and settlements discussed in The Hague over US and Iranian assets in each other's countries following the revolution. These were remarkably successful, and the truth was that Iranians and Americans worked together constructively on a professional level. The difficulty, as always, was politics; and this too the Reformists sought to ameliorate by tackling the very issue that they felt was at the core of America's grievance: the hostage crisis.[12]

It is remarkable how much reflection had occurred in Iran over the hostage crisis. On one level, people simply accepted it as an event that defined the early revolution and a debt paid for the Mosaddeq coup in 1953. It was in the past and everyone ought to move on. There was a recognition that this was the singular grievance at the heart of America's problems with the Islamic Republic, but few people appreciated the depth of this grievance or the fact that Iranians had done anything wrong. Throughout the 1990s, however, it was increasingly accepted as a regrettable incident, one that was nonetheless defining but was apposite to the time and could not be repeated. This was not a view encouraged by hard-liners, who sought to institutionalize the event as an almost sacrosanct part of the revolutionary calendar. However, the anniversary held on November 4 each year was attended by fewer and fewer people. Eventually, some Reformists thinkers were bold enough to suggest that the episode had in fact been an understandable mistake.

Conservatives derided this revisionism, reminding people that some prominent Reformists were the very students who had taken the embassy and that it was too late to show remorse. This was a view also held by many American skeptics, although the idea that people cannot change their positions over a generation strikes this writer as unreasonable. Among the most prominent revisionists were Asgharzadeh, the leader of the seizure, and Abbas Abdi, a leading Reformist journalist. Asgharzadeh made it clear that they had not intended to seize the embassy for more than a few days, that the initiative had been their own, and that they had been overwhelmed by the political response and its ramifications. In short, he and his colleagues had been caught up in a revolutionary whirlwind of youthful zeal and idealism. He was adamant that they had never treated the hostages harshly—a statement contradicted by the evidence. And while he could not regret it as an event of its time, the passage of that time allowed him to reflect more soberly on the consequences of his actions and to recognize that these had not been entirely beneficial for the Islamic Republic.

Abdi went considerably further and sought out a meeting with one of the hostages, Barry Rosen, which was held in Paris. It is a matter of debate how much was achieved—it was, after all, an informal meeting insofar as there was no direct official sanction—but it was nonetheless a sincere attempt to resolve differences and lay ghosts to rest.

Not all these ghosts related to foreign affairs. A major driving force behind these moves came from a desire to lay to rest the internal obsession with the United States. Whether in the form of cultural imitation among the country's youth or dogmatic hard-line antipathy, the United States remained a central feature of political and cultural life in the Islamic Republic. One of the motives for a detente between Iran and the United States was to settle this obsession once and for all, to move away from the vicious cycle of myth by engaging instead with reality.

Iranians made great efforts to invite foreign journalists to visit and report on the realities of their country, but there was also a clear need for Iranians to confront their prejudices and fears about the West. Hard-liners and their traditional followers held a deep disgust for what they considered to be the moral degradation of the West, obsessed as they believed it was with pornography and homosexual rights. However, for many Iranians, even those who espoused dialogue and were enthusiastic of social and cultural interaction, a healthy skepticism of the West's political motives remained.

The points of suspicion were raised by Khatami in his CNN interview, but the importance of these doubts were heightened because the Reform Movement itself made much of tracing its intellectual and political roots back to the Oil Nationalization Crisis and the National Front of Dr. Mohammad Mosaddeq.[13] In fact, the Reformist Islamic Participation Front in many ways sought to model itself on its illustrious predecessor. With the reemergence of nationalism as a political force, so too did Dr. Mosaddeq reemerge as the icon of a movement. The spectre of Mohammad Mosaddeq and the manner of his fall cast a long if complicated shadow on the political landscape. Mosaddeq's fate encouraged caution among the Reformist leadership, especially Khatami, fearful that populism could lead, as before, to dictatorship. The flourishing myth of Mosaddeq and the pursuit of democracy seemed to sit uneasily with the desire to build bridges with the United States.

Why, asked conservatives, do you seek assistance with democracy from the very country that crippled its development? It was a salient point that highlighted the complexity of the issues being confronted. Khatami decided these issues could best be addressed by placing them in an overall framework of reconciliation. He labeled this the "Dialogue of Civilizations," a direct response to the pervasive thesis of a "Clash of Civilizations," emphasizing the importance of cultural, *meaningful* communication. Derided by his critics both at home and abroad for yet more woolly liberalism, Khatami was serious and genuine about this enterprise.[14]

The United Nations was sufficiently impressed with President Khatami's attempt to bridge the widening cultural divide to adopt the idea as its own. For many Iranians, it seemed that their country was finally coming in from the cold, and there was particular pride in their embattled President's achievement. The process of engagement seemed set; 2001 would be the "Year of Dialogue Between Civilizations."

IRAN-US RELATIONS IN THE SHADOW OF 9/11

Crassus took Syria and the nearby regions because he was keen to conduct a war against the Parthians which he thought would be simple glorious and profitable.

APPIAN—The Civil Wars, Book II, 18

FOR MANY OUTSIDE OBSERVERS, the key to any rapprochement between Iran and the United States lay with the stability and durability of Khatami's project for development. For the first few years, it would be fair to say that skepticism reigned. Few were willing to concede that Iran might be capable of indigenous change, and the notion that Islam and democracy could be compatible seemed an exercise in semantic acrobatics or simply delusional. These prejudices were founded on decades of subjective experience in the Middle East, and themselves reflected a trend in Western intellectualism about the role of Islam in political development.

A generation earlier, Arnold Toynbee and Elie Kedourie had clashed on the intellectual merits of proposing a democratic solution to the politics of the Middle East (in this case, the Arab world), and it would be fair to say that Kedourie's realism triumphed over Toynbee's idealism. For Kedourie, the notion that democracy could be transplanted or cultivated in an Arab world that had recently emerged from the Ottoman Empire was a classic case of the Western imagination overreaching itself and indulging in romanticism. This view increasingly predominated the mindset of generations of Western bureaucrats, including trained Arabists largely sympathetic to the Arab cause, and was reinforced by the disillusion of experience, as successive Arab regimes gave way to dictatorships.

Nevertheless, Arabists who justified autocracy emphasized it as a necessary transitional phase that would allow for the development of good governance, which would then provide the firm basis onto which democratic accountability could later be added. In the case of Iran, the lack of Persianists following the Islamic Revolution meant there were few sympathetic parties to make this case. Any proponents—in some cases diplomats who had been held hostage in 1979—were treated like the thesis they espoused, as delusional.

Arabists were equally skeptical of the case for democratic development in Iran. This view reflected the vested interests of the states they represented (the autocratic rulers in the Middle East), for whom the prospect of a democratic model emerging from Iran was a political nightmare. Indeed, many regional countries, having benefited from the rupture in Iran-US relations, were deeply antithetical to the loss of investment, prestige, and importance that would result from a rapprochement between the United States and an Iran engaged in a process of democratic transition.

Many were obsessed with the idea that Iran and the US would settle their differences. Such underlying fears were expressed in terms amenable to the United States: Iranian objections to the peace process and the fictional Iranian threat across the Persian Gulf, the consequence of an imperial legacy not helped by the tendency of Iranians to patronize their Arab neighbors. With respect to the peace process, Iran consistently protested that any assistance it offered to resistance groups was focused largely on Hizbollah—not an advantage as far as the Americans were concerned—that its support was largely moral, an argument not sustained by the facts, and intriguingly, that if Iran was such an obstacle to peace, why not invite her to participate in the peace negotiations? This invitation was clearly anathema to the Israelis, although more perceptive minds would have recognized that an underlying motive for Iran's continued obstructionism was the fact that it had not been invited to the table.

The counterargument was the fact that Europe was already engaging with Iran, an experience that was tedious, frustrating, and pointless. This was due, in part, because the Iranian diplomatic machinery had focused its attention on cultivating the expatriate community for much of the 1990s and was unprepared for a meaningful dialogue. A good example of Iran's diplomatic incoherence was the fact that a fluent English speaker could be dispatched as an ambassador to Tajikistan (a Persian-speaking country), while finding a diplomat with a modest level of English competence in the embassy in London was difficult. In this way, the Islamic Republic crippled its own diplomatic efforts. Yet in fairness, much depended on the energies of individual diplomats, and in Europe as well as in the UN mission in New York, a new cadre of diplomat was in the making, active to engage and participate. The task was formidable, though the advent of President Khatami made the process easier. Khatami was the first president to be invited to a succession of state visits to Western countries, visiting France, Germany, and Italy, including a highly publicized visit to the Pope, who Khatami asked to pray for him.

And pray he might, because Khatami was finding resistance both at home and abroad. The Europeans, for all their generous welcome to the new smiling Iranian President, seemed less enthusiastic about matching words with deeds. As Khatami's domestic difficulties mounted, he anxiously looked for a meaningful foreign policy success to bolster his position. And while Iranians basked in their newfound celebrity, Iran's mercantile elites were eager for access to markets, technology, and investment. Investment was particularly important, yet European companies and businessmen were keener on trade than investment, and their caution was well founded. The legal and political climate was unstable and obtuse, the shadow of American sanctions loomed large in the minds of many European companies, and most importantly, the two business elites lacked meaningful communication.

The industrial capitalism of the West may have used the same words as the mercantile capitalism of Iran, but they meant wholly different things.

Consequently, many European companies came away disappointed from their encounter with Iran. Where they wanted legal transparency and accountability, Iranian merchants preferred personal ambiguity; where one wanted laws, the other needed flexibility. Iranian Reformists wanted European companies to take the risk of investment and consequently kick start the process of economic rationalization—much the same, they pointed out, as had happened in Russia. However, the very experience in Russia had reinforced caution among the Europeans—and Russia had been supported by the United States. Europeans justifiably argued that the change had to come from within Iran first, and noted that few Iranians seemed to be willing to invest in their own country.

What was really required in Iran, as in Russia, was a political decision, but Iran was hamstrung by its poor relations with the United States and the unenviable task of negotiating with the incoherence of the European bureaucracy. If individual European bureaucracies proved slow to respond to change, the collective might of the European Union was positively glacial, with political pitfalls at every stage as decisions had to be ratified by home governments. This was a reality that irked many Europeans, and arguably had less to do with the eurocrats than with the complex network of political checks and balances that ensured no one got carried away. On one level, this incoherent complexity was something the Iranians could readily deal with. It was familiar, and the procrastination it encouraged was admirable. Iranians on the whole relished the intrigue of the European Union and the ability to manipulate its members to get the desired effect.

Of particular use in this respect was the rotating EU presidency. Iranians noted how the tough human-rights position of certain northern EU states would be replaced within six months by the more flexible and amenable attitude of a southern presidency. For Iran's Reformists, determined to push through a rationalization of the state along with the cultivation of civil and human rights, this incoherence was frustrating. Faced with mounting conservative resistance at home, they frequently, if privately, urged the Europeans to take a more robust line on a number of issues, so that at the very least they could use it as leverage against the opponents at home. But in the absence of carrot or stick, the Europeans appeared impotent, if not incompetent, and drew the derision of not only both political factions in Iran but also the United States.

One critical example will illustrate this process. During the first Rafsanjani administration, Iranian agents had been involved in targeted assassinations throughout Europe. For one reason or another, many of these agents managed to get away. (In the case of the murder of the Shah's last Prime Minister, Shahpour Bakhtiar, the French police proved extraordinarily complacent.) The notion that the Europeans were turning a blind eye—the victims were after all Iranians—gained credence among the Iranian public. This interpretation did not escape the notice of the leadership, who themselves grew increasingly complacent in covering their tracks. In 1992, a hit squad was sent to kill a number of Kurdish dissidents as they sat in the Mykonos café in Berlin. That a Middle Eastern country should send a hit squad to Europe was bad enough. That the hit squad should act with reckless abandon in spraying a Berlin café with machine-gun fire was beyond contempt, and the German government was forced to act.

Iran-German relations soured markedly and the protracted trial raised the prospect that senior leadership figures would be indicted on charges of murder. Whether such charges could be proved was debatable, but the trial was intended to send a signal to the Iranians that such behavior was no longer acceptable. Even now, however, as dissidents at home and abroad relished the embarrassment accruing to the Iranian political establishment, ambiguity pervaded the process. Iranian Intelligence Minister Ali Fallahian—the man apparently responsible for the affair—was invited for private consultations with his German counterpart in Bonn. What transpired at this meeting remains unknown, but the general public concluded that much of what was going on was a charade for public consumption. Meanwhile, the date of the verdict coincided with the election of Mohammad Khatami and the promise of better relations. This coincidence softened the practical impact of the severe verdict. The leadership of the Islamic Republic proceeded to express indignation. The EU ambassadors departed from Iran en masse, only to return a week later without the German ambassador, who was instructed to come last.

Iran had successfully turned a political crisis into a humiliation for the

EU. It was a humiliation that nobody would forget, least of all the Iranians. Conservatives laughed at the meekness of a Europe determined to maintain its commercial links, while Reformists enthusiastic for a new start balked at the ease with which Europe had crumbled. Europe's reasoning was in fact less cynical than some of its American critics argued. It recognized the importance of Khatami's election and took the political decision to engage with the promise of a better relationship. In fact, no further attacks occurred on European soil. Nonetheless, it was an expensive leap of faith, and one that the EU was not prepared to repeat in the absence of clear reciprocity. Perhaps the only country to move with alacrity on the diplomatic front was Britain, with the settlement of the Rushdie affair in 1998. But this simply brought Britain up to the same level of diplomatic representation as its EU partners.

One of the reasons there were no more attacks on European soil was that President Rafsanjani in 1992 decided that the cost for Iran's position overseas was too high. He thus persuaded hard-liners in the regime to divert their attentions elsewhere. Unfortunately for Iranian intellectuals, the Minister of Intelligence, Fallahian, decided to unleash his most radical elements against home-grown dissidents. One notorious character was Saeed Islami (alternatively named Emami), who was rumored to have been recruited following studies in the United States on account of his impeccable zealotry and loyalty to the system. This sojourn in the United States, which has never been confirmed, was later used to argue that he had been a CIA plant all along, with the avowed purpose of discrediting the Islamic Republic. Whatever the veracity of this point, those who knew Islami argued that he was far too dogmatic and inflexible to have been given the responsibility of dealing with internal opposition. Others agree on this point but argue that he was only following orders.

Operational matters aside, in 1998, four gruesome murders in Tehran caused outrage among the Reformist press and public alike. Some alleged that these murders were the tip of a large iceberg.[1] It is worth remembering, however, that many former intelligence officials were campaigning on the Reformist ticket and many sympathizers were in the Ministry, which was composed of different factions.

Khatami ordered an immediate enquiry and indicated that action would be taken to purge the Ministry of rogue elements. This was not the way the President was expected to behave, and Khatami's decision caught hard-line conservatives by surprise. The result was a radical reorganization of the Intelligence Ministry, with a new Minister known for his Reformist leanings, Ali Yunessi, replacing the conservative incumbent (Fallahian had long since gone). Islami was arrested and charged, and he conveniently committed suicide in prison. He was a expedient scapegoat, a shadowy figure who could no longer be questioned. Some commentators even alleged that Islami had been behind the Mykonos murders in an effort to disrupt EU-Iran relations.

The main casualty was the conservative establishment itself, and two people in particular came in for damaging public criticism: the former Minister of Intelligence, Fallahian, and his boss, President Hashemi Rafsanjani, for having in the very least turned a blind eye. State and society were at loggerheads. The latter sought to further explore the extent of the murders, while the conservative establishment was determined to suffocate further discussion.

In 1999, these tensions erupted when the flagship Reformist paper *Salaam* published a letter allegedly from Islami outlining a policy of press repression with a view towards destabilizing the Khatami government. Appalled by these new revelations yet also sensing an opportunity, the conservatives moved to have the paper closed down. Frustrated students, galvanized by Reformist rhetoric, decided to hold a small protest outside the University of Tehran in defense of the newspaper. Hard-line vigilantes known as the *Ansar-e Hizbollah* (Helpers of the Party of God) attacked the demonstration, and at least one student died. What followed was to shake the foundations of the Islamic Republic. Long used to having a monopoly of violence, the conservative establishment was shocked by the students' anger not only in Tehran but throughout the country.

The conservative establishment had no response to these demonstrations, which were carefully orchestrated and organized through the use of mobile phones and the Internet. The Supreme Leader Ayatollah Khamenei was so disconcerted by the student chants accusing him of murder that he failed to make any formal response for days, leading some to suspect that he had lost his nerve. Eventually, following gentle encouragement (and the protests of the Revolutionary Guard, whose veiled threat to launch a coup was indignantly dismissed by Khatami, quoting Ayatollah Khomeini's injunctions against military interference in politics), Khamenei emerged to turn the other cheek. This proved a misplaced act of humility that served only to encourage the demonstrators and dismay his supporters. Finally, Khamenei came out fighting, performing the role of "oriental despot" to perfection and demanding that the transgressors be punished.[2]

Those overseas were almost as startled as the conservatives in Iran, with some commentators leaping to the conclusion that Iran was on the verge of a revolution. Appeals went out for Iranians to revolt en masse, while foreign journalists, particularly at the BBC, interviewed members of the Mojahideen-e Khalq Organization (MKO), who proudly announced that the students were their supporters and were seeking the overthrow of the regime. For all the disaffection that did exist and the popular desire for change, revolution was not on the minds of the students at that time. In fact, the term *revolution* brought back memories of the traumas of 1979–1980, and this was precisely what the vast majority of Iranians did not want to relive. One revolution in a lifetime was enough, and the strategy had to be reform through concerted pressure, not a thorough revolution. Even if such aspirations had existed at this stage, vocal Western support de-legitimized it at a stroke.

Within Iran, anxiety grew about matters spiraling out of control. Although political ambiguity was a hallmark of Iranian life, political anarchy brought forth shudders from all walks of life. The students themselves, faced with the prospect of the demonstrations turning to riots, decided to avoid the potential loss of public support by toning down the demonstrations. Khatami urged a return to calm, warning students not to precipitate a full-scale conservative backlash, which might derail the reform program altogether. Pursue change through legal means, he argued; look towards the parliamentary elections of the following year, 2000. Extensive arrests nevertheless followed as the conservative establishment feverishly sought to stamp out what amounted to a youth rebellion. Foreign readings of this event were largely misplaced, focusing as they did on the reaction rather than on the views and strategies of the students.[3]

Throughout the summer of 1999, the leadership of the main student union was buoyant, in stark contrast to the image painted in the West. Repression was to be expected, they had anticipated a backlash, and the casualties were within acceptable limits. The gains achieved in terrifying the conservative establishment were worth the pain, and Iran's students would prove the naysayers abroad wrong. The target was the seizure, through legal electoral means, of the legislative house, the nation's Parliament, to which the Constitution had allocated all responsibility for the ratification of new laws. Control of Parliament would remove the last obstacle to serious reform, and a coalition of the media and students were determined to lead the movement that would seize it. The one remaining obstacle was the Guardian Council, a body of twelve religious lawyers who had acquired the power to vet candidates. The students would approach this problem by proposing so many candidates that the Guardian Council would be overwhelmed.

The Council turned out to be far more lenient than many had anticipated, and Reformist candidates began to drop out so as not to split the vote. The Reformist campaign had one last-minute blessing in disguise, and this was the sudden decision of former President Hashemi Rafsanjani to run for a seat. So hated had Rafsanjani become among Reformists, especially in light of his alleged culpability in the murder of dissidents, that his presence gave Reformist strategists a personal target. Much to the chagrin of the conservatives, the Reformists swept to power, defying their critics and proposing a dramatic agenda for change. Yet at the very moment of their triumph, the Reformist leadership lost their nerve.

The euphoria that characterized the mood on the streets was matched by anxiety among the political establishment. This anxiety was expressed in an assassination attempt on Saeed Hajarian, the strategist behind the election victory. Hajarian had always argued that the various vested interests would never give up power but had to be coaxed out of it through a mixture of persuasion and pressure. The bullets did not kill him but did cripple him for life, in a cruel metaphor for what was to happen to the Reform Movement over the next four years.

Khatami was stunned. Hajarian had been a personal friend, and he immediately arranged for him to have surgery abroad. Khatami began to reflect whether the entire project was worth it. At this crucial time, when the masses were calling for change and for their leaders to capitalize on the success they had engineered, the leadership chose to seek compromise. This compromise had a view to more durable gains later, but the effect was to take the sting out of the movement and deprive it of much needed momentum.

The conservatives could hardly believe their luck. They were in no mood for compromise, because the threat was too serious. The new Majlis deputies were not only discussing the possibility of further liberalization in the social and cultural arena but also demanding political and economic accountability. This last demand hit a nerve because most members of the conservative establishment were complicit in the complex web of commercial corruption that increasingly defined the elite structure of the Islamic Republic.

For many in the mercantile elite, who may have been sympathetic to the reform movement and the prospect of new markets abroad, the fear of a left-wing assault on the sources of their wealth (through taxes, accountability, and transparency) was too much to contemplate. Consequently, they moved into a tighter alliance with the Islamic authoritarians. In securing a landslide in the Parliamentary elections, the Reformists had not only raised their own expectations of what could be achieved but also recklessly if inadvertently galvanized the conservative elites into a swift reaction. The proper response at this stage would have been for the Reformist leadership to ride the tide of reform. In prevaricating, they allowed a reenergized conservative opposition to hit back, while deflating their own side. When the hard-line conservative Judiciary moved to close down Reformist newspapers, in an unprecedented cull of the progressive press, the Reformist leadership called for calm and urged their followers not to take to the streets but to instead await the inauguration of the new Parliament, after which new legislation would be passed.

This determination to use legal channels wherever possible was high minded and commendable, but it was a characteristic flaw in the Khatami strategy. His political strategist, Hajarian, had been a ruthless political realist in understanding that popular pressure was a necessity against a hard-line conservative establishment that was impervious to meaningful dialogue. Concomitantly, Khatami's decision to go exclusively through the Parliament made sense only if everyone was playing by the same legal rules. For conservatives, however, especially the more hardline and authoritarian elements, the law existed to serve their political interests, and as such it was flexible. As a result, when the new deputies energetically drew up a liberal press law enshrining freedom of the press (something that had always been guaranteed in the Constitution), the Supreme Leader Ayatollah Khamanei took the unprecedented step of publicly intervening to prevent its ratification. His predecessor had never been so bold, at the very least maintaining the fiction of an independent legislature (the House of the Nation). Khamenei's action tore away this veil in an authoritarian gesture applauded by his supporters and derided by his critics.[4]

Up until this point, the Constitution had always been flawed but reformable. Now, even this expectation had been removed. The conservative establishment, in successfully protecting their interests, had done incalculable damage to the long-term credibility of the system. Some remained optimistic that the Parliament could still push through meaningful change, but a pattern of repression was now getting into its stride, helped in large measure by the Reformist determination to be rigorously legal in their procedure. Not only did they manage to contain the Reformists in the isolated cocoon of Parliament (where they gradually lost touch with their constituents), but they handed the political initiative back to the conservatives, who held the two levers of legal control: the Judiciary, which interpreted the law, and the Guardian Council, which vetted legislation for compatibility (politically defined) with Islamic law.

Some suggest that Khatami was persuaded upon this path by a promise from his opponents that they would ultimately respect the legislative will of the Parliament, even if there had to be compromise on particular pieces of legislation. If so, the next four years were to prove the hollowness of that promise. Instead, the Guardian Council repeatedly blocked legislation. The Judiciary, newly reinforced by staff recently purged from the Intelligence Ministry, moved to harass and imprison key Reformists, always being careful to locate the balance between selective repression and reckless provocation. The strategy was to de-politicize a boisterous and tempestuous public, to both bore and exhaust them into submission. The political public of 2000 was leaderless and bewildered.

Into this political quagmire ventured the United States. Their initial response to Khatami's overtures in 1998 had been confused and incoherent. This may have reflected a lack of direction from the top, President Clinton being preoccupied with domestic affairs. However, for all the problems that the first Clinton administration created for Iran-US relations, Clinton in his second term was to prove an enthusiastic proponent of exploring the possibility of better relations.

The geopolitical reality of the benefits of better relations was not lost on the professional bureaucrats in the State department and the Pentagon, particularly those with an eye on the strategic picture. Politics could eventually be transcended; the obvious coincidence of interests would remain. Not only did the United States and Iran share common enemies in the region—Iraq and Afghanistan—but a friendly Iran would make US policy easier in Central Asia and the Caspian littoral and provide a balance for US policy in the region. It was even predicted that Iran-Israeli relations would eventually be settled, a view espoused by a number of Israeli analysts who were aware of the debate going on in Iran.

The realist core of the US foreign policy establishment was daring to raise its head over the Iranian parapet. This act of political boldness was facilitated by the changes being observed in Khatami's Iran. Such views were not voiced publicly; these were professional assessments not for public consumption. Yet they must have had an influence on Clinton's decision to take a more constructive approach towards Iran. In his second term, with no electoral contest and in search of a foreign policy legacy, Iran appeared ready and full of Eastern promise. The change in direction was Clinton's, and it was generally acknowledged that Iran policy was being driven by the White House. This could be seen in the fact that Clinton made a point of appearing at the United Nations when Khatami appeared and deliberately remaining in place to listen to the Iranian President's speeches. In 1999, Clinton even went so far as to acknowledge that Iran may have been justified in some of the grievances it held against Western countries, an acknowledgement Khatami described as courageous.

The tentative thaw was confirmed the following year when Secretary of State Madeleine Albright formally responded to the Khatami overture. This was to prove the most constructive public statement from an American official for the better part of two decades. Albright officially pronounced not only on the regrettable actions of 1953 but also, and this was a major step forward, on the short-sightedness that had led to the United States supporting Saddam Hussein in the Iran-Iraq War. In many ways, this latter admission was more significant in that it spoke directly to the veterans of the Iran-Iraq War. Although it was a relatively small gesture, its significance lay in the fact that it talked *to* the Iranians and their fears rather than *at* them about American concerns. Rather than being about "what we want," it was about "what we can do for you."

In addition, Albright announced that sanctions would be lifted on a selection of traditional Iranian goods, including carpets and pistachios. The efficacy of this last gesture is a matter of debate given that it tended to assist the segments of society (the mercantile classes) who were least disposed toward the United States, leading some cynics in Iran to argue that America was supporting the elites over the people. It could equally be argued that it was a strategy intended to convince and persuade the skeptics in the Iranian political system that the United States was not an instinctive antagonist. Some joked that the decision to lift sanctions on pistachios was an attempt to win over Rafsanjani—one of the leading pistachio merchants in Iran. However, because customs duties remained exorbitantly high, this gesture had little practical consequence, leading the most hard-line opponents of the United States to argue that this was another public relations exercise. But it was not a meaningless exercise, and it was known that Khatami understood and appreciated the gesture. In his eyes, it was a good start.

Yet in international relations as in politics, timing is everything. Just as the United States failed to swiftly respond to the initial overtures, so too Khatami, in the aftermath of the triumph and tribulation of the parliamentary elections, was in no position to react. Some of his supporters had been critical of his failure to respond to the earlier, more discreet American reactions. But by 2000, Khatami felt unable even to make supportive comments, let alone engage in a symbolic handshake with the US President, whose urgent desire for a result was dictated by the fact that his final term in office was coming to an end. Clinton reportedly went so far as to send a letter through the Swiss Embassy in Tehran (which represented US interests) outlining a program for the normalization of relations. It was, as Khatami was to later admit, a huge missed opportunity.

While Khatami had to contend with his conservative critics at home, so too did Clinton. For every positive step taken, opponents provided ample room for dissent. This reflected the nature of the political system and also the fact that neither President possessed sufficient authority to transcend their critics at home. By 2000, Khatami, faced with contradictory positions coming out of the White House and the US Congress, felt unable to move. This prevarication was in part justified by the consensus in Iran that if the Democrats, who had traditionally been hostile to Iran, were offering terms, it would be better to hold out for a Republican victory in November 2000. Ignoring the fact that it had been a Republican Congress that had been responsible for much of the hostile legislation towards Iran, Iranian analysts simplistically concluded that a Bush victory would herald the return of oil and realism to American foreign policy, both of which played to Iran's advantage. It was a fatal miscalculation.

As President George W. Bush settled into the White House in January 2001, Khatami faced his own reelection campaign in June of the same year. Beset by critics on all sides, he seriously considered stepping aside. But at the last minute, he decided that his continued presence on the political center stage would shield the reform process from an even worse fate and allow the social development of the country to continue. His resounding reelection victory, with more than 20 million votes, confirmed his personal popularity along with the popular conviction for change. It seemed as though whatever the mounting pressures from the conservative establishment, the people of Iran were resolute in their determination to pursue change. The election campaign supported the view that young people in particular were prepared to sacrifice economic gains in the interests of political progress.[5]

Khatami was gradually realizing that his opponents were not willing to give ground despite his electoral mandate. For all his determination to pursue the legal path to reform, most if not all the state's legal resources were at the disposal of his opponents. Moreover, Khatami had been deprived of his most able lieutenants. Hajarian had been shot and crippled; the revolutionary Abdullah Nuri was now languishing in prison; and his only other minister of political note, Ataollah Mohajerani, the Minister of Culture, was being pursued. Domestically, the Reform Movement was being effectively blunted. Some complained that they were witnessing a silent coup. Parliament, far from being the legal vehicle for change, was becoming a Reformist prison, encouraging a dangerous disconnect between Reformist politicians and their constituents.[6]

Facing gridlock at home, Khatami decided to turn his attention abroad, where a significant success might allow him to tip the balance at home. Reformists argued that all political factions (beyond the most extreme elements) had accepted that relations with the United States would be beneficial, but that the conservatives simply did not want the Reformists to take credit for the breakthrough. Khatami therefore wanted to deliver this breakthrough and return triumphantly, and politically renewed, to Iran. Europe had proven somewhat lacklustre and incoherent in its response. Britain was perhaps the most effective European power in Iran between 1998–2003, in large part because of the excellence of its staff both in Tehran and London. But Britain labored under a historical legacy that would always constrain what could be achieved, and it was notable that Britain was the one major European country not visited by Khatami during his presidency.

America, meanwhile, appeared to be indulging in a period of navel gazing. Contrary to expectations in Iran, the new Republican presidency, with its clear oil interests (Halliburton, Vice President Dick Cheney's former employer, had an office in Tehran), seemed to be paying little attention to international affairs, let alone Iran. Rather than pursue the Clinton policy, Bush was defining himself against Clinton in every possible way. Anything Clinton did was bad, and this clearly, and with little difficulty, applied to Iran. An early example of this approach was the resuscitation of a dormant allegation linking Iran to the bombing of the Al-Khobar towers in Saudi Arabia in 1996, in which US personnel had been killed. A number of senior US investigators had been convinced of the involvement of militants connected to Iran (a group known as Hizbollah

Gulf). As in many similar cases made against Iran, there was a paucity of credible evidence. American investigators were frustrated by the lack of apparent cooperation from Saudi Arabia, and Clinton had chosen not to pursue it. At the time, Clinton's unwillingness to pursue this was seen as a political decision reflecting the emergence of the Reform Movement in Iran. More likely, Clinton was unwilling to move on the basis of a suspicion. In this, he may have been influenced by the rush to judgement in the aftermath of the Oklahoma bombing, where some pundits were likewise anxious to blame Iran or Islamic militants.

Nonetheless, the Bush administration decided to revive this allegation and issued a public indictment that was treated with contempt by commentators who bothered to read beyond the first paragraph, in which Iran was mentioned. The rest of the indictment detailed individuals with little or no association with Iran, and as one US diplomat privately conceded, it was more a political than a legal document. This approach—guilt by suspicion—was not a Republican innovation. The Democrats had in their time been past masters at this game, and in many ways Clinton's last administration was a temporary, and somewhat forced, aberration against the overwhelming (structural) consensus.

This structural consensus was at the same time reinforced by the personnel Bush was introducing into his foreign policy establishment. Just as Warren Christopher privately berated Iran for having derailed his career by contributing to President Carter's election defeat in 1980, many of the new Republican officials of 2001 carried with them the scars of Iran-Contra. Among the luminaries of note with responsibility for Middle Eastern affairs in the Bush White House were Elliot Abrams and Douglas Feith.[7] Another prominent individual was John Bolton, who entered the State Department and was generally known for his uncompromising world view. If the potential influence of these people on the direction of Iran policy was yet to be felt, another development did raise some eyebrows: the cultivation of links with the Taleban.

Iran did not have good relations with the Taleban, whose ascent had raised sectarian tensions. In 1998, following the murder of Iranian diplomats by Taleban militia, the Khatami administration had seriously considered taking military retaliation, mobilizing up to two hundred thousand troops on the Afghan border. For many observers, animosity towards the Taleban regime in Afghanistan was the ideal coincidence of interests by which US-Iran relations could be gradually mended. The Taleban represented a type of political Islam both sides could condemn. The Islamic Republic of Iran was one of the few, if not the only, Islamic country to criticize the Taleban for having perverted Islamic values and teachings. However, the Taleban were largely the product of the hard work of US allies in the region, notably Pakistan, and it seemed as though the anticipated realism of the Bush administration might go as far as contemplating oil deals with the Taleban.

9/11

Then came 9/11. Of all the countries in the Islamic Middle East, Iran's reaction was the most extraordinary, expressing an empathy with the US position that contradicted the stereotype so frequently presented to the American people. Rather than celebrate, as some insensitively did in the full glare of the Western media, or indulge in formal pronouncements of commiseration, both state officials and important sections of Iranian society publicly expressed their solidarity with the victims of the outrage.

The first to express his condolences was Khatami, followed by the Mayor of Tehran and the municipality Fire Chief. On Iranian streets, young people showed their sympathy by demonstrating against terrorism—a demonstration that had a firm eye on analogous developments in Iran. The Iranian response compared well with those that took place in the Western world. This was in part a reflection of the broader sympathy for the West and the United States that had been enhanced by the existence of an extensive diaspora community. Even the ritual chants of "death to America" were suspended at Friday Prayers for several weeks as a show of respect, although some argued that this conservative gesture was more out of fear than respect.[8]

In the immediate aftermath of the attacks, some American commentators attempted to pin the blame on Shias, and by extension Iran. Journalists were disappointed when experts told them that the names of the hijackers were not characteristic of Shia Muslims. Khatami, anxious that the blame not be associated with Iran, summoned Hizbollah leaders to Tehran to make sure they could confirm that they were not involved. Reassured, Khatami recognized the opportunity that could emerge from the catastrophe. Americans had been traumatized by the attack and had spent the better part of the following month collecting their thoughts and reflecting on what had happened. In many ways, the psychological impact of the attack was more profound than the material damage. Prejudices had been challenged and stereotypes shattered. The leaders of the attack were not Shia or Hizbollah but Sunni, and most hailed from two countries long held up as staunch allies of the United States: Egypt and Saudi Arabia. With old dogmas being revisited, the potential for a diplomatic revolution on par with 1979 seemed in the cards. Khatami aimed to make the most of the window of opportunity afforded to him.

The United States, with the full support of the international community and the United Nations, intended to seek redress against the Taleban in Afghanistan. Khatami sensed the moment was at hand and persuaded skeptics in the conservative establishment that assisting the Coalition war in Afghanistan would be in Iran's best interests. The hated Taleban would be removed, striking a blow against Pakistan and enhancing Iran's regional reach, and the hard task of building bridges with the United States would be facilitated. The key to the argument was this: the United States *needed* Iran, and Iran should be gracious enough to assist. Events had effectively served to balance, at least at a particular and regional level, the nature of the Iran-US relationship. It was an egalitarian moment that should be seized. According to some Iranian sources, this was not noticed by their American interlocutors, who continued to demand access to facilities in a manner not calculated to win them friends in the Islamic Republic.

It is the nature of secret discussions that we will never know how particular negotiations were conducted. Success or failure is often determined by not only words but also the way in which those words are delivered. Whether American negotiators demanded anything from the Iranians is a matter for debate, but we can be fairly certain that for all the Iranian admiration for Anglo-Saxon frankness, their appreciation soon dissipated when it was directed, occasionally aggressively, at themselves. Many a negotiation has failed because of American arrogance and Iranian pride. Nevertheless, it would appear that some arrangement was reached, even if this was negotiated by Britain—the British Foreign Secretary Jack Straw had been among the first visitors to Iran in the aftermath of 9/11, well aware that Iran's support in the ensuing struggle would be useful.

The visit seems to have settled some nerves in Iran because the ritual anti-American chanting restarted soon after, leading some local wits to point out that Perfidious Albion (Britain), envious of a possible US-Iran rapprochement, had moved quickly to get things back to normal! It was the first visit by a British Foreign Secretary since 1979 and the clearest indication yet of the impressive progress made in Anglo-Iranian relations since their formal reestablishment in 1998. While Iran officially criticized any impending attack on a fellow Muslim country, few people in Iran shed tears for the Taleban, which had long been mocked in popular slogans as the epitome of all that was wrong with political Islam. Hard-line militants in Iran were regularly derided as being the Taleban of Iran, and this characterization of the conservative opposition had been an effective electoral tool in the Reformist political lexicon.

It was made public that because this was a UN-led mission, Iran would assist with the rescue of any Coalition pilots who found themselves in Iran, an allusion perhaps to the fact, never acknowledged, that overflight rights were being granted. Far more important, however, was the assistance provided in the form of the Northern Alliance, led by the charismatic Ahmad Shah Massoud. Massoud had been assassinated, but the Northern Alliance was to form the backbone of the Afghan resistance to the Taleban, and its participation hastened their fall.

Iran similarly played a constructive role in the subsequent negotiations in Bonn about Afghanistan's future, negotiating with a skill and diplomacy that impressed a number of their American interlocutors, who conjectured that perhaps the moment had arrived for a thaw in relations. After all, never was the US and Iranian coincidence of interest so blatantly apparent to all. Here was a situation that eschewed the need for affection but depended entirely on a realistic assessment of mutual interests. In short, it was a realist dream made in heaven. Unfortunately for the bureaucrats at the table, politics would soon ensure that this sweet moment of detente was an anachronism that belonged to an earlier, simpler age. Khatami's gamble, which appeared so close to success, proved to be no more than a mirage.

THE AXIS OF EVIL

During the autumn of 2001, Iranians would have been forgiven for believing that their country had not only weathered the storm but had managed the crisis of 9/11 so effectively that hitherto unforeseen windows of opportunity were revealing themselves. American officials were talking in constructive terms about Iran—the problem was Sunni not Shia, and the Al Khobar indictment miraculously vanished. In addition, there were tentative indications that tensions with Israel might be relaxed. It was a surreal moment that some conjectured might presage a diplomatic revolution. In truth, it proved to be the calm before the storm.

For hard-liners in Iran, as well as hawks in Israel and the United States, this rapprochement was an unhealthy venture that needed immediate attention. For the Israeli government, the prospect of a US-Iran rapprochement would put a cap on a difficult year in US-Israeli relations, made worse by the fact that Bush needed quiescence on the Israeli-Palestinian front if he was to successfully maintain his coalition against Afghanistan. The fear of being sidelined in favor of much needed Muslim allies appears to have encouraged the Israelis to engage in an intense round of lobbying with the United States. If the United States required the support of Arab states for its war on terror, everyone could still agree that Iran remained a problem. Extensive efforts were made to remind Washington of Tehran's continued enmity towards the Israeli state and prevent any reassessment of US relations with Iran. Initial attempts to do this in the aftermath of the attacks had failed miserably, ensuring redoubled efforts in November. In this the Israelis were assisted by supreme advantages: the Iranians had no comparable lobbying machinery in Washington, and more importantly, hard-liners in Iran were more than willing to oblige the Israelis with their Iranian stereotype.

The first problem to arise was the issue of fleeing Al Qaeda and Taleban fugitives across the border into Iran. An overt link between Al Qaeda and Iran would have been a gift to hawks who were determined to see Iran as the root of all evil. As with other allegations directed against Iran, this one was going to be difficult for the US to prove, not least because of the sectarian tensions existing between the radical Sunni Al Qaeda and Shia Iran. Iran at first denied that any fugitives from the Afghan war were moving into or through Iran—a bold claim given the nature of the border. As fugitives turned up in Iranian prisons, the Iranian Foreign Ministry conceded that some had come across the border but were in custody.

The next problem related to the final destination of these fugitives. The United States wanted to extradite them. Iran refused, returning some to their native countries. Iran's caution in this regard may have been dictated by the need to balance their assistance to the Coalition against the threat of Al Qaeda retaliation. Khatami had reportedly cautioned the Coalition that if they must go into Afghanistan, they must do it correctly. In other words, any unfortunate consequences were likely to affect Iran, which after all could not leave the region after the job was completed. Consequently, Iran sought to manage its relations with Al Qaeda by employing a rationale that was antithetical to the philosophy of the war on terror. For Americans, this was simply another example of Iranian duplicity.

At the same time, rumors abounded in Iran of new networks being cultivated between Iran's hard-liners and Bin Laden's associates. Such a relationship is difficult to verify and was the subject of some conjecture in Iran. Another allegation was that some members of Iran's revolutionary guards (IRGC) were facilitating the flight of Afghan fugitives for money. It was generally acknowledged that Rafsanjani and Khatami had to intervene to put an end to this act of entrepreneurial spirit after it had been brought to their attention by disaffected members of the IRGC protesting the stupidity of such a venture. Such rumors, whatever their veracity, fed the neoconservative imagination in the US, particularly the argument that Khatami, for all his personal attraction, was not in charge of Iranian policy. For those in any doubt, the next discovery was to provide the much needed hard evidence.[9]

In January 2002, the Israelis made a sudden and fortuitous seizure of the *Karine A*, a ship full of weapons, destined for the Palestinian Authority and reportedly dispatched from Iran. The discovery was so timely that even Israel's allies in the West viewed it with suspicion, and for several days there was a marked reluctance to acknowledge Israeli claims. Certainly, the shipment was curious. Iran was not a novice when it came to the shipment of arms to its protégés and allies, and the normal route for such deliveries would have been through Damascus or Lebanon. Moreover, shipments would have traditionally been by air, not by boat around the Arabian peninsula. Western observers may have expressed doubts because they were well aware of Iranian methods in light of Iranian shipments to Bosnia, which as far as the Iranians were concerned had been managed with the tacit approval of the West.

Prime Minister Sharon relished the propaganda coup that the seizure offered and paraded the weapons, replete with Persian lettering, for the benefit of the camera. No amount of Iranian denial could dent the effect, and the air of self-congratulation in Israel was palpable. The Americans were more irritated by Arafat's persistent political incompetence in having apparently sought the shipment. In political terms, a useful connection between Iran and terrorism had been reestablished in the American mindset, and again at the very least it could be argued that Khatami was not in charge. Detente was off.

At the end of January 2002, President Bush delivered his State of the Union address in which he described Iran, along with Iraq and North Korea, as part of an axis of evil. Rarely has such a rhetorical device had such devastating consequences. While many in Iran could empathize with the preamble that condemned the un-elected minority in Iran, few Iranians could reconcile themselves with the notion that they belonged in the same category as their old foe Saddam Hussein or the totalitarian regime in North Korea. More crucially, however, was the impact that the speech had on Khatami's own credibility. Having failed to effectively transform the domestic agenda, he had now shown himself incompetent on the international stage. When he made the argument for Iranian support for Coalition efforts in Afghanistan, he had stressed, in the face of concerted hard-line opposition, that the potential rewards would be worth it. Arguably, the fear that Khatami's gamble was about to pay off led to the sabotage that was the *Karine A.*

The State of the Union speech unashamedly announced a return to a familiar track. The speech was as startling for what it left out. References to Bin Laden and Al Qaeda were minimal in contrast to the list of terrorist groups related to the Arab-Israeli conflict. Certainly, none of the three members of this new axis had connections to Al Qaeda or 9/11. The allusion certainly seems to have caught some American policy makers off guard as well. They struggled to come to terms with its implications, and commentators posited a number of theories as to how the speech was constructed. It was generally known, for instance, that Bush had an affection for Churchill's skill with rhetorical devices, but other than that, Iran's inclusion in the list was either deliberate or accidental depending on one's sources.

Almost all that could be concluded was that the heart of American policy towards Iran was confused, as befits a position that has been emotionally constructed rather than rationally thought through. In the months that followed, the incoherence of American policy (in the loosest sense of that term) became apparent as officials struggled to reconcile the rhetoric with reality. Was Iran really in the same category as Iraq and North Korea? Was it possible to have a dialogue with a state that was evil? Even Bush seemed to stumble on this particular incongruity, while others pondered the irony of the United States adopting theological motifs usually associated with the mullahs in Iran. While commentators attempted to dissect the implications of Bush's speech, the real and immediate casualty of the speech in the West was Great Britain. Tony Blair had been the only European leader to endorse Bush's comments at a time when Britain had been engaged in tortuous negotiations over its nominated candidate for ambassador, David Redaway.

Redaway was a fluent Persian speaker with considerable experience in Iran and was the natural choice to maintain and extend the considerable diplomatic momentum that Britain had built up with skill since 1998. Anglophobes in the Iranian establishment opposed his appointment on the perverse grounds that he was too familiar with the country. Blair's unqualified support for Bush's categorization of Iran provided hard-liners with the final justification they needed. British diplomatic momentum was blunted. The virulent nature of hard-line criticism, particularly against Redaway's wife (who was Iranian), was not only offensive but a breach of diplomatic protocol. The general sense of goodwill was replaced with a justifiable feeling of bitterness. Persianists were in short supply in Western bureaucracies, and Iran could ill afford to alienate them. Many in the Iranian Foreign Ministry establishment were aware of the loss, and bitterly resented the way in which hard-liners in the regime consistently sabotaged their efforts.[10]

The hard-liners in Iran could barely contain their delight at the opportunity Bush had afforded them. Khatami, well on the way to being a lame duck president, was now confirmed as such. Although hard-liners had always argued that nothing was to be gained from negotiating with the West, even moderates reluctantly accepted the notion that the only approach was to be tough and confrontational. Clearly Khatami's strategy of dialogue had failed. In Iran, the Reformists were put on the defensive, as hard-liners in the Revolutionary Guard urged the imposition of martial law and an end to the Reform process. This was their third attempt to decisively overturn the Reform Movement. Previous threats had been made during the student demonstrations and in the aftermath of the parliamentary elections.[11]

Those in Reformist circles feared that the hard-line establishment was determined to launch a coup. The hope, expressed through a variety of channels, was that Europe would vigorously oppose such a development. Europe enjoyed an authority in Iran that America did not, and the belief, not unjustified, was that hard-liners would back down if faced with overwhelming resistance.

Hawks in the West drew their own conclusions from this development, ignoring the fact that they had been complicit in the effective suffocation of the Reform Movement by stubbornly refusing to acknowledge its seriousness. By not engaging in dialogue with those who were willing to participate, they had facilitated a hard-line backlash. For the hard-liners, tough posturing rather than negotiation was the only way forward. It was a deteriorating, absurd, vicious cycle in which the rigid obstinacy of the hawks on both sides produced a self-fulfilling prophecy and its own justification.[12]

Yet if the moral certainty of neoconservatism had moved into the ascendancy in the United States, their counterparts in Iran had yet to complete their victory. Khatami was down but not out, and his continued existence was an irritating reminder of their failure to dominate. More interesting was the popular reaction in Iran, particularly among parliamentary deputies. From 2002, domestic politics stalled in Iran as the latent obsession with the United States came to the fore of political discussion. But it was the nature of this discussion, largely missed by the United States, which revealed how fruitful a coherent policy of engagement could have been. Iranian policy makers were left bewildered by the axis of evil speech and proved far more critical of their own foreign policy establishment than that of America. In a curious reversal of policy debates in the United States a quarter century earlier, the dominant theme was "who lost the United States?" For some Reformists, the American rebuff was too much to handle and clearly could be traced to other more manipulative agents: "By taking such a stance, George Bush is trying to test public opinion. And when the public opinion would correspond to his, he would then act. [The] European Union and a number of Asian and European countries have criticised Bush's position describing it as inappropriate and wrong. Only England has supported Bush. . . . England is behind those crises created in our country and the outside movements that support them. England is the one who motivates America to act brutishly. We must discover England's footprint in these events. In truth, England is the one who fuels events." Old habits die hard![13]

For all the indignation, the prevailing discussion revolved around whether or not negotiations were desirable, and opinions were based on the normal political divides. Hard-liners were opposed. Reformists, and some moderate conservatives, argued that flexibility had to be retained. The debate grew lively, with some deputies arguing that the record of the United States compared favorably with that of Russia, whose aggrandizements against Iran over the past two hundred years had been far more damaging to Iranian interests but did not prevent reasonable relations. As one reader noted in the letters page of a newspaper, "In my opinion America has provided the greatest help to Muslims and Iran." Politicians, echoing this public mood, noted that America had at times been supportive of Muslim causes (again contrasting favorably with the Russian experience in Chechnya). A clerical deputy went so far as to draw a religious analogy by pointing out that the Imam Ali (the first Imam of the Shias) had deigned to negotiate with his arch opponent the Umayyad Mu'awiya, and that the United States was surely not worse than Mu'awiya! Reformists stated that engaging in dialogue allowed Iran to better represent its interests and did not mean that the two parties had to have any affection. In addition, US and Iranian diplomats had negotiated on a variety of disputes and interests, the most recent case being the Bonn discussions on the future of Afghanistan. In the words of one Reformist journalist:

"There is no rational strategic explanation for refusing to hold talks with America. The sooner Iran begins to hold public and official talks with America, the sooner it will be able to further its own interests. However, the longer Iran postpones the talks, the greater the losses it will incur. In fact, if we had started to hold official talks publicly a few years ago, we would not have faced many of the problems in the bilateral relations between the two countries. Postponing the talks means that Iran has hardened its position. Eventually, Iran and America will have to negotiate. The longer such talks are postponed, the greater the losses Iran will incur and this will primarily serve America's interests."[14]

The debate became so intense and obsessive that by the summer of 2002, the head of the Tehran Judiciary, taking his lead from a speech by the Supreme Leader, issued a directive outlawing "discussions about discussions with the United States." This absurd initiative broadcast on state television took some time to digest because it was not clear what the remit of such a decree might be or on what authority the head of the Tehran Judiciary had issued it. Reformist politicians and university professors were furious about its implications and roundly condemned it. One professor suggested that if discussions were to be banned, the government might as well close down the universities. Some Iranians remarked sardonically that the best thing to do was to decamp to the provinces and discuss the United States beyond the jurisdiction of the Tehran Judiciary. Finally,

Khatami himself intervened, lampooning the Tehran Judiciary for its stupidity (the decree was quickly rescinded) and pointing out that the timing for talks with the US was incorrect. Khatami abhorred the politics of the bully either at home or abroad, and to offer talks now would be to send the wrong message to the US administration.[15]

The level of debate far outshone that taking place in the United States, where the focus was firmly fixed on Iraq. Although some neoconservative commentators argued that the focus of US attention should be on Iran, this attention did not entail a nuanced policy of engagement. The only intervention the Bush administration made during this intense period of discussion was to brazenly support the resignation of Ayatollah Taheri, the venerable and highly respected Friday Prayer leader of Isfahan. Taheri had resigned in protest of the rampant political and economic corruption of the Islamic Republic, and the failure of the revolution to deliver on its promise of political freedom and social and economic justice. His resignation speech, delivered in the summer of 2002, sent shockwaves through the political establishment in Iran, in light of the ruthless condemnation he heaped upon the corruption of the Revolutionary organs of power. President Bush's clumsy intervention in support of Taheri revealed a woeful ignorance of the political dynamics of Iran and effectively consigned Taheri's thunderbolt to the political margins. The press was forbidden to reproduce the speech, which hard-line conservatives argued had been drafted by the CIA.[16]

It is now generally acknowledged that not only was the Bush administration firmly focused on Iraq, but its strategy was almost exclusively one of force. For all the protestations of diplomacy, the military juggernaut was mobilizing. If some insisted on the diplomatic route, the window of opportunity was a good deal shorter than the public face of the administration cared to admit.

All war is deception. The decision to pursue Saddam Hussein and Iraq was a blunder of extraordinary proportions. Many of the reasons for this have been cited in numerous other works. Two will be reiterated here: the failure to provide for postwar planning with the potential opportunities provided to Iran, and the disdain for international law represented by the invasion.

Yet these reasons are particular rather than general, and the real failure was one of grand strategic myopia. There was a failure to see the bigger picture, to recognize an obsession for what it was and to deal with the core of the problem. Just as the United States continues to be blinded by its loyalty to Israel, so too was it determined to avoid the difficult, emotional issue of Iran. Both Iraq and Afghanistan became American problems as a result of a determination to contain revolutionary Iran, and yet the greatest superpower on the planet could not bring itself to engage in a meaningful way with its core problem in the region. Instead, it hid behind a veil of hubris, presenting rhetoric as policy and pretending all along that America had no need for Iran.

Had the United States been serious about spreading democracy throughout the Middle East, one must question the judgement that decided to target the very countries with little or no democratic architecture. The invasion of Afghanistan could be justified on the basis of 9/11. But Iraq was pursued because it was militarily possible, and Iran was ignored because it was politically too difficult. Rather than pursue the military solution in Iraq, the United States should have taken the opportunity to pursue the political solution in Iran. The democratic architecture, for all its flaws, was in place, and the audience was receptive. The events of 9/11 and subsequent polling throughout 2002 had shown a population eager for dialogue. They were ignored.

The reasons for this neglect were both ideological and structural. The ideology was underpinned and reinforced by decades of historical mythology, which neither side had the political will nor mechanisms to challenge. In the United States, these ideas were becoming so rigid as to impose a structure. In Iran, fluidity was likewise solidifying in the wrong direction. Moreover, these ideas were being reinforced by bureaucratic structures, which were naturally given to inertia but were now reinforced by individuals who had neither the will nor the sense to confront the challenge. In American this development involved the return of personnel scarred by Iran-Contra; in Iran this was reflected by the sheer exhaustion of Reformist politicians and the sense of betrayal Khatami felt.

Now the impending Iraq war exacerbated an already difficult situation by redirecting all personnel with any experience of the Middle East to work on the immediate crisis of Iraq. From 2002, the West took its collective eyes off the Iranian ball, while Iranian hard-liners prepared to contain and ultimately close off the window of opportunity. Their first targets were the political pollsters who had dared to proclaim that Iranians were interested in a dialogue. The pollsters protested that the survey had indicated the sophistication of an Iranian public who remained distrustful of American intentions but nevertheless regarded exploring a dialogue to be in the national interest.

For hard-liners, however, animosity towards the United States was an article of faith, opposition to which was tantamount to treason. At the same time, they moved to sabotage any attempts by pragmatic conservatives, particularly Rafsanjani, to open a covert channel of negotiation with the United States. Indications are that a number of routes were being investigated with a view to negotiating a "grand bargain" that would resolve all outstanding issues between Iran and the US. Reformists along with their hard-line opponents were contemptuous of any unofficial approach, and it would appear that likewise the United States was incredulous that old Iran-Contra contacts were being activated. Yet at the same time, there were strong hints that a formal diplomatic representation had been made to the United States in the aftermath of the Iraq invasion through the offices of the Swiss ambassador in Tehran. The precise details of this offer remain classified, but we do know that the United States rejected it. In the run-up to the invasion of Iraq, the impression was of a superpower high on hubris. If the Iranians were seeking to deal now, just think what they might offer following the triumph in Iraq.[17]

Iran's conservative elite—broadly divided into the mercantile community, rich traders, and Islamic authoritarians—were experiencing considerable anxiety over the impending war in Iraq. But it was not necessarily an anxiety that would work in America's favor. Confronted with the implications of reform, they tended to side with each other against the Reform Movement. Now that the Reform Movement was crippled, fractures in the elite began to reappear, particularly between the traditional conservatives (pragmatists and moderates) and the hard-liners, who may be defined as neoconservatives. Whereas traditionalists at least paid lip service to the notion of democracy, the neoconservatives had no such urges. Although the former eschewed the woolly liberal hypocrisy of the Reformers, they likewise detested the dogmatic inflexibility of the hard-liners. Trade, after all, depended on a certain amount of flexibility, and the emergence of an Iranian neoconservative movement was something to be concerned about. But the traditionalists did not take the neocons seriously as a political force, despite the fact that they were making them-selves felt over the past few years.

Perhaps as long as the traditionalists and neoconservatives seemed to share the same ends, the latter were simply not perceived as a threat. Even in 2003, the traditional elite was more concerned about the apparent threat from abroad. In this way, they too failed to see the threat emerging before their eyes and ignored the changing patterns of politics in the country. Khatami and his supporters warned of the impending danger, but this was dismissed as political hyperbole. The elite was more preoc-cupied by America's intentions and the lack of any clear policy, particu-larly with respect to the concept of regime change. Many members of the elite with no affection for the hard-liners, or the Supreme Leader around whom they tended to congregate, were nonetheless anxious that regime change meant that they too would be subject to eviction. Some even went so far as to argue that regime change entailed the dismemberment of the Iranian state itself.

In the absence of any clear statements from the United States, these fears accumulated to the point of forcing together reluctant elements of the elite. They were acutely aware that the regime as a whole, following several years of systematic repression, was losing its social foundation. The cost of promoting apathy and disillusionment with the political process was that the people might not rally round when you needed them most. But dislike for the regime did not necessarily translate into support for a foreign government whose ambitions with respect to Iran remained un-clear. In this respect, although Iranians were impressed by the strength and purpose of American leadership (Rumsfeld's can-do attitude was favorably compared with the procrastination of Iranian leaders), the one card that the regime kept up its sleeve was that of nationalism. Whenever interna-tional tensions increased, state broadcasting would play the highly emotive unofficial national anthem (*Ey Iran*) or broadcast a short television piece on the history, mythology, or sheer beauty of Iran. These were calculated to convince Iranians that America posed a challenge to the nation, not simply the regime. Reckless American rhetoric did much to reinforce this impression.

It says something of the opportunity squandered by the United States that such views took time to permeate through the wider society. In the run-up to the Iraq war, Iran held no major demonstrations against the war (in marked contrast to Western countries) and politicians openly protested the anti-American bias of state television! Iranians could barely disguise their glee at their old foe finally receiving its just desserts. Some even felt that an American occupation of Iraq would force the Americans to the negotiating table. After all, Iran and America were finally neighbors, and not just on one border.

NUCLEAR POLITICS

The aggressor is always peace loving; he would prefer to take over our country unopposed. To prevent his doing so one must be willing to make war and be prepared for it. In other words it is the weak, those likely to need defence, who should always be armed in order not to be overwhelmed. Thus decrees the art of war.

CARL VON CLAUSEWITZ—On War

IT SAYS SOMETHING of the resilience of a society that it can continue to see light at the end of the deepest tunnel. As with Afghanistan, many Iranians regarded Iraq as an opportunity. Some saw it as an opportunity to procrastinate further. Others viewed Iraq as an opportunity to extend Iranian influence and power. Still others believed that the opportunity of a new power dynamic would enable a dialogue to emerge between the United States and Iran. Put simply, America might know how to get into Iraq, but it will need Iran's help to get out. This last position would obviously require America to recognize its predicament, and this was not going to happen in the immediate aftermath of the invasion. The invasion in military terms was so successful that there was little prospect of

American ambitions being reassessed downwards. If anything, America's neocons were feeling bullish. This worried the Iranian elite. It also worried the Europeans.

In 2002, leaks within Iran's nuclear establishment had resulted in a dissident Iranian opposition group, the National Council of Resistance of Iran (NCRI), exposing Iran's nuclear developments. Quite how this leak occurred remains unknown, but some suggest the information was provided by a third country (Israel), who had offered the information to other opposition groups before it was finally seized upon by the NCRI.[1]

The NCRI was traditionally recognized as the political wing of the Mojahideen-e Khalq Organization (MKO/MEK), which had been banned as a terrorist organization in several European countries and the United States. Despite these associations, it continued to enjoy good access to a number of lawmakers in the United States and Europe. They urged governments to recognize the NCRI as the official opposition to the Islamic Republic, an ironic position given the anti-American pedigree of the organization (it began as an Islamic Marxist movement deeply antithetical to American imperialism) and its involvement in the assassination of US personnel in Iran during the 1970s.

The MKO had much to be angry about in its relationship with the political elite of the Islamic Republic. Having been deeply involved in the overthrow of the Shah, the movement found itself at odds with the religious wing of the revolution, who made much of the movement's Marxist pretensions to orchestrate and justify a widespread suppression of the movement. The MKO leadership first fled to France and then, somewhat imprudently, relocated to Iraq in 1986. There, in the words of one historian, they completed their transformation from a political movement into a cult. More important, as far as ordinary Iranians were concerned, was their decision to enjoy Saddam Hussein's patronage at a time when Iran and Iraq were at war.[2]

This simple fact made their claim to be the official opposition difficult to justify. Most Iranians, whatever their feelings towards the Islamic Republic, could not side with an organization that was effectively committing treason. This political problem aside, the MKO remained the most organized of all Iranian opposition groups, with a highly effective public relations machinery. These two facts help explain their effectiveness among legislators. Journalists and analysts, who were regularly bombarded with MKO press statements, grew more skeptical, as it became increasingly apparent that their profound animosity—fully reciprocated by the political establishment in Iran—consistently colored their judgement.

Some legislators fully endorsed MKO/NCRI views. Others supported them only for the irritation they would cause the Iranian leadership rather than for any practical change they might encourage in Iran. Paranoia about the MKO played right into the hands of the hard-liners in Iran (as had happened during the student riots in 1999). As a political strategy, this was to prove (and continue to be) one of the more facile aspects of Western policy.

The periodic polemics of Western legislators with respect to their support for the NCRI was to cause considerable frustration among Western diplomats, who argued that the negative consequences far outshone any benefits such support might bring. At the very least, Iranian politicians could point to the contradiction and hypocrisy of Western countries who condemned Iran as the foremost sponsor of state terrorism while offering support to a group they themselves had classified as terrorists.

It was in this general atmosphere that the revelations provided by the NCRI came to light. And just as doubt precedes faith, the initial skepticism made the subsequent veracity of the substance of their claims all the more damning. The revelations proved a double blow to the Islamic Republic by providing details of hitherto secret nuclear developments and dramatically enhancing the NCRI's international credibility.

By stripping away the hyperbole that accompanied the disclosure, we can better understand the nature of the problem. Far from revealing a secret program hidden from the International Atomic Energy Agency for eighteen years, the disclosures dealt with two plants, in Natanz and Arak, that had been developed in 2000 and 1996, respectively. What the information pointed to, but could not confirm, was that Iran was further ahead in its nuclear research than expected.

It was well known that Iran had a nuclear program. (Cheney, Rumsfeld, and Wolfowitz, key members of the Bush administration, had also held senior positions under President Ford. It would have been impossible for them not to know of Iran's nuclear ambitions. In addition, a new member of the team, Ambassador Zalmay Khalilzad, wrote his doctoral thesis on nuclear proliferation using Iran as a case study.) But the program's continued development after the Islamic Revolution had been a matter of concern for successive presidents, including Clinton. It was a matter of public knowledge, for instance, that Iran had discovered deposits of uranium estimated to exceed 5000 tons in 1985.[3]

At the same time, it was also true that Western intelligence agencies were more concerned with the development of biological and chemical weapons, and had paid less attention to nuclear developments. The focus of their nuclear concerns was the power plant in Bushehr, which was being erratically developed by the Russians. Iranians joked that they hoped the US would bomb Bushehr, allowing them to sue and get a proper reactor. Some evidence suggests that Rafsanjani was so unimpressed with Bushehr that he had contemplated reaching an agreement with Clinton by which the United States would supply the technology to build a natural gas power plant. It seems, however, that this proposal never moved beyond preliminary discussions.

The revelations of 2002 were as much an embarrassment to Western intelligence agencies, who could be accused of having been insufficiently diligent, as they were to the Iranians, who had denied the truth of the revelations. The characteristic procrastination of an Iranian establishment that had been caught off guard exacerbated Western suspicions, especially when a planned, November 2002 visit to Natanz by the head of the IAEA, Mohammad El-Baradei, was postponed. The Iranian view was that they had nothing to apologize for, because their actions were fully compatible with the safeguards laid down by the Nuclear Non-Proliferation Treaty (NPT), which stated that they needed to alert the IAEA only when they intended to enrich uranium. The existence of Natanz and Arak suggested that this was what they *intended* to do, and that furthermore they intended to develop the facility to highly enrich uranium through the development of a heavy water reactor, which is not strictly necessary for power generation. Nonetheless, Iranian officials argued that they had to inform the IAEA only after they were about to start enriching, in other words, after all preparations had been completed.

The secrecy of the preparations, they argued, was a result of the nuclear powers themselves not fulfilling their NPT obligations by facilitating the development of civil nuclear power in Iran, one of the benefits of having signed the treaty. Why, argued Iranian officials, was Iran constantly under the microscopic gaze of the West, when both Israel and more recently India and Pakistan had gone nuclear? In fairness to the Iranians, the Western argument that none of the aforementioned powers had been signatories to the NPT, while legally valid, remained politically (and ethically) dubious. It suggested that countries who signed international treaties were at a greater disadvantage than those who flouted international convention. Neither India nor Pakistan had suffered greatly from their decision to become nuclear weapons powers, and it was probably this development (in 1998) that persuaded the Iranians to accelerate their program. For Iranians, the pressure being felt was wholly political.

This was true, but it made the situation far more serious. The growing confrontation over Iran's nuclear program could not be understood outside the general political malaise that characterized Iran-US relations. Nor could it be fully appreciated outside the changed international atmosphere inaugurated by 9/11. The Europeans understood the latter but failed to appreciate the depth of the former. The Iranians, on the other hand, were dismissive and contemptuous of the situation as a political exercise that had been witnessed and surpassed many times before. They might have been able to see the bigger picture, yet they failed to appreciate the totality of the crisis confronting them. Instead, they chose to view it as one of the many manufactured crises that had to be navigated. The fact that it was essentially political made it solvable and by extension less critical. However, in the wake of Khatami, they lacked the tools to engage and deal with the problem. Instead, the realist approach predominated, inasmuch as Iranian negotiators considered that the US simply had to be placated by pandering to its interests. It was even suggested, for example, that the US be invited to participate in Iran's nuclear program.[4]

NUCLEAR NEGOTIATIONS: PHASE ONE

In short, this new crisis was routine rather than extraordinary and could be overcome with imaginative diplomacy. Khatami was perhaps the only leading figure in the Islamic Republic to appreciate the depth of the problem, but even he was now cynical about Western intentions and their reliability as a partner. Nonetheless, the mounting international crisis in Iraq, and gentle encouragement from the Europeans, convinced the Iranians that it would be better to be as transparent as possible about their nuclear program. Consequently, the developments in Natanz and Arak were publicly affirmed by Khatami in February 2003. Anxieties increased in the aftermath of the fall of the Bath regime in Iraq, the speed of which surprised even hard-liners in Iran. This was followed by an IAEA report that condemned Iran for violating its obligations under the NPT by not providing a full disclosure of its activities. The pressure was mounting, and in the aftermath of a successful invasion, the timing was opportune.

The United States was likewise anxious to move quickly to pin down its old foe in the legal quagmire of the NPT. The Europeans, meanwhile, also spotted an opportunity, but in their case the challenge was slightly different. By acting forcefully and with alacrity, Old Europe (in this case joined by Britain) could prove the merits and efficacy of diplomacy, bring Iran to heel, restrain the United States, and heal trans-Atlantic wounds. In many ways, it was a diplomatic opportunity too good to miss, especially because it appeared that the Iranians were now amenable to some sort of negotiated settlement. Unfortunately, the European's enthusiasm to secure an agreement clouded their judgement.[5]

The European strategy was essentially this: Iran was in breach of its NPT obligations and US pressure was mounting to report it to the United Nations Security Council. The European Union (EU) would offer Iran a negotiated settlement by which the Iranians would promise to come clean on all their activities and sign and ratify the Additional Protocol, which would allow for more intrusive inspections of Iran's nuclear facilities. In truth, the Additional Protocol represented an attempt to strengthen a treaty that many people considered anachronistic in light of modern technological developments. It sought to add an element of compulsion to what was a voluntary agreement. Many hard-liners in Iran were arguing that Iran should withdraw from the NPT rather than subject itself to humiliating inspections. After all, Iran, unlike Iraq, had not invaded anyone, nor had it been defeated in war.

The Europeans sought to take a tough line, in part to convince Iran of the seriousness of the situation but also to deflect criticism from a highly skeptical US administration. Its strategy was essentially legal: Iran had to fulfil its treaty obligations pursuant to international law. In the words of one European diplomat, "This is about meeting your responsibilities. It is not about haggling."[6] This was neither personal nor political but simply a matter of law and order, and the Europeans were not suggesting that Iran should be prohibited from having a civil nuclear program. It just had to provide the required guarantees that it would not seek a military option. The precise nature of these guarantees remained diplomatically ill-defined to ensure agreement.

Nonetheless, this ambiguity was a harbinger of difficulties to follow, especially in light of the historical distrust Iranians had for Western legalism. Had treaty after treaty not proved that international law was simply a political device to ensure Western control? Iranian negotiators tended to subscribe to the argument that, in the absence of strength, Iran was likely to be ignored and abused as it had been in the past. The difference among Iranian factions was the degree of trust and compromise one could afford the Europeans (the US was generally viewed with suspicion). Traditional conservatives and Reformists argued that some sort of agreement needed to be reached with the Europeans, if for no other reason than to divide them from the United States and ensure European support in deflecting US ambitions towards Iran. Hard-liners remained far more skeptical of Europe's capabilities in this regard and tended to view the EU3 simply as lacklustre US surrogates who could not deliver. Given the hard-liners' ideological antipathy towards the United States, it was not clear just what their own strategy might be. The notion that it takes hawks on both sides to ultimately bridge the divide is nonsense; you need decisive leadership willing to take risks (the "Nixon goes to China" or "Sadat goes to

Jerusalem" model). Given the lack of such leadership, these views reflected the wishful thinking of well-meaning observers rather than a realistic assessment of the position of both sides.

Despite the absence of any constructive strategy, the hard-line interpretation of Western unreliability gained momentum in light of the legal fiasco that preceded the invasion of Iraq. Just where was international law and adherence to due process in the run-up to the invasion, asked Iran's conservatives? Did the differing treatment of Iraq and North Korea not prove that might was indeed right, and that weak powers could not rely on a legal defense if the United States chose to ignore the law? This view was reinforced by the American neoconservative argument that the only law that prevailed in the international sphere was that of the jungle.

Moreover, hard-liners were convinced that the ultimate aim of Western powers since 1979 was the overthrow of the Islamic Republic. In other words, the nuclear dispute was simply a particular means to a general end, a position reinforced by the unwillingness of the United States to reject the notion of regime change. These arguments fuelled the view that Iran should not allow itself to be shackled by an international legal system that was inherently unjust. Nor should it depend on Western partners, who were unreliable and whose aims had always been to refuse the Islamic Republic's desire for nuclear technology.[7]

The failure of trust was therefore mutual, and it ensured, in the first instance, that Iran's nuclear negotiations were removed from the hands of the very individuals who would have been more amenable to a diplomatic solution: the Reformists. This shift in political emphasis was effectively endorsed by the Europeans, anxious to get results. Consequently, they proceeded to ignore the elected government and deal almost exclusively with the conservative and technocratic National Security Council, headed by Hasan Rowhani. It is a matter of conjecture whether Khatami was anything more than a lame duck president at this stage, but the European approach was deeply insensitive to all Iranians and gave succour to the conservatives (along with the hard-liners), who were further encouraged to marginalize the Reformists. So enamoured were the Europeans with Rowhani, for instance, that his imminent succession to the presidency was taken for granted. This became a matter for general political discussion in the West but a signal that would not have been missed by political pundits in Tehran.

In October 2003, the foreign ministers of Britain, France, and Germany suddenly departed for Tehran to crown their negotiations with a triumphant agreement, signed with much fanfare and against the expectations of critics in the United States, Europe, and Teheran. Iran agreed to sign and ratify the Additional Protocol and to suspend its plans to enrich uranium pending further final-status negotiations. Europe, meanwhile, recognized Iran's right to develop peaceful nuclear energy and to assist in its development, along with the promise to enter a more general dialogue about regional security and stability. It was a theatrical moment in the best sense of the term: a showpiece event, intended to prove to the world that diplomacy and the methods of Old Europe could yield results. Such was the mutual cynicism that some Iranian diplomats privately conceded the psychological importance of achieving even the most modest treaty agreement with the West. Yet far from being the crowning success, it contained the seeds of future difficulties.

For all the concentration on detail, individuals neglected the political context and ignored the core of the problem: the lack of trust, a consequence of a bitter political malaise between Iran and the United States. Without sorting this problem out, any settlement of the nuclear dispute could be only temporary. Although most of the participants appeared to recognize this reality, they seemed unable to grapple with it in any meaningful sense. At the very least, they drew different conclusions, and some argued that a solution to a particular problem might ultimately lead to a more general peace. The absence of a broader framework concerned the Iranian negotiators, who worried that concessions on the nuclear issue would simply result in the United States moving to another matter of contention (terrorism, Israel, or now Iraq). They wanted a broader agreement but were unsure how to secure it, and they did not help matters by being divided and incoherent. They might complain that Khatami's attempts at detente had been rebuffed, but many traditional conservatives who now led the negotiations were themselves guilty of undermining Khatami's strategy. In failing to recognize the cultural dynamics of the political problem, their own attempts to broker a grand bargain fell largely on deaf ears.

Yet if divided opinion was hampering a coherent Iranian strategy, much the same could be said of their Western interlocutors. In Iran at least, the overwhelming trend had continued to be towards some sort of dialogue. In the United States, certainly in the aftermath of 9/11, the preference was for confrontation. Huntington's "Clash of Civilizations" thesis had returned with a vengeance. The European negotiators had to contend with a variety of different constraints: the critics in their own countries, members of the European Union who were not consulted by the Big Three when they went in haste to Tehran, and the hawks in the United States and Israel.

All this made for a complex and layered dynamic that was open to sabotage at many levels. Strategic vision, intellectual effort, and decisive leadership would be required to overcome these enormous structural and ideological obstacles to communication, let alone agreement. All these were lacking in almost all quarters, as Europeans and Iranians rushed to surmount the immediate crisis with a view to placating critics and achieving ends that had little to do with the overall problem. It was as if the structures of confrontation were so powerful that the individual actors could do little more than patch up the periodic crises that resulted from this dangerous environment. Such a pieced together approach, in the absence of a clear strategic perspective, could have unfortunate consequences. Nothing illustrates this better than the immediate consequences of the agreement signed with much anticipation in Tehran in October 2003.

THE PARLIAMENTARY ELECTIONS OF 2004

The publicized Tehran agreement of November 2003 in itself was indeed a matter for considerable self-congratulation. A major crisis appeared to have been avoided: Iran and the United States had been contained. While the Europeans trumpeted the success of old-style diplomacy, the Iranians also announced the agreement as a significant achievement that had secured concessions from the other party. (The model for this was the Rushdie affair solution, although the significant difference in that case was that Britain had no one else to answer to.) The Europeans regarded the agreement as the beginning of a process of confidence building; Iran viewed it as an immediate crisis that was overcome. Europe considered the negotiations complete. Iran regarded the process of negotiation as continuous, and if the political environment became more favorable, negotiations should be re-opened.

More significant than any of these particular differences in interpretation was the tacit agreement apparently reached between the Europeans and their traditional, conservative Iranian interlocutors. Europe wanted the Additional Protocol signed and ratified. Security was paramount, and there was a sense of urgency in the aftermath of the Iraq invasion to settle the Iran crisis amicably, if not for the sake of Iran than for the future of trans-Atlantic relations. This unstated agreement seems to have involved the notion of nonintervention in Iran's politics, a sensitive issue regularly raised by Iranian politicians. It may have been the securement of such an assurance that convinced conservatives in all factions to buy into the agreement of October 2003. But nonintervention in an era of globalized politics and media dissemination is nonsense. As has been shown, America's physical absence from Iran did not prevent it being involved in Iranian politics. The consequences of this understanding were felt in the parliamentary elections of February 2004.

Ever since the sixth parliamentary elections had resulted in a landslide for the Reformists, the conservative establishment had been fighting to recapture the political initiative. They had rigorously and ruthlessly sought to forestall and constrain the Reformist Parliament through judicial harassment and the vetting of legislation by the supervisory Guardian Council. One of the more absurd examples of this was the 2002 bill outlawing torture, which Reformists attempted to pass in an effort to bring current practice in line with the Constitution. The Guardian Council considered this both un-Constitutional and un-Islamic and argued that torture had to be retained for use in exceptional circumstances, using arguments that were ironically becoming increasingly frequent in the West. Ultimately Khatami's frustration at the powerlessness of the presidency to confront the conservative legal machinery resulted in him seeking a legal amendment to enhance his powers. This move was also quashed. Having contained the Reform Movement and frustrated the public will, the conservatives were determined to prove they could do even more by seizing elected offices.

This process began, discreetly but surely, with the municipal elections of 2003. Khatami had made much of the development of local council elections as a mechanism for bringing democracy to the people and getting them involved in local issues. This was a theoretically sound idea with unfortunate political consequences. The Tehran municipality, dominated by Reformists, became the focus of intense, if somewhat theatrical, political infighting. This was broadcast almost nightly by the conservative-led state television service. Consequently, people became disillusioned with the political process, viewing the debacle of the municipality as a microcosm of the wider gridlock in government. Partly because of this disenchantment but also because the elections were local, the turnout in 2003 was pitifully small, around 15 percent, most of whom were core conservative voters. The result was a conservative council for Tehran. But this was no ordinary conservative council. It was full of hard-line religious radicals, who admired the ascendancy of the can-do neoconservatives in the United States—never underestimate the role of imitation in Iranian politics.

The new mayor was Mahmoud Ahmadinejad, better known for his unorthodox religious views than his political acumen. Ahmadinejad's principle achievement as mayor of Tehran was to be denied a seat at Khatami's cabinet table, a privilege accorded to most of his predecessors. The political ascent of Iran's neoconservatives (like those in the US) had begun, but this rise was achieved in the full glare of popular ignorance and the contempt of their opponents, who could not take their political views seriously. Some Reformist strategists warned of the danger ahead and argued that the Reformists were losing their popular base. Traditional conservatives considered themselves the natural party of government, to whom people would turn in a crisis, and such developments failed to concern them. But the failure of Reformists to address this hemorrhaging of popular support was inexcusable.

Civil servants with Reformist sympathies grew anxious at these developments and had privately warned the West, particularly Europe, that the hard-liners were determined to orchestrate a coup. In the absence of resistance at home—the public was disillusioned, but the greater concern was a lack of bold Reformist leadership—a concerted and unified European protest would have an impact.(An American protest would simply encourage the hard-liners.)

It is debatable whether a European protest would have deterred the hard-liners by the end of 2003 because the political environment had changed. Not only were neoconservatives in Iran increasingly bullish about their domestic position—reformism had effectively been crushed—but Iran's regional and international position was also looking less daunting. Iran was the chief beneficiary of the US war on terror. The triumphalism of spring 2003 was beginning to dissipate. America was finding Iraq and Afghanistan indigestible, and Iran's political leverage was growing. Prospects from Tehran looked extraordinarily good as the demolition of two of Iran's most difficult enemies had created a geopolitical vacuum, making Iran the regional power.

The Iranian imperial mentality moved quickly to take advantage of the unique opportunity afforded by the myopic policies of the Bush administration. It achieved this not by confronting the West but by quietly and tacitly working with the Coalition. In Shia-dominated southern Iraq, the British needed Iranian compliance and support to ensure a peaceful occupation. Iranian nongovernmental organizations and religious charities flooded southern Iraq with social services the Coalition could not deliver (the Revolutionary Guards were not far behind). On the eastern frontier, Ismail Khan, the Lion of Herat, who had spent much of his time in exile in Iran, was restored to his nominal patrimony. Not since the early nineteenth century had Iran's political reach been so extensive. They were seemingly on the cusp of empire, and even staunch nationalists found this tonic intoxicating.

Power so easily attained is rarely appreciated, and the consequence of these developments was complacency. Traditional conservatives congratulated themselves on the recurring luck that always seemed to come to Iran's aid at the most difficult times, dismissing the warnings of Reformists and convincing themselves of the justice and correctness of their policies. Clearly they must be doing something right if things always worked out. Neoconservatives had no mystery about this; it was proof of

Divine Provenance. Such convictions provide the believer with a moral certainty that is difficult to challenge. The political consequences of this self belief were to be witnessed in the run-up to the seventh parliamentary elections.

Secure in the knowledge that the West would not protest and aware that Iran's regional position was strengthening every day, the supervisory Guardian Council ruthlessly vetted a list of prospective candidates for the forthcoming elections. Some three thousand candidates, many of them sitting Reformist deputies, were barred. It was an act of extraordinary electoral vandalism and was openly described by senior Reformists as a constitutional coup. Most did not believe that the Guardian Council decision would be allowed to stand, and some argued that the political process needed space to work itself out. At the very least, Supreme Leader Ayatollah Khamenei would intervene to urge the Guardian Council to show more balance. He did, but his intervention was lukewarm and insincere. To much subsequent incredulity, it was revealed that the Guardian Council was acting on the advice of Khamenei, who in a dream had apparently been provided with a list of acceptable candidates by the Hidden Imam himself. Khamenei's refusal to deny this assertion by one of his senior lieutenants spoke volumes. In the words of one Reformist "Presently some try to turn the Islamic Republic into an Islamic monarchy."[8]

Reformist deputies organized a sit-in of the Parliament building to rally support, but by this stage bolder leadership would have been required to galvanize a skeptical public. Khatami had hoped for a compromise but was rebuffed and could barely disguise his sense of betrayal. His decision to nonetheless encourage participation in the elections merely increased his isolation from a public contemptuous of his leadership. The public divisions within the Reformist leadership, with some arguing for a boycott and others for participation, simply increased popular rancour and ensured that there was no coherent internal protest.

Meanwhile, traditional conservatives viewed the developments with trepidation. Their contempt for the naiveté of the Reformist deputies dissuaded them from protesting, but they were also privately concerned that so blatant a fraud would damage the long-term authority of the system. Many more moderate conservatives simply withdrew their candidacies, noting that there was no honor in winning an election with no competition. In many constituencies, the choice was reduced to one hard-line nominee.

The Guardian Council unprecedently and unconstitutionally shadowed the Interior Ministry's management of the elections by dispersing forty thousand election observers of their own. This was a rigged election even by recent Iranian standards. The real significance of what was taking place was the attempted reversal of eight years of popular democratization. It was achieved on the back of poor leadership and popular disenchantment, but it was interpreted abroad in a more convenient manner.

Iranians would have rallied had the Reformist leadership been united and robust in confronting the challenge of the hard-liners. If Khatami and his cabinet had resigned in protest, a constitutional crisis would have probably resulted in the hard-liners backing down. The experience of the last five years indicated that the one thing the hard-liners feared was a popular backlash. It was important for them to show that, at the very least, the people had turned against the Reformists. Yet some Western pundits went further and argued that people were not only against the politicians who had failed to deliver but also against reform as an idea. This interpretation was used to justify the deafening silence emanating from Western politicians. In an extraordinary rewriting of the last eight years, it was simply concluded that Iranians were not interested in democracy, an analytical exercise that was reassuringly stereotypical and obviated the need to think.[9]

Iranians were stunned to discover that far from condemning the electoral farce, Britain had decided that this was an opportune moment to send Prince Charles on a humanitarian visit to the earthquake-shattered city of Bam in southeastern Iran. As the first visit by a British royal since 1979, the humanitarian dimensions of this visit were lost on most Iranians, who convinced themselves that Prince Charles had come to bestow a particularly British blessing on the coup that was transpiring. (An American delegation was more prudently planned for after the election, but then that proposal fell victim to the election results.) Britain's motives were sincere, but the visit resulted in a loss of credibility among Iran's democratic activists. The timing showed an uncharacteristic lack of attention to detail among Britain's foreign policy establishment. Some European diplomats privately complained that the lack of response and absence of a democratic agenda in favor of an exclusive focus on the issues of security and proliferation had handed the moral high ground to the US neoconservatives. Britain's priorities, and by extension its foreign policy resources, were directed towards solving the unfolding crisis in Iraq. Arguably, democracy in Iran was a victim of the West's pursuit of democracy in Iraq. Rarely have scarce resources been so misdirected and opportunities so recklessly squandered.[10]

The juxtaposition of the Bam earthquake and the subsequent parliamentary elections showed the complexity of Iranian politics. The Reform Movement may have been suffocated, but this did not automatically mean a de-politicization of the public or a desire for more autocratic religious rule. Far from it. People were disillusioned with the process and exhausted by the effort. They were appalled by the their leaders' lack of courage, which failed to match the convictions they apparently held. They were equally disdainful of the contempt shown by the hard-liners towards their views, and the Guardian Council was harshly criticized. In the words of one Iranian official, the Council was not a generation out of touch; it was at least a century behind the times.

In seeking to restore their power, the conservatives (and their hard-line allies) had sacrificed a considerable amount of their authority, and many conservatives recognized this problem. Indeed, none but the most extreme authoritarians considered the problem insignificant. But they did regard it as manageable. The population might be disgruntled now, but nationalism would serve, where perhaps an appeal to Islam would not, to rally the people behind the Islamic Republic. For this they needed a well-defined enemy and a crisis.[11]

THE NEOCONSERVATIVE REACTION AND CONFRONTATION IN IRAQ

For the hard-liners in the regime, the enemy was clear and well defined. It was and continued to be the United States in particular and the West in general. There was no point in building bridges or fostering detente. Of certain eternal truths, one was the animosity between the United States and the Islamic Revolution. To think otherwise was to sully the purity of the Revolution and hasten its demise. For this reason, engagement was an act of treason. It was a view that dove-tailed neatly with the perspective of American hawks, who likewise considered any form of compromise with the Islamic Revolution tantamount to treason. Engagement would, by necessity, affect the nature of the Revolution, but Reformists regarded this process inevitable in the modern world and felt that the best one could do was to manage it effectively.

Even traditional conservatives accepted this principle; they simply wanted to manage the process in their interests rather than leave it to the Reformists. In rejecting meaningful engagement, American hawks played into the hands of Iran's neoconservatives: more so because America's failure to even recognize the Revolution encouraged many members of the elite who had little sympathy for the political developments in the country to stick with the devil they knew. Thus, when American commentators and politicians talked loosely of regime change, without defining what they meant, members of the Iranian political establishment saw themselves as the target. The consequence of regime change was obvious for all to see in Iraq.

Moreover, it was argued, the Americans not only were interested in regime change but also sought to challenge the integrity of the Iranian state itself. Again, the evidence was clear for all to see in the fractious debacle emerging in Iraq, which through 2004 was separating into preordained constituent parts. In failing to define their policy, America allowed rumors to circulate among members of the elite, who were themselves disenchanted with the radicalization of politics.

What matter if the people are with us? Such was the view that seemed to dominate American thinking. The belief that most Iranians were inclined to be sympathetic towards the United States—a view reinforced by the experience of American emergency workers during the Bam earthquake (the first time Americans had been actively engaged in helping ordinary Iranians on the ground)—resulted in more complacency rather than serious reflection. Certainly most Iranians (including many of the elite) had struggled to find any reason to oppose the Iraq war and particularly the decision to topple Saddam Hussein. In light of the aftermath of Afghanistan, it is remarkable how popular sympathy leant towards the United States, even to the extent of parliamentary deputies publicly denouncing the bias of state television against the United States.[12]

American observers, however, often oversimplified or misread these signals, with a view to justifying the continued US opposition to the Islamic Republic in general rather than aspects of its behavior. With attention focused on Iraq, much of the responsibility for engagement was privatized and delegated to the expatriate community largely resident in Los Angeles, whose political mantra was the pursuit of another revolution and the encouragement of a popular uprising—themes that Iranians in Iran viewed with contempt. It was easy to call for revolution from the comfort of Los Angeles or London; there was no price to be paid for failure. Some of the delegation of this responsibility stemmed from the erroneous belief that Iranians instinctively knew more about their country than foreigners, even though the closest some of these Iranians had been to Iran was the local Persian restaurant.

There was no reason why Iranians (in Iran or outside) should know more about their history and politics than, say, the average Americans knew about theirs. Most expatriate Iranians knew little about the history of Iran beyond the most perfunctory knowledge of particular great kings. What they lacked in serious knowledge they made up for in emotion, and this in turn was fed by a rich political mythology. Consequently, Iranian expatriates reinforced the historical mythology that divided Iran from the West.

Views and perspectives need to be addressed, but historical myths are too layered and profound to be treated on a superficial plane. This is the real meaning of *engagement*. But in truth, little engagement was occurring. On the contrary, some mythologies were accepted without critical inquiry or assessment, such that the popular mythology of Mosaddeq in reinforcing the belief in nonintervention gave hard-line repression a free hand. What may have been applicable in 1953 does not necessarily apply to the globalized community of 2004, when the very act of nonintervention may be paradoxically interpreted as an act of intervention. The circularity of the process may be bewildering to the uninitiated, but the trick is to know where and when to enter the circle, a task requiring professional expertise.

For example, in the parliamentary elections of 2004, the West apparently placed security concerns above democratization and human rights, and chose not to protest the fraud perpetrated against the Iranian people, ostensibly in an effort to show sensitivity to the legacy of 1953. Iranians interpreted this act of nonintervention differently. For a decade, reformist intellectuals and politicians had argued for serious reflection on Iran's historical relationship with the West. Books and articles urged Iranians not to instinctively blame the West for the ills of the country, while the influential lay religious philosopher Abdolkarim Soroush had even argued that part of Iran's intellectual heritage was derived from the West.

The task of reassessment was undeniably huge, but at least a start had been made. Now, in the aftermath of the elections, Iranians wondered whether reassessment was little more than wishful thinking, as the hardliners had said all along. Many Iranians had interpreted the European determination not to intervene as acceding to the electoral manipulation that had taken place. It did not help that far from condemning what had transpired, the West seemed to prefer the conservatives. In the words of one somewhat naive Western diplomat: "These are issues that we have to deal with security people on—in other words the conservatives. . . . The reformists have never been in the loop on these kinds of things. Having conservatives running everything may not be a reflection of the will of the Iranian public, but it will probably make our job as diplomats trying to deal with the people that matter much easier."[13]

So much for democracy in the Middle East. Hitherto, most Iranians expressed cynicism of the West's desire to promote democracy because of their intervention in overthrowing Mosaddeq. Now it seemed that the West was speaking yet again with forked tongue, at least where Iran was concerned. More damaging was the hard-liners' view that their contempt for the public will was supported by the West. Some even had the audacity to argue that the Guardian Council had done no more than the US Supreme Court in 2000. In sum, in the absence of any coherent American strategy, the myth of Mosaddeq had been compounded by the myth of the 2004 parliamentary elections. The West could no longer take popular sympathy for granted.

The situation after 2004 became more complicated on a number of fronts. The new Parliament, stacked with hard-line deputies, had no intention of ratifying the Additional Protocol. On the contrary, they believed that the negotiating team was too soft with the Europeans and should insist on the retention of all Iranian national rights. This emphasis on nationalism was important because, in the absence of authentic electoral legitimacy, the new Parliament had to resort to emotive nationalist rhetoric to both rally the people round and blind them to the fraud that had occurred.

Just as those in the United States who dared challenge the legitimacy of the war in Iraq were labeled traitors, so too were those in Iran who dared query the details of the nuclear issue. Nuclear development, particularly the need to enrich uranium, became an iconic issue that would brook no questions, not even those relating to the cost of the venture. It became an exercise in vulgar nationalism, a hijacking of an ideology in the interests of power that disguised the supreme irony: a Parliament elected on the basis of contempt for the national will presenting itself as the protector of that nation.

Furthermore, the team in charge of the negotiations, led by Hasan Rowhani, faced a different type of challenge at home. Hard-line critics had always exerted pressure, but this had been balanced by the more moderate position of the Reformist deputies, some of whom were reportedly just as anxious as the West to find out what was going on with nuclear development. (There were reports that the Parliament intended to set up an investigative commission.) Now these Reformist deputies were gone, and Rowhani found himself trying to secure an agreement to contain further hard-line gains, while the neoconservatives sought to ensure the opposite. In other words, the nuclear negotiations became subject to political pressure of a wholly different nature, which began to mirror more closely Europe's relationship with the Bush administration. Neither group of neocons was interested in an agreement. The context of the debate was also changing.

Although the negotiations had begun in an atmosphere of anxiety for the Iranians, the developing quagmire in Iraq provided them with re-newed confidence. This confidence was enhanced by the revelations of the abuses at Abu Ghraib. The broad sympathies that Iranians held for the West and the United States had been damaged by the electoral fiasco. Now with Abu Ghraib, the image of the Great Satan was given greater public impetus. It is difficult to overestimate the impact of the Iraq War on Iranian perceptions of the West. For all the criticism, there had always been a grudging admiration for the rationality and political freedoms that the West represented, bound together by a respect for the law. These were contrasted favorably with the situation in Iran. Now this respect was coming under serious strain. The development of democracy in Iraq would have been music to the ears of Iran's political activists; anarchy and disorder played straight into the hands of the neoconservatives.

This disorder was more than a matter of perception, immensely dam-aging as that was. Iran's political system had always thrived on ambiguity and calculated disorder. Custom and the pervasiveness of extensive per-sonal networks, rather than any adherence to a transparent legal system, was the order of the day. Khatami's attempt to kindle a change in this sys-tem had faltered. Now the Iranian traditional elites found a new play-ground in Iraq.

The Coalition forces found the fractious anarchy of Iraq difficult to manage, but Iranians were well equipped to take advantage of the oppor-tunity. While the Coalition was determined to normalize political life, Iranians thrived on a crisis, viewing it as an opportunity to be seized (es-pecially the potential for commercial gain). This reflected the mercantile character of the Iranian political state—short term, volatile, and domi-nated by opaque personal networks. Iraq was the ideal extension for the Iranian political system. In contrast to the occupying forces, Iranians had access to the networks (largely through the Shia seminaries but also through Shia Arabs in general and the Kurds in the north), tended to speak the relevant languages (Kurdish and Arabic), and had considerable experience of organizing in a crisis situation.

Nevertheless, the Iranian position should not be oversimplified. Offi-cial policy was and remains the desire for a stable and secure Iraq, with its territorial integrity intact. The only red line that Iranian officials insisted upon was that no military threat should emerge from Iraq again, which entailed seeking political stability at the expense of military strength. But this overall policy objective does not necessarily contradict the means and methods used by Iranians agencies. The ideal for Iran would be a sympathetic Iraqi government with strong economic ties to Iran. With economic penetration came the reinforcement of an economic (and political) culture. If Iranians were more successful than the Coalition, it is because they were working with what they found, rather than attempting the harder task of changing it.

The consequence of this policy was that throughout 2004 and 2005, the Iranian presence in Iraq increased dramatically, to the point that some American commentators were becoming hysterical about the implications. The British took a more sober attitude to the Iranian presence, at the very least viewing it as a necessary evil, although some regarded Iranian participation as constructive. British planners did not enjoy the same missionary zeal as their American counterparts with respect to Iraq, and there was considerable disquiet among British officials over the venture and the lack of post-war planning. As a result, if the Iranians would enable a more manageable occupation and an easier withdrawal, so be it.

As far as the Iranians were concerned, the British presence was considered useful in shielding them from trigger-happy Americans. In many ways, British forces sat uneasily between two largely antagonistic forces, especially when the infiltration of Revolutionary Guard forces was taken into account. Britain viewed such infiltration with justifiable concern but felt that they could impress the need for restraint through political channels.

This restraint was soon to be sorely tested. In the summer of 2004, British troops patrolling the Shatt-al Arab waterway, which divides Iran from Iraq, were seized by a team of Revolutionary Guards. The seizure of the eight servicemen, along with their boats, provided the first clear indication that politics were changing in Iran. It was a fiasco in public relations terms. The British press began to question the *modus vivendi* that had governed British-Iranian relations to date, with diplomats hurriedly defending a relationship that seemed nonsensical in popular and populist terms. The tabloid press had a field day, dusting off the tried and tested image of mad mullahs and terrorists with depressing ease, and providing evidence that the Khatami presidency had barely dented the popular image of Iran in Britain.

The more populist of Britain's journalists advocated a strongly confrontational posture. This stance was counterproductive to Britain's overall strategy, which was to avoid unnecessary tensions. Nevertheless, democratic politics being what they are, Her Majesty's opposition (the Conservative party) leapt into the fray, demanding to know why the government was not being more robust against this key member of the axis of evil. All this made the job of the diplomats far more difficult, and in this they were mirrored by their Iranian counterparts, who were likewise confronted by an unhelpful piece of political theatre.

The Iranians had claimed that the British soldiers had a tendency to recklessly cross the border, and on this occasion they had had enough and decided to make a point by arresting the individuals involved. What seems more likely is that hard-line elements in the Iranian political establishment—the local Revolutionary Guard Commander—wanted to make a point. Part of this was for internal political consumption, but the major audience was abroad, specifically the British and the Arabs, because a film of the captured soldiers was broadcast only on the Arab satellite network of Iranian state television.

One suggestion was that the abduction was retribution for the abduction and humiliation of Iranian fishermen by the authorities of the United Arab Emirates (UAE). Because Iranian hard-liners regarded the UAE as a British client state, the decision was to retaliate not against the UAE but against the puppeteer. This justification was an interesting indicator of the political views of the Iranian neoconservatives. But something more sinister was afoot. The released film depicted the soldiers blindfolded in a fashion reminiscent of the US Embassy hostage crisis in 1979. Had this footage been broadcast in Iran, it would have received a mixed reception, particularly because the imagery suggested a nostalgia for a past most Iranians had no intention of returning to. The crisis itself was over in two weeks (although the boats have yet to be returned), in large part because useful channels were available to effectively lobby for the soldiers' swift release. But it nonetheless revealed a number of worrying trends.

First, it indicated the complex nature of Iranian politics and the decentralized way in which power worked. The local commander may have been prompted to take some action, but the details of that action were up to his own initiative. This prompting probably came from colleagues in the Revolutionary Guards and their allies in the hard-line establishment, rather than from the elected government. Curiously, despite repeated reassurances, the Iranian Foreign Minister was powerless to impose his will or the government's on the command structure of the Revolutionary Guards. Basically, the Iranian government had to negotiate with the Guards, like any other interlocutor, although they clearly possessed advantages that the British government did not. The Revolutionary Guards (much like the Army under the Shah) were administered through a parallel structure to the regular government and were keen on their independence of action. This structure was also being replicated in Iraq, and concerns grew that local commanders might start to operate more independently of government there too.

Second, it indicated that elements in the regime wanted a tougher stance towards the West and were not afraid of provoking a crisis. The abrupt seizure of the British soldiers also drew attention to the fact that the anarchic situation in Iraq, far more than the clumsy diplomatic dance that constituted the nuclear negotiations, would probably provide the spark to ignite Iran's continuing Cold War with the United States.

But most importantly, the episode revealed an unhealthy nostalgia for the halcyon days of the early revolution among key sectors of Iran's neoconservative movement. The full implications of this development were felt later, with the emergence of Ahmadinejad. The new Parliament and the confrontational attitude of its allies in the Revolutionary Guards did nothing to enhance Iran's international image or improve its chances of negotiating a favorable settlement on the nuclear issue. As the political situation deteriorated and the landscape became dotted with minor crises, the possibility of mutual trust diminished. The terms of any agreement became tougher, leading to a further radicalization of political opinion. The transformation of the negotiations into political theatre began in earnest in 2004, when the new Parliament viewed the prospect of a compromise deal with disdain. Instead of a compromise, they were determined to redefine Iran's relations with the West and turn to the East.

This essentially meant fostering relations with Russia and especially China, although the new Speaker of the Parliament announced to much press ridicule that his agenda was to pursue policies that would turn Iran into the Japan of Islam. None of these models of development showed an awareness of history, even recent Iranian history. The business culture in Russia might appeal to the Iranian mercantile community, but Russia had not been a reliable political ally. Apart from the historical legacy was the more recent experience of the legal status of the Caspian Sea, in which Russia peremptorily abandoned its show of solidarity with Iran after it received favorable terms from the West. As for China and Japan, their economic success depended in large part on their relations with the United States, a prospect Iran's neoconservatives did not even venture to contemplate. The allusion to Japan, given that country's especially turbulent relationship with the United States over the previous century and a half, seemed particularly ignorant.

NUCLEAR NEGOTIATIONS: PHASE TWO

In immediate terms, the appeal to Eastern models of development meant less attentiveness to the needs of Europe, who then spent a year catching up with the events they had unwittingly encouraged. A number of areas of dispute belied the triumphal tone of the October 2003 agreement. Indications were that the Additional Protocol was not going to be ratified. Although Iranian officials insisted that the terms of the agreement were nonetheless being implemented (inspections were occurring), these were not to the level expected by the Europeans—and the Americans, who were watching with a skeptical eye. The provision of adequate safeguards was proving a difficult case to answer inasmuch as no amount of inspections seemed to satisfy the Americans (or the Israelis), and Iranian officials rightly argued that they were not going to subject the country to the sort of spot inspections inflicted on Iraq, which had after all been defeated in a war. To submit to such a regimen would have been tantamount to national suicide.

Other areas of dispute revolved around the precise meaning of the terms of the agreement. For example, both sides believed that the definition of *suspension* had been agreed to. However, while the Europeans believed the meaning to have been clear and unambiguous, the Iranians argued that the voluntary temporary suspension allowed for exceptions, particularly for limited uranium enrichment for research. The Europeans insisted that there could be no room for exceptions, because exceptions allowed doubt to creep in and the aim was to build confidence. The Iranians, on the other hand, sought to push the limits to show their own people (and critics in particular) that they weren't soft with the Europeans; to pressure the Europeans to broker a more comprehensive final agreement; and to exhaust the European negotiators by showing themselves to be more pedantic.

While Iran's diplomats showed an attention to detail that impressed their European counterparts, the concern remained, heightened by the occasional comment from an Iranian hard-liner, that the Iranians were involved in a verbal scorched-earth exercise designed to give them enough time to fulfill various aspects of their nuclear research. Iranian negotiators accused the Europeans of prolonging the discussions and procrastinating for their own ends. It was unclear what these ends might be, but it is true that the Europeans did not move with alacrity. This probably reflected the nature of European bureaucracies and the fact that Iran was dealing with a collection of bureaucracies rather than a single one, who in turn had to look over their shoulders at the United States. It was soon apparent that the Europeans were not united in their position (as they sought to argue) and did not agree with the United States.

The United States, for all its eagerness to delegate responsibility to the Europeans, proved an excellent back-seat driver, periodically intervening to jeopardize the negotiations.[14] America made no secret of their lack of faith in the success of the negotiations, but they set such a high standard for good faith that they effectively proved their own skepticism. America intimated that it would not be happy unless Iran dismantled its nuclear program. The US also indulged in the language of regime change, which went straight to the heart of Iran's security concerns.

Iran soon came to the conclusion that no agreement with Europe would be worth the paper it was signed on unless America was involved to guarantee it. Yet this contradicted a basic tenet of hard-line dogma in Iran: no compromise with the United States. And for most hawks in the United States, compromise was anathema. What was the point of compromising with and by extension legitimizing a regime that was ideologically bankrupt and, it was argued, on the verge of collapse? The irony of this position was that hard-liners in Iran considered that any compromise with the United States would delegitimize the Islamic Revolution and therefore presage collapse.

The negotiations were a minefield of contradiction and misunderstanding. Sincere and genuine individuals on all sides were seeking a solution, but in many ways they were seeking the solution to the wrong problem. Consequently, every step forward was easily sabotaged, leading to further distrust, which made additional progress more difficult to achieve. The critical mass of goodwill on both sides proved insufficient to surmount the monumental obstacles in the way of a durable agreement. These obstacles were political and practical, in that the negotiations were a trilateral affair (Iran and the EU and the US), with each side seeking to placate multiple parties, some of whom were ideologically ill-disposed to any agreement. The farcical nature of this dynamic became clear in 2005, when the Europeans congratulated themselves on having softened the American position from one of denying the Iranians any nuclear technology (a position blatantly contravening the NPT) to one that simply demanded they abandon uranium enrichment. To date, the public face of the negotiations had emphasized the need for Iran to temporarily suspend enrichment until a permanent agreement could be reached. This was no easy task, because a permanent settlement was dependent on Iran providing objective guarantees that it was not seeking a nuclear weapons capability.

Doubts persisted because of Iranian obtuseness and a determination to negotiate terms that Western diplomats considered to be a nonnegotiable legal obligation to be transparent. Accepting this, it was nevertheless true that any sort of nuclear power program would provide the host country with the option to break out and develop weapons. This fact of scientific life, acknowledged by the NPT, was a voluntary agreement that could function only on the basis of trust. It is doubtful whether the Americans were ever serious about the functionality of the NPT with or without the Additional Protocol. No amount of detailed negotiation could get either party away from this vital reality, and if anything the process of negotiation had made matters worse.[15]

While Iranians sought creative ways to achieve this objective guarantee, the Europeans made it clear that the only objective guarantee that could work was a permanent cessation. As a negotiating tool, this position had some merits. However, once the position became public, following a leak from one of the European participants (suspicions fell upon the French), the transformation from diplomatic negotiation to political theatre was complete. The already small prospects of an agreement vanished. In seeking to placate the Americans, the Europeans had barred the door to a diplomatic solution. This need not have been the case had the Americans showed more political will earlier in the negotiations.

When the Americans finally came on board with the Europeans—to the latter's immense satisfaction—it proved to be far too little too late. Trust was dwindling, opinions were polarized, and domestic pressures were mounting. The Americans had been persuaded to fully support the European initiative and to prove their newfound enthusiasm by providing Iran with spare parts for its civilian airliners and by removing the veto on Iran's desire to join the World Trade Organization. This last offer was both imaginative and novel (although negotiations to enter the WTO would have taken years and could easily be prolonged further). But the Americans chose to whisper rather than shout about it, almost in hopeful anticipation that the Iranians would turn it down. That they did reject it revealed the surprise with which the Iranians greeted the offer but also reflected the derisory nature of the other aspect of the deal.

For a country seeking a grand bargain, being offered the technological scraps from the American table was too much. The Americans must have known this. The Europeans assured the Americans that if the Iranians backtracked on the November 2004 agreement (which effectively recon-firmed the agreement signed a year earlier, albeit with clearer language and particular emphasis on proving that suspension had actually taken place), they would join with the US in insisting that Iran be referred to the UN Security Council. Arguably this deal had more to do with heal-ing the wounds between Old Europe and the United States than it did with finding a solution with Iran.

For the Iranians, it was almost as if the Europeans had concluded that a solution was not possible and that they would be best served by seeking an accommodation with the United States. For the Europeans, unity was the byword, and it was vitally important that Iran be confronted with the reality of an international consensus. Nonetheless, the scars of Iraq had to be healed, and if Mohammad would not go the mountain, the mountain had better go to Mohammad. So the Europeans moved towards the American position, and no country moved more quickly than France.

AHMADINEJAD

Faced with political pressures at home and the end of the Khatami presi-dency (his second term), the Iranian team sought one final time to offer a comprehensive deal in March 2005. Rebuffed, they threatened to restart uranium enrichment and then recoiled, deciding instead to await a European counteroffer in August. By then it was clear that even the Eu-ropeans were becoming exhausted with the process.

The sticking point remained the right to enrich uranium on Iranian soil. The Europeans insisted that they should simply supply the required uranium. A more imaginative offer along the same lines subsequently of-fered by Russia never materialized because reportedly the only European country with the capacity to offer such a facility was France. And this was an offer that France, for one reason or another, was unwilling to counte-nance. By then, however, the political situation in Iran had taken another turn for the worse.

The election of the hard-line former mayor of Tehran, Mahmoud Ahmadinejad, to the presidency of the Islamic Republic was as much a surprise to the victor as it was to the horde of political analysts—Iranian and otherwise—who had completely failed to read the runes. The natural inclination of international punditry is to blame their failure on the obvious unpredictability of the Iranian people, who were clearly all mad for having elected a religious zealot. Conclusions of this nature reflected poorly on the pundits who made them and echoed similar comments made in the aftermath of the Islamic Revolution in 1979 (and by the British during the Mosaddeq crisis).

Astonishment of this nature, which tended to look for extraordinary reasons behind ordinary events, also complimented and confirmed the providential views espoused by the religious leadership in Tehran. While Westerners might conclude that Iranians were clearly deranged, the victors in the election might as well take the astonishment and surprise as a sign that God works in mysterious ways. A careful look at the facts would unsurprisingly reveal more sober reasons behind Ahmadinejad's victory. These may be divided into three unequal parts: fraud, astute political tactics, and the incompetence of his opponents.

Ahmadinejad contested a vigorous and at times vicious election. But few people could argue that the election was free or fair. It was conducted in a political environment that had seen the Reform Movement crushed, in part through their own failures of leadership, but mostly because the conservative establishment had launched a concerted campaign of repression. The result was a Reform Movement that was fractured and broken and had lost its constituency. That said, of the six candidates who contested the election, four ran on an overtly Reformist platform (with varying credibility) and collectively garnered twice as many votes as the two conservative candidates. This was despite the fact that between forty to fifty percent of the electorate chose not to vote. Had there been but one Reformist candidate, the evidence suggests he would have won.

Furthermore, Ahmadinejad, who had hitherto barely registered in the polls, received substantive logistical support from Revolutionary Guard and militia units in the final week before the election. This provided him with a nationwide reach he otherwise had not enjoyed. Finally, evidence suggests that blatant ballot rigging ensured that he managed to secure a run-off in the second round. By Iranian standards, the extent of this rigging was low. But in a race with six candidates, the difference between coming in second and third was no more than several hundred thousand votes (there are forty-two million possible votes to be cast).

At least three of the six candidates were so outraged by the rigging that they threatened to withdraw from the election, while a fourth registered his unhappiness at proceedings. The one who forfeited his second place proceeded to resign all his posts in the Islamic Republic. The other two were persuaded to stay in the interests of national unity. The sum of this is that Ahmadinejad's core vote numbered around five million. This number is not insignificant, but it was nowhere near the twenty-two million votes achieved by Khatami in the first round in two successive election victories.

Ahmadinejad ran a slick counterintuitive campaign that showed that the neoconservatives had learned the lessons of the Khatami era. In many ways, Ahmadinejad's campaign mirrored that of Khatami's in 1997. He campaigned on change, social justice, a fairer distribution of the country's wealth, and greater resources for young people. Notably absent from his campaign material were references to religion and social conservatism, with his campaign team making a point of rejecting allegations that he would be preoccupied with the length of a women's head scarf. On the contrary, Ahmadinejad was presented as a war veteran who enjoyed an austere (revolutionary) lifestyle, possessed the common touch, and was profoundly nationalistic with a policy that could be best described as Islamic socialism. Moreover, he was relatively unknown—and therefore should be given his chance—and crucially, he was not a cleric.

All in all, Ahmadinejad was an attractive option given his opponent in the second round. Hashemi Rafsanjani was the choice of the technocrats and the mercantile elite. He had also attempted to present himself as a reformer, although with little success because of his obstinate opposition to the economic reforms presented by Khatami. Given the skepticism facing him in Iran, his strategy of presenting himself as the one senior statesman who could solve the crisis with the international community tended to play better with that community than it did with his own. In a curiously mismanaged campaign, Rafsanjani barely traveled beyond Tehran, and most of his campaign literature seemed to be in English rather than

Persian. As campaigns go, it proved successful. The international community was convinced, but unfortunately they could not vote.

He failed to convince traditional Reformist voters that he had indeed reformed himself. Most of these people, having voted for Khatami in two elections, switched their allegiance to Ahmadinejad. They did this not because they were devotees of Ahmadinejad's ideological world view but because they distrusted Rafsanjani and, crucially, because Ahmadinejad seemed to be promising change and a better economic future. In other words, the Iranian electorate that voted in June 2005 made their choice on the basis of sound domestic and economic reasons. In this respect, they were no different than their counterparts in Europe and quite distinct from the religious electorate that voted President Bush back into office in 2004. As repeated government polls indicated, the secularization of Iranian society continues to gather pace, with fewer and fewer people showing an interest in organized religion. The latest such poll reportedly conducted by the Ministry of Intelligence revealed that less than twenty-five percent of Iranians considered religion to be an important factor in their lives.

This simple fact meant Ahmadinejad could not sit secure in the knowledge that the majority of the population shared his views. On the contrary, as the inauguration of the new President approached, it became apparent that Ahmadinejad's power base was both small and fragile. During his campaign, he had made extraordinary promises that would have required him to confront some of the country's most entrenched vested interests, including many of his own supporters among the hard-line establishment. Some argued that the realities of government would moderate his views and force him to compromise. After all, he had to administer the country with the help of officials who had emerged into prominence under Rafsanjani and Khatami and who reflected the more internationalist posture of these two Presidents. Some senior officials would have to go as a natural consequence of political change. The level of professional opposition to Ahmadinejad was unprecedented; most of the Iranian ambassadors in Europe had signed a letter in favor of Rafsanjani and at least one left his post to actively campaign on behalf of the former President. But surely Ahmadinejad would not remove middle-level managers, who were generally competent and essential for the day-to-day running of the country.

The first indication that Ahmadinejad would pursue a different strategy to consolidate and extend his base came with his cabinet nominations. His nominees had little or no experience of senior administration, which could be construed as a good thing. However, their background in security and intelligence worried observers. Moreover, far from introducing a cabinet based on merit and technical ability, Ahmadinejad seemed determined to nominate old friends, either from the Tehran municipality or the Revolutionary Guards.

As far as the nuclear negotiations were concerned, Hasan Rowhani was replaced by failed presidential candidate Ali Larijani, who had formally headed state television and radio. Larijani was not a popular figure and was regarded as a technocratic ideologue whose loyalties were with the Supreme Leader Ayatollah Khamenei. His tedious program schedules, designed to emulate and praise the Leader, were legendary, as was his blatant bias against the Reformists. More worrying, however, was his enthusiasm for portraying Ayatollah Khomeini as the new Prophet Mohammad and portraying his successor Ali Khamenei as the new Ali of the Age. Such an analogy was considered blasphemous by many Iranians, including conservative clerics, and indicated that Larijani had more in common with the unorthodox views of the new President than may at first have been apparent.

The reckless nature of the choices and the flippant way in which Ahmadinejad decided to introduce them only increased the profound contempt the newly disenfranchised elite were developing for the upstart President. The condescension of the elites, which in many ways had facilitated Ahmadinejad's election, was compounded by a fear that the new President was about to undo much of the good work of the previous decade, especially with respect to Iran's international relations. Far from continuing a policy of engagement begun by Rafsanjani and pursued with some vigour by Khatami, Ahmadinejad was determined to follow a radically different route that sought to increase rather than diminish tensions.

Like his erstwhile allies in the Parliament, Ahmadinejad was convinced that negotiating with the West was a fruitless exercise and that the only approach of any merit was that of robust confrontation. The West, after all, only respected strength. If some of his allies viewed such a position in tactical terms, as a means of forcing concessions out of the West, Ahmadinejad's perspective was more straightforward. In simple terms, he was not interested in whether the West conceded anything. On the contrary, a state of continued tension and confrontation was desirable, and the criticism of the West was to be actively sought. This was a return to the early glory days of the revolution, when Iran had stood alone and "America could not do a damned thing." If Iran drew criticism from the West, it merely confirmed the righteousness of Iran's position. For those who found the religious rhetoric too much to handle, the myth of Mosaddeq was once again drafted into service to portray the new President as a latter-day national hero and the nuclear crisis as another Oil Nationalization crisis.

Too many people have sought to find the method in Ahmadinejad's madness, but the secret to his success has always been his simplicity. He may have a doctorate in engineering but he does not have a doctorate in philosophy. For all his pretensions to out-philosophize Khatami, Ahmadinejad's world view is simple and Manichean in its duality, a duality between which there can be no compromise or engagement. Having ridiculed Khatami's attempt at dialogue, American neoconservatives had found an opponent who shared their belief in the Clash of Civilizations.

Unsurprisingly, none of this augured well for the nuclear negotiations. The Europeans provided a less than enthusiastic presentation of their new terms in August 2005, reflecting their despondency with the political turn of events in Iran. The European offer was not quite as bad as indignant Iranian politicians would have had us believe. It was a solid offer that interestingly avoided the language of "permanent cessation," opting instead for a lengthy "temporary suspension. " It certainly did not warrant the demand for an apology that the new Iranian negotiating team apparently issued. (Questions remain over the source of the highly indignant response, with some Iranian diplomats suggesting that the demand for an apology was an act of sabotage by the departing team.)

But the offer was couched in labored bureaucratic language intended to offend no one and satisfy everyone. Already heightened Iranian national sensibilities were offended, with bullish retorts from Iranian neo-conservatives dismissing European weakness and contemptuous of Western options against Iran. Indeed, Iranian politicians seemed to relish the position of splendid isolation towards which they were taking the country, insisting that the West needed Iran more than Iran needed the West.

In truth, no one in the West had a good idea how one was to deal with the new President, whose unorthodox religious views and hard-line politics were a matter for serious concern. The very sanctions that could be used as leverage against the previous administration, including referral to the UN Security Council, were apparently welcomed by the new team. Indeed, Ahmadinejad enjoyed taunting the West. Iran seemed to be raising the stakes. Some argued that this was to force a decision, but others worried that Ahmadinejad had no strategy within which he was basing his escalation.

It would not be too cynical to note that many considered Ahmadinejad's election to be a useful moment of clarity. No longer was there any doubt or ambiguity about the Islamic Republic of Iran. The system was clearly ideologically bankrupt and indefensible. The departure of many of the professional negotiators and diplomats—some forcibly, others voluntarily—was a pointed reminder that the face of the Islamic Republic was changing.

It is easy to romanticize the state of relations before Ahmadinejad's election—the decision to restart limited uranium enrichment had been taken before Ahmadinejad's inauguration in August 2005. But at an immediate political level, there can be no doubt that his arrival marked a qualitative change, not simply a change in tempo. For all the problems the previous administration had with the West, they at least believed negotiation was possible and relations desirable. Only stability could provide Iran with the basis for the economic growth the country so desperately needed. For Ahmadinejad, relations are not desirable and the possibility is irrelevant. Iran could seek other friends or thrive in splendid isolation. With oil prices so high, there is no need for foreign relations that ultimately could only pollute the purity of the revolution and the perfection of the nation.

Ahmadinejad has begun his presidency as he means to go on: with a heady mix of populism and religious nationalism. He is a man of conviction reinforced by firm religious beliefs and the good fortune of experience. That experience has taught him that perseverance in the face of apparently insurmountable odds will pay dividends in the end; that the Iranian nation, if it stays united and resolute, can face all enemies; that force provides its own justification; and that he will triumph. The collapse of the Reform Movement and the transformation of Iran's regional position all serve as testament to these facts, which are not simply the expression of material determination but the manifestation of the Divine Will.

This last aspect of Ahmadinejad's character has been the cause of the most concern among his domestic opponents, especially the clerical leadership, and is likely to be his undoing. Charismatic leaders, or those who aspire to be, need an event or a crisis to surmount to convince doubters. In the absence of a sign, no amount of extraordinary and populist behavior will suffice. In the end, the people will become bored; and Iranians, twenty-seven years after the revolution that transformed their lives and sent them to war, bore easily. To counter this, and secure his position, Ahmadinejad may be tempted to take risks and provoke a confrontation. It is all a world away from the modest, moderate Muslim personality of Mohammad Khatami. The West may yet rue the day they neglected the opportunity for dialogue and engagement.

CONCLUSION

For as long as Khatami is in office and the 6th Majlis' term has not ended, America will not take military action against Iran, since it will face problems from both the world and public opinion, but in view of the recent [local] council elections results, they anticipate that the next elections [the Majlis and Presidential elections] will have the same results as the council elections. And based on that premise, they are preparing the ground for any kind of action against Iran.

EMADIN BAQI, REFORMIST JOURNALIST, JUNE 2003

STUDENTS OF international relations have a tendency to look at states as actors—rational or otherwise—with an occasional foray into the domestic political context of their foreign policy making. Rarely do we look at the ways in which these actors relate and communicate with each other or the ways in which they have influenced the behavior and perceptions of the other. When we do, more often than not any assessment of influence tends to be one way—looking, for instance, at the way in which the West, and America in particular, has imposed its culture, values, and economic system on the global community.

In the age of the global media revolution, to consider that a relationship might be reciprocal is tantamount to heresy in some quarters. Yet the parallels between Iran and the United States are as striking as the influence they seek to impose on each other and the world around them. Both are imperial powers, in a cultural if not in a political sense. Iranian youth culture is heavily influenced by the imagery and culture of the West, and most Iranians seek both an education and a vacation in the Western rather than the Eastern hemisphere. At the same time, people in the West enjoy the fruits of Persian culture, be it carpets, handicrafts, or poetry. In the United States, for instance, one of the most widely read poets is the Persian medieval mystic Jalal al din Rumi. Few other non-Western cultures have enjoyed quite the same impact on the Western imagination.

This cultural relationship underpins a more immediate political encounter. America's encounter with Iran began as an observer, anxious to expand trade but appalled at the way in which European powers seemingly fought over the spoils of a nation. Iranians at the turn of the twentieth century viewed the United States as an opportunity to break free from the political manipulations of Russia and Great Britain. But as the United States moved to replace Britain on the international stage, it fell victim to a poisoned legacy in Iran. Iranians felt betrayed by America's complicity in the overthrow of Mosaddeq in 1953, and the strength of their feelings reflected a change in Iranian political culture and life, particularly the growth of political consciousness in the latter half of the twentieth century. What might have passed for a political event of little consequence to the majority of the population became a founding myth of national culture.

The coup of 1953 ensured that henceforth America was part of domestic Iranian politics. This negative image was compounded by a series of mistakes made throughout the following twenty-five years, both on a personal and a political level, as the number of American workers in Iran grew exponentially. What is remarkable about the anti-Americanism that emerged in this period is that it was driven by the groups of people who should have been most sympathetic to the American position: the professional and educated classes who were offended at the slights to national sensibilities, be it on a broader political level or a particular social one.

In 1979, Iran and the United States were participants in a crisis that thrust Iran into the living rooms of America. The radio ensured that the United States became a matter of domestic importance in Iran after 1953. The television served a similar purpose for the United States, by providing the means by which the Islamic Revolution and Iran penetrated American society and permeated its imagination. Henceforth, Iran was no longer simply a foreign policy issue handled by professionals but an issue of domestic political importance. Paradoxically, at the very moment that formal diplomatic relations were severed, the intensely personal nature of US-Iran relations was crystallized. This cycle was completed with the trials and tribulations that defined the Iran-Contra affair. The Republican loophole was closed, and Iran became a bipartisan affair in American politics. The nature of this relationship, compounded as it has been by the revolution in global media, makes the policy of noninterference or nonintervention nonsense. In the modern media age, boundaries are vague and frontiers ill-defined such that even the most determined isolationist is confronted by the reality of engagement. Best, therefore, to be prepared for it.

America's professional bureaucracy shares much in common with her European counterparts, but her politics—popular, personal, and replete with networks—have more in common with those of Iran. The sense of mission, the possession of an imperial culture, and above all a deep sense of religious purpose are characteristics more familiar to Iran than contemporary Europe. And it is in politics that the parallels between Iran and the United States have become explicit. In 1979 the West looked in horror at the consequences of a revolutionary Iran, imbued with religious zeal and determined to export its particular idea of freedom to the world. Twenty-five years later, the roles had reversed, only in this case the United States was able to convincingly defeat Saddam Hussein. Whether it will win the peace in Iraq is another matter, the likely beneficiary ironically being Iran.

This political relationship should facilitate communication and understanding, but the truth is that these similar political cultures have been moving in different directions. Perhaps the only moment of meaningful contact was the last two years of the Clinton administration. With the advent of the Bush administration, the two political cultures were increasingly defined by a shared belief in confrontation. Politics, therefore, define Iran-US relations. Populist and rich with emotion, this narrative of confrontation has permeated the popular imagination and driven the elites. The structure of the political mythology this process has created is profound and has been subject to regular intervention and disruption by a variety of vested interests for whom the continued US-Iran antipathy serves a useful political purpose. Although attempts were made to deconstruct this powerful myth during the Khatami presidency, the task remains beyond the ability of one party to the dispute. One cannot have a dialogue with the deaf.

The first step, therefore, must be to confront these myths, recognize their importance and potency, and begin their deconstruction. They cannot be dismissed as mere politics; they are the engines that drive our perceptions and must be handled carefully and critically. Nothing so affects individuals as their beliefs. This is a long-term and methodical task that should be interrogated by those with professional expertise. Indeed, few relationships so effectively highlight the problems created by the politicization of government and foreign relations as the relationship between the US and Iran. Short-term solutions and the dependence on the electoral cycle have inhibited the development of a coherent long-term strategy—a policy that can be achieved rather than a list of rhetorical devices. Foreign policy lacks continuity and initiatives are sabotaged before they have a chance to be tested. Although the Iranians have misread the political situation in the United States, the rate of political turnover in the United States is so frequent as to prohibit coherence. Iran cannot even work with a four-year electoral cycle because limits are often set by the biannual Congressional cycle. For a nation that tends to view developments in the long term, such a limited cycle of opportunity is oppressive.

Yet the steady hand of European bureaucratic rationality is itself not free of problems. European bureaucracies, much like their counterparts in the United States and Iran, are large, cumbersome, and slow to react. Their inability to adapt to modern circumstances has been in part the justification for the politicization of government, and this certainly has been the case with the intelligence and foreign policy communities in the

United States, where the impatience of politicians has barely been disguised. The solution is not the politicization of the bureaucracy but its managed reform. As the experience with Iran has shown, the professionals on the whole have been correct in their assessments. If policy mistakes have been made, it is normally because the professionals' judgements have been overruled or their voices have not been heard in the political and bureaucratic cacophony.

As a complex political system, decisions on Iran cannot be entirely delegated to politicians with no particular competence in the field. The important task is to address the structural and cultural problems within the bureaucracies, to streamline the process of decision making, to ensure that voices are heard, and most importantly to re-professionalize the bureaucracies themselves. Perhaps a valuable lesson can be learned in the way in which various military organizations, always at the sharp end of a diplomatic encounter, have sought to adapt themselves to the vagaries of modern realities. They regularly challenge the tendency towards consensus and mediocrity that bureaucracies impose, and seek to streamline and coordinate their ability to react swiftly and coherently.

The desire to populate foreign policy establishments with generalists may be genuine in its attempt to guard against those who may discover too much affinity with their subject matter, but the system of rotation every three years is self defeating. With only a short supply of trained Persianists—those who can not only string a sentence together, but are culturally attuned, know the context of a statement, and understand the underpinning myths—it is astonishing to find that they are allocated tasks for which they have no specialized training. Although this decision has sound and sane reasons, the banality of bureaucratic rationality taken to its absurd extremes is bewildering. The singular case of this occurred in the run-up to the Iraq War, when specialists were sucked into the black hole of Iraq with no appreciation of the consequences this might have for broader regional issues. And in this case, understanding Iran was vital to the successful resolution of Iraq. Only the British Foreign Office has actively sought to address this structural deficiency.

Post-revolutionary Iran has been a poor career option for most diplomats. By the mid-1990s, the prerevolutionary cadre of foreign service specialists discovered, somewhat belatedly, that they had no one to hand over to. This unfortunate gap coincided with the period of greatest inactivity—dual containment—when myths were reinforced and stereotypes confirmed. But the gap is also indicative of changing priorities and poor planning. Area specialists require long-term training, and their absence cannot be easily compensated for, as the United States found to its cost after 9/11. Neither Arabists nor Persianists can be created at will. We may never return to the heyday of professionalism, but concerted and determined measures should be taken to address the deficit in knowledge, a deficit that produces a vacuum rapidly filled by myth, sound bites, and empty rhetoric.

A network of politicians, propagandists, and journalists have all been complicit in the creation of a consensus that has suffocated debate and obstructed knowledge. This consensus is far more than a military-industrial complex. Those who seek to challenge the consensus are dismissed as irrational, even though they adhere to the Western tradition of knowledge more resolutely than the carriers of myth. Few statements have exemplified this trend more clearly than Donald Rumsfeld's comment that "the absence of evidence was not the evidence of absence." By such standards, one must conclude that the Western enlightenment is over and we have entered a post-modern age in which belief and conviction tolerate no scrutiny.

How refreshingly familiar this must sound to the religious hard-liners in Iran. All the criticisms that have been applied to the West can be applied equally to Iran, whose capacity for mythic construction and consumption traditionally outstrips anything the West can offer. For all the changes and reflection that have taken place, it is remarkable how little scholarship about the West and Western civilization has occurred. For example, Iran has no institutes for Western studies, and although individual academics may pursue the study of the languages and literature of the West, knowledge of the Western historical experience remains piecemeal and fragmentary. If Iran is truly interested in a dialogue with the West, it needs not only to know itself but likewise to know its interlocutor, and in particular to understand the political complexity of the states it seeks to engage with. An impressive if hasty start was made with Khatami, whose familiarity with Western philosophy far outshone any reciprocal knowledge of those he engaged with in the West. Furthermore, Iranian society and a large part of the political establishment are moving in a different direction than their counterparts in the West, who remain blissfully unaware and uninterested in the reality of Iran and the Iranians.

This knowledge deficit, and in particular a manifest failure and unwillingness to recognize the historical context and founding myths of Iran and its relationship with the West, has been tragically evident in the current crisis. Quite apart from the lack of strategic vision that led to the invasion of Iraq, it is now apparent that the Americans, and to some extent the Europeans, are struggling to find ways in which to solve the Iranian question. The consequence has been an overdependence on rhetoric and demagoguery that has been confrontational rather than constructive, punitive rather than a means to a defined end. There has been a marked failure to distinguish between the state and the nation, and to recognize social changes and the political dynamic. Instead, much like Ahmadinejad, the preference has been to analyze Iran in the framework of a revolution that occurred more than a generation ago, as if all that has transpired since is inconsequential. More damning has been the failure to engage with Iran as a distinctive actor, as opposed to an extension of the Cold War or intra-Western rivalries. Particularly ineffective has been the tendency to view Iran through the familiar analogies of the Western experience, defining it as totalitarian and ignoring the complexities it represents. Such intellectual indolence may reflect a justified frustration, but it does not assist in the effective formation of policy.

Nothing has exemplified this trend more than the sudden flood of literature and commentary accompanying the current nuclear crisis. The titles themselves leave no doubt about the political agenda behind the particular polemic, with Iran and the Iranians implicitly or explicitly associated with terrorism and fanaticism, illogical and irrational and at best duplicitous. Where no evidence exists to substantiate the more outrageous claims, evidence is simply invented or the absence of evidence is taken as evidence of guilt. Iranians are justified in their bewilderment at this inversion of Western judicial practice and of their need to prove a negative. They are in part to blame for this lack of trust. The hostage crisis clearly had a major impact on US perceptions of Iran, and even though many Iranians have sought to explain this unfortunate lapse in judgment, many others continue to consider it an achievement. Still others, like the Americans and 1953, cannot bring themselves to understand why the Americans were so affected!

Yet at the same time, we should remember that this particular perception of Iran as a regional menace predated the Revolution and enjoyed its modern genesis during the final years of the Shah. Those harbingers of doom that profess Iran as a great threat to humanity and civilization would do well to remember that the last Shah was considered in some quarters to be a megalomaniac with imperial ambitions. In the 1976 novel by Paul Erdmann opportunely titled *The Crash of '79*, these latent anxieties were given prosaic and popular expression. The tale is remarkably apposite for the current crisis, involving as it does the development of a nuclear weapon with a view to the Shah projecting Iranian power in the region and, through the use of oil, to the wider world. The characters and national stereotypes, be they French, Israeli, Russian, or American evangelical Christian, are remarkably familiar. The thriller revolves around the failures of Western policy makers to grasp the devious ambitions of the Shah, whose aim is to detonate a nuclear device over the Saudi oil fields, thereby rendering them useless, before invading Iraq to secure those oil fields and complete Operation Sasanid. The only solution for a West panicking over its future is a preemptive strike that results in the detonation of the Iranian nuclear device, with similarly catastrophic results for the world oil market! The novel was underpinned by and evoked the general fear of Iranian imperial ambition.

Although subsequent events were to prove that the invasion was to take place in the other direction (Iran has been on the strategic defensive for two hundred years), such realities were but a minor inconvenience to the ideologically determined. The fear of a resurgent Iran remains. Rather than grapple with the question, some have sought to eliminate it. Consequently, a recent tendency is to talk of the fragmentation of Iran into its constituent ethnicities. The idea of Iran transcends ethnicities; it is defined by a cultural cohesion. Nothing shows more ignorance of recent history and contemporary politics as the suggestion that the United States ought to encourage the territorial disintegration of the modern Iranian state. Nothing would galvanize the nationalist constituency more than the suggestion that the very fabric of the nation is at stake. And by extension, nothing would please Ahmadinejad and his supporters more than to be able to argue that the nuclear issue is only a thinly veiled attempt to do to Iran what appears to be happening to Iraq. This fear is at the heart of the political inertia that has constrained political debate and allowed a hard-line reaction to take hold. No serious internal challenge will be contemplated while the very idea of Iran is considered under threat. Many in the West are too easily impressed by the Islamic rhetoric that periodically emanates from the Islamic Republic to recognize that at core what matters is Iran. Islam may be the means for some, but for the vast majority Iran is the end.

That such ideas are even being discussed should remind us that the nuclear impasse is a consequence of a far wider problem between Iran and the United States, not its cause. A solution to the nuclear issue will only defer and not solve the Iranian question. That question, which has been inherited by the United States, can trace its roots further back than 1979 or 1953, to the humiliation of Turkmenchai in 1828 and the gradual realization that Iran had suffered an imperial fall from grace. Our current preoccupation with the nuclear issue should not deflect us from the fundamentals of this historical situation and the political myths it provides.

If confrontation turns to conflict, it is unlikely to be deliberate, nor is it likely to emerge from the nuclear crisis. Iran and the United States are now neighbors on several difficult frontiers, so the opportunities for conflict are extensive. More importantly, as this book has shown, the cultural structure of their relationship is such that it encourages conflict. To surmount this culture and to overcome the consensual momentum will require leadership of extraordinary imagination, vision, and courage. America in particular must think in terms of not only winning the war but winning the peace, by recognizing that Iran-US relations in the twentieth century have been defined as much by collaboration as confrontation, even after the Islamic Revolution of 1979, and that compromise has and continues to be possible. A preoccupation with conflict is blinding us to the opportunities for the future. The alternative is to be carried by this momentum towards a conflict that nobody desires but which no one will be able to avoid, the consequences of which will make Iraq look like the cakewalk it was prophesized to be.

AFTERWORD

THE PUBLICATION OF THE FIRST EDITION of *Confronting Iran* in the summer of 2006 coincided with the Lebanon war fought between Hizbollah and Israel. Few conflicts can have better exemplified the central thesis propounded in this book: the centrality to U.S.-Iran relations of competing narratives founded on a profound sense of mistrust. As an observer of the political process in the United States, I found it quite remarkable how quickly the blame for the struggle was laid at Iran's door—complete with an elaborate rationality that brooked no criticism, and more strikingly, that was developed on an internal agenda with no recourse to the Iranians themselves. Indeed within two hours of the news of the abductions of the Israeli soldiers by Hizbollah, the narrative of Iranian responsibility had been dictated by the White House to the press, which dutifully reported it for mass consumption. The war in Lebanon, we were told, was triggered by Hizbollah opportunism that had been prompted by an Iranian attempt to deflect attention from the growing pressure on its nuclear program. Evidence for this correlation was provided by the fact that Ali Larijani, Iran's top nuclear negotiator, had stopped off in Damascus en route back to Tehran, after yet another difficult round in the negotiation process.

The American narrative of the Lebanon war was predicated on the belief that the Hizbollah leadership took direct orders from Tehran on a day-to-day basis. The narrative also relied heavily on well-worn stereotypes about "Persian cunning" and the Iranian propensity to cause mischief. Iranians, of course, themselves assisted the process by providing a suitably one-dimensional president (Ahmadinejad), whose views on the legitimacy of Israel were well known, as well as repeated denials that they had in fact armed Hizbollah with a range of rockets, when the evidence in this particular regard suggested otherwise.

Of course, the American narrative was deeply flawed—beginning with the fact that there was no evidence that Larijani had precipitated the war in any way. It was certainly true that the Iranians had warned that any attack on its nuclear facilities would see a swift response against American interests, including Israel. Indeed Iranian military planners had long since come to the conclusion that the security of Israel was the political Achilles' heel of U.S. strategy in the Middle East, and that only the threat of retaliation against Israel would make American politicians think twice about attacking Iran (from the American perspective, of course, it was this very threat that made action against Iran an increasing imperative—an alternative logic that the Iranians simply did not grasp). It seemed absurd, therefore, that Iran would expose its valuable deterrence to an Israeli onslaught on the basis of another failed nuclear negotiation.

In reality, Iran did not feel under pressure for its nuclear program in the summer of 2006. On the contrary, most Iranians had allowed themselves to be convinced by their rambunctious president that Iran was in the driver's seat. Not only was nuclear progress being made—enrichment was announced with all the operatic stage management familiar to Morgan Shuster, complete with fake tubes of enriched uranium and doves—but Iran's regional position appeared to be strengthening by the day.[1]

The shine of Ahmadinejad's presidency had yet to fade in the summer of 2006. The populist president continued to enjoy his period in the political limelight, and for the latent criticism from the elite, his liberal dispensation of cash, he appeared to be reinforcing his popularity with the masses. Ahmadinejad thus had no overriding political need to distract popular attention by instigating a war. And while coverage of the Israeli devastation of the Lebanese infrastructure proved useful in reinforcing an Iranian sense of injustice against the United States and Israel, there are indications that, unusually, coverage of the war was moderated so as to not excite any unnecessary further anxiety among the Iranian population, who might draw parallels between the war in Lebanon and the continuing confrontation with the United States.

Indeed, viewed through a different lens, Israel's assault on Lebanon could be interpreted in an altogether different manner. While Hizbollah may have been opportunistic in its capture of two Israeli soldiers, this opportunism had less to do with Iran, and more with Israel's growing difficulties in Gaza, where Palestinians had abducted another Israeli soldier. And the Israeli response can scarcely be considered spontaneous; increasingly, it is clear that Israel had been planning for some time to deal with Hizbollah. It was perhaps Prime Minister Olmert's folly that he was persuaded to take this opportunity to put them into operation.

The war did not come about because Iran wished to send a message to the West about its power in the Middle East. If anything, the war was an attempt by the West to send a message to Iran about the limitations of its power in the Middle East, with the added bonus of Israel successfully eliminating Iran's carefully built-up deterrence in the region.

Such an analysis would help explain why so much American and Israeli attention during the war was focused on Iran. It was only the increasing recklessness of the rhetoric within the U.S.—declarations of World War III, and calls for an immediate air strike against Iran—that prompted some within the United States to reflect on the emerging hysteria.[2]

Arguably one of the remarkable consequences of this thoroughly internal dynamic—to the best of my knowledge, no Iranian official was actually interviewed throughout the conflict by a mainstream American media outlet—was the return of the neoconservative agenda in some force. The Iran threat seemed to breathe new life into an ideology that had been temporarily subdued due to widespread criticism of the administration's prosecution of the Iraq war. Neoconservatism erupted into a frenzy of apocalyptic rhetoric. Speculating as to why President Ahmadinejad had chosen August 22, 2006, to formally respond to the E.U.'s latest offer to resolve the nuclear impasse, Professor Bernard Lewis cautioned his readership that the date coinciding as it did with the anniversary of the night flight of the Prophet Mohammad to heaven, "might well be deemed an appropriate date for the apocalyptic ending of Israel and if necessary of the world." He added reassuringly, "It is far from certain that Mr. Ahmadinejad plans such a cataclysmic events precisely for August 22. But it would be wise to bear the possibility in mind."[3] When August 22 passed relatively uneventfully, others helpfully pointed out that the date also coincided with the end of the Iranian calendar month. Nonetheless even mainstream media who had shown public remorse for their uncritical acceptance of the Bush administration's justification for war in Iraq, were shamelessly scrambling aboard the latest war bandwagon, much to the surprise of some of their European colleagues. It was a salutary reminder of the depth of mistrust that characterised Iran-U.S. relations, and the pervasive sense that open conflict, however undesirable, was probably inevitable.

*   *   *

Public opinion in Tehran was as polarized as it was in the United States. The war in Lebanon was widely regarded as yet another victory for the president and his policies. Lebanon had suffered and Hizbollah was badly bruised, but the latter had survived against apparently all the odds, and the public relations triumph reverberated around the region. For Ahmadinejad, the victory was particularly sweet since it seemed to reinforce his conviction that faith and determination could overcome the most intractable odds. The victory offered further justification for Iran's robust policy towards the West—like Hizbollah, Iranians could resist, survive, and ultimately triumph.

Of course, Ahmadinejad's narrative was based on a highly selective reading of the evidence. It ignored the very real damage done to Lebanon's infrastructure by the Israeli air force (the likely blueprint for any U.S. air strike against Iran). It was also predicated on the idea that Iranians harboured the same will to resist as the forces of Hizbollah. More experienced hands, including some in the Iranian military, were less sanguine about the consequences of an American attack, and were less convinced that "Iranian nationalism" would rush unwavering to the aid of the Islamic Republic, especially if Ahmadinejad was seen as having invited an attack.

Ahmadinejad's reported enthusiasm to rekindle the spirit of the Iran-Iraq War unnerved many of his political rivals, but in the summer of 2006, there was little that could be done to dent the president's self confidence. Indeed Ahmadinejad appeared to be intervening more extensively than ever in the nuclear negotiations, anxious that no one should steal his thunder, or indeed undermine the direction of his policy. His emerging sense of invincibility led directly to the collapse of the ongoing negotiations between Ali Larijani, chairman of the National Security Council, and the E.U.'s high representative for foreign affairs, Javier Solana.

The protracted negotiations over the course of the summer of 2006 had by no means been entirely constructive. Larijani was generally regarded as a hard-liner in matters of nuclear policy; like the president, he was openly contemptuous of his predecessor's record in the negotiations, arguing that Hasan Rowhani had been too soft. At the same time, Larijani was a tactical rather than an ideological hard-liner—he was open to discussion if the right concessions were made. And he was particularly amenable to any deal that could enhance his standing within Iran. Larijani had been Ahmadinejad's rival for the presidency in 2005, and the rivalry between the two men was ongoing. For the very same reasons, Ahmadinejad—reinvigorated as he was by the war in Lebanon—remained emphatically opposed to any deal that might overturn Iran's "red lines". Earlier that summer he had taken nearly three months to respond to the E.U. offer on the nuclear program. Indeed the decision to respond with a willingness to continue talks appears to have gone down particularly badly among European diplomats. Larijani on the other hand, while publicly supporting the government's position, seemed to have a better appreciation of European patience and decided to continue negotiations with Solana.

Larijani appears to have taken UNSCR 1696—the resolution demanding complete cessation of uranium enrichment by August 31, 2006—more seriously than Ahmadinejad, and was more fearful of the consequences of disobeying it. His anxieties were shared by many within the Iranian elite that Ahmadinejad's triumphalism in the wake of the Lebanon war was blinding him to diplomatic defeats elsewhere. However, when it was alleged that Larijani was contemplating a compromise that included a temporary ninety-day suspension of uranium enrichment in return for a move away from the Security Council and possible sanctions, the Ahmadinejad administration weighed in with an emphatic rejection of any such possibility, in a move that deftly pulled the rug from under Larijani. Iran's top nuclear negotiator was left to reflect on his "constructive" talks with Solana.[4]

Throughout the fall of 2006, Ahmadinejad appeared by all accounts to be in charge of government policy on all its fronts, while his opponents were limited to bemoaning his reckless rhetoric and incoherent populism from the sidelines. Yet almost on cue, Ahmadinejad's confidence began to overreach itself. His flippant attitude to the West and the nuclear negotiations was matched by an increasingly dismissive attitude to his critics at home. In part, this attitude was a product of his inherent populism and his consequent distaste for the "establishment". But Ahmadinejad's contempt extended even to those who had supported him, causing consternation among hard-line conservative allies within the Majlis who found his disrespect for them too much to handle. Ahmadinejad's manner was hardly new, but eighteen months into his presidency, it was beginning to grate. Moreover, critics among reformists and traditional conservatives argued that his foreign policy was ill served by an exclusive domestic policy, which pandered to the pious masses at the expense of many other segments of the population. Indeed, even his allies were pointing out that while he had consolidated his base, he had singularly failed to extend it, and vulgar nationalism founded on a simmering international crisis was a poor substitute for coherent economic policies. Fresh from his foreign policy successes however, Ahmadinejad was brooking no criticism, and with characteristic self assurance he moved to secure more gains in the municipal elections that had been scheduled along with those for the Assembly of Experts, for December.

Municipal elections were traditionally among the least significant in the Iranian electoral calendar, and it was generally assumed that turnout would be low. Indeed, Ahmadinejad had first come to prominence as mayor of Tehran in the municipal elections of 2003 with a paltry turnout of 15 percent. Similarly, the elections for the Assembly of Experts were popularly regarded as an esoteric affair in which a somewhat symbolic "college" of aged clerics were elected every eight years to provide constitutional supervision over the Supreme Leader. The assembly did in fact enjoy significant constitutional powers—in particular the right to elect and if necessary impeach the Supreme Leader—but the fact that the assembly rarely did anything contributed to its popular image as little more than a retirement home for otherwise redundant ayatollahs.

In 2006, however, the constitutional prerogatives of the Assembly of Experts seemed more relevant than usual. Given that the assembly was elected every eight years, there was a good chance that the new assembly would elect the next leader. Furthermore, it was widely rumored and generally assumed that Ahmadinejad's theological mentor, the extreme hardline and highly authoritarian Ayatollah Misbah-Yazdi, was mobilizing his followers to ensure a clean sweep in the elections and the domination of the assembly. Such a victory would put him in prime position to succeed Khamenei as leader, and given his political and religious views, this was not an outcome many Iranians, including many in the elite, viewed with excitement.

In order to generate some excitement among a public that had grown disillusioned with increasingly rigged elections, it was decided to hold the elections on the same day, with a view to ensuring a high turnout and overturning the hard-line constituency within the electorate. Ahmadinejad's opponents began to mobilize, organize, and campaign. Ahmadinejad remained confident. He controlled the levers of power and access to government funding, which he could spend liberally on publicity, and he was able to control the political process to some extent by restricting the ability of his political rivals to disseminate information. But to a large extent, Ahmadinejad remained confident simply because he *believed*. Such was his belief that he refused the advice of his hard-line allies and submitted a separate list consisting of his own nominees (including his sister) to campaign on his platform, poetically called "The Sweet Scent of Service."

As a result of Ahmadinejad's hubris, the hard-line conservatives entered the elections divided. The opposition, however, was united: the traditional conservatives under Rafsanjani, and the Reformists, under Khatami, combined their resources, platforms, and candidates. It marked yet another shift in the changing political alliances of Iran, but also was representative of the seriousness with which both Rafsanjani and Khatami considered the nature of the challenge. Rafsanjani was considerably assisted by the fact that the Guardian Council—with the probable sanction of Khamenei—prevented many candidates from both right and left running for the assembly, sharpening the contest between Rafsanjani and Misbah-Yazdi. The result was a landslide for Rafsanjani, who more than doubled the votes gained by Misbah Yazdi, topping the lists for the assembly. The victory was all the sweeter for Rafsanjani because the turnout was unusually high at about 60 percent.

The scale of the turnout combined with the new alliance of Reformists and moderate conservatives had a resounding impact on the municipal elections. The hard-liners, including Ahmadinejad's own faction, lost control of virtually every council in the country, including, most importantly, that of Tehran itself. By some accounts, Ahmadinejad's own list gathered no more than 3 percent of the total vote, in what one prominent moderate conservative described as, "a big NO to superstitious sentiments, irrational expectations, delusions, and thoughts with no relation to experience or expertise."[5] The seizure of the Tehran city council by moderate conservative supporters of the mayor, Mohammad Baqer Qalibaf, was a particular blow for Ahmadinejad. Qalibaf was defeated in the 2005 presidential elections, and was a vocal critic of the president.

Ahmadinejad's humiliating defeat meant that it was open season for public criticism of the president, and those for whom discretion had been the better part of valor now unleashed their fury. Quite apart from the growing criticism of his idiosyncratic views, Ahmadinejad's critics assailed him for his mishandling of the economy, made more acute by the international crisis for which no resolution seemed to be at hand[6].

Having effectively announced victory at the end of summer, Ahmadinejad was by winter struggling to explain how Iran was now on the brink of sanctions, the threat of which over the past year had effectively brought Iran's mercantile economy to a standstill. Iran's merchants were becoming restless, and even the much heralded turn to the East (China) was not providing the dividends anticipated. Ahmadinejad's boundless optimism, infectious to begin with, was increasingly being characterized as either naïve or delusional, while his economic policies, insofar as they could be defined, were beginning to inflict dangerous inflationary pressures upon the economy[7]. Inflationary pressures have often been closely linked with political upheaval in Iranian history; in this case, Ahmadinejad's economic populism had resulted in a massive cash injection into the economy (by some estimates five billion dollars was injected through cash handouts to the poor), which the poor gratefully received and promptly spent, pushing up the price of basic commodities. These inflationary pressures were compounded by his decision to somewhat arbitrarily cut interest rates, thereby encouraging the middle classes to withdraw their money and spend it, along with the simmering international crisis, which encouraged the rich to send their money abroad. All of these factors further weakened the rial, thus causing yet further inflation.

On December 23, 2006, the threat of sanctions had become real with the ratification of UNSCR 1737, which froze the assets of organizations and individuals listed as being involved in Iran's nuclear program. It was in many ways a symbolic if significant move on the part of the UN— and one that Ahmadinejad characteristically dismissed as a mere scrap of paper. His arrogance infuriated the elite, who pointed out that other associated sanctions to the banking system were beginning to bite. Critics also point out that Ahmadinejad's expenditure of the oil reserve fund, which had been carefully built up by Khatami, had effectively made Iran more vulnerable to sanctions.

With all the certainty of religious conviction, however, Ahmadinejad appeared oblivious to the criticism. He rebuked his parliamentary critics who noted the high price of tomatoes and urged them to shop in his own district, where tomatoes were apparently cheaper.[8] Likewise, in a protracted interview with state television, he denied that Iran was facing any serious international pressure; paraphrasing Ayatollah Khomeini, Ahmadinejad claimed that America could not do a damned thing.[9] This was the conclusion reached by government experts—men who understood such things—he explained condescendingly.

He added for good measure, in answer to a question about his method of policy making, that he believed instinct to be much underrated.[10] It was perhaps this instinct that persuaded him to host a Holocaust conference—

imposed on the foreign ministry—that inevitably drew the ire of the international community[11].

The elections in Iran exposed the serious divisions within the Iranian political establishment over the direction of policy and the management of foreign affairs.[12] It also revealed a president increasingly detached from the reality that he had created. Much the same conclusion could be drawn from the mid-term elections in the United States. Here too, President Bush had suffered an electoral reverse, but here, as in Iran, he refused to be deflected from the course he had chosen.

The superficial similarities of these setbacks should not, however, mask the significant differences. The American political establishment is divided over the issue of Iraq, to be sure, but considerably less so over the issue of Iran. Differences have arisen over the method, but there is less political debate over the substance. Many are concerned about the prospect of war with Iran, but politicians of rank generally agree that Iran is a serious problem. The emerging divisions within Iran are more substantive—many senior political figures are urging a fundamental reassessment of Iran's stance towards the United States.

Most Iranian foreign policy analysts, not just those surrounding President Ahmadinejad, continue to fatally misread the American political process. They possess an almost naïve faith in American "rationality," and resist the idea that Americans might in fact be just as stubbornly ideological as they are. Yet the indecent haste with which the White House sought to bury the Baker-Hamilton report was surely the clearest indication of the suffocating weight of the structure of confrontation that binds the United States to Iran. The report's recommendations as they pertained to Iran were, to be sure, concise. But in urging some form of dialogue with Iran, Baker-Hamilton had ventured bravely into the no-man's-land of Iran policy, only to find the hail of fire (a significant amount of it "friendly") sending them straight back into the trenches for cover.

Both Democrats and Republicans vocally objected to the idea of engagement with Iran, arguing that with Iran in the driving seat, this was the wrong time to talk. Indeed, the reasons given for not engaging in some manner with Iran became at times convoluted, if not contradictory.

The report argued that since Iran played an important role in Iraq, it was important to engage Iran to facilitate stability in an Iraqi state that was clearly "breaking down", if not "breaking up". Politicians on both sides of the aisle rejected this idea because they didn't want to go begging to the Iranians for help, and simultaneously because the Iraqi insurgency would continue whether the Iranians were engaged or not. In other words, the Iranians were not responsible for the insurgency. The bipartisan dismissal of the Baker-Hamilton report's recommendations on Iran precluded any further discussion of America's policy toward its longstanding foe, or indeed absence of it.

Bush went many steps further by rejecting wholesale the recommendations of the report, and seeking counsel instead from the archconservative American Enterprise Institute. He committed the United States to a "surge" in Iraq, and, curiously, to confronting Iranian mischief in Iraq. In other words, Iranian responsibility was dismissed when engagement was suggested, but reintroduced when a "surge" needed to be justified. This would be supported by a strengthening of American naval and air power in the Persian Gulf, most obviously the dispatch of a second carrier group.

The rhetoric of confrontation had returned with a vengeance. But in a way that was truly remarkable, the existing narrative of U.S.-Iranian relations had been reconstructed to fit America's Middle East policy priorities. The great anomaly in America's policy toward the Middle East since 9/11 had been the fact that the hijackers on that fateful day had been Sunni, and had come from two of America's strongest allies in the region. But the overthrow of Saddam ensured the establishment of a Shia government in Iraq and brought to power—through democratic elections—a regime comprised largely of individuals who had lived in or were sympathetic to Iran. Indeed one of the major arguments working against the notion that Iran wants to destabilize Iraq is the fact that there has never been a more pro-Iranian government in Baghdad.

The emergence of an Arab Shia government has always been problematic for America's traditional allies in the region, some of whom have sizeable Shia minorities, who may now agitate for their own rights to be recognized. The potency of Shi'ism has only been exacerbated by the war in Lebanon, and the overwhelming popularity in the Arab world of Shia

Hizbollah's resistance to Israel. Some Sunni *ulema* even believe that the popularity of Hizbollah has encouraged the conversion of Sunnis to Shi'ism. Fearful of their waning power, Sunni Arab states have taken the unprecedented step of discrediting Shi'ism by blaming Hizbollah for the conflagration in Lebanon. Sunni Arab leaders, wary of a Shia Iraq, urge America to be tougher on the Shia's, who they now conveniently described as Iranians/Persians by any other name; an ethnic identification that basically focused attention firmly on Iran as the source of the region's ills.[13]

In order to placate their Arab allies, Western leaders also warn of a Shia ascendancy—conveniently ignoring the fact that it was the Western invasion of Iraq that facilitated it. President Bush, somewhat caught up in the rhetoric, even talks of an "epic" struggle between Shia and Sunni.[14] This is clearly a simplification of the struggle in the Middle East, but a convenient one, which manages to reunite the United States with its Arab allies, while simultaneously offering Israel a sense of solidarity in a shared struggle against the Shia "arc of crisis" driven by Iran. It also allows the United States to blame the fiasco of Iraq on the Shias, and conveniently conflates the two narratives of confrontation—"nuclear" and "Iraq"—into one tidy confrontation, either of which can facilitate escalation.

*   *   *

President Bush has authorized American troops to capture and kill Iranian operatives that the United States believes are fomenting insurgency. Politicians and pundits in both Iran and the West have convinced themselves that this conflict can be contained within Iraq and that it will therefore not escalate further into greater war with Iran itself.

The logic of confrontation dictates otherwise. On one level, it is inconceivable that Iran will sit back and watch as the United States goes after the Shia militias and effectively attempt to dismantle the structure of Iranian influence in Iraq. This would be considered tantamount to defeat, and given the extensive network of connections, the propensity for Iran to be drawn into the conflict in Iraq is high. And while there are sharp divisions within the United States over a potential war with Iran, what would happen if Iran were thought to be responsible for the deaths of U.S. servicemen? In that case, retaliation against Iran would not be a difficult sell to the American public.

Both sides have drawn red lines over Iran's nuclear program. Both sides know that a climb-down is tantamount to political suicide. Both sides suspect that the other is unlikely to be magnanimous in victory. This means that both are likely to take this argument to the very brink of a confrontation. In ordinary circumstances this would be a dangerous game to play. In the absence of direct diplomatic representation, it becomes reckless.

To date, neither side has truly made the effort to understand the other. Politicians spew aggressive rhetoric while continuing to rely instead on a vague belief that rationality will prevail in the end. To be fair, there have been commendable strides in the development of the State Department, with an "Office of Iranian Affairs" being formed to bring together a coherent team of specialists. But their task is a daunting one, made all the more acute by the fact that as the crisis with Iran grows, a shortage of experts has been replaced with a surfeit of expertise. Faced with this cacophony, Bush is just as likely to stick with what he is familiar. The truth is Americans like their politics simple while Iranians like their politics complex. It is a combustible mix. There have, to be sure, been some tentative moves toward a modest engagement, but the structures of confrontation remain emphatically in place, and the political leadership required to overcome it has yet to materialize. Further escalation is by no means inevitable "but we would be wise to bear the possibility in mind."

Ali M. Ansari
1 May 2007

ACKNOWLEDGMENTS

W HEN I WAS FIRST ASKED to write a short book on the current state of US-Iran relations, I viewed the task with trepidation. The writing of contemporary history is a difficult river to navigate, given the paucity of available archival sources and the problems inherent in writing history from within. It is all the more difficult when the subject is as emotive as that of Iran-US relations. However, the experience has been not only challenging but also enlightening, and I thank Michael Dwyer at Hurst for encouraging me to seek answers to the questions that had intrigued me about the nature of US-Iran relations.

In the United States, my heartfelt thanks go to the team at Basic, who managed the production of the book and ensured that my ideas were effectively translated into an accessible and coherent narrative. Particular thanks go to my editor, Lara Heimert, my production manager, Christine Marra, and my copyeditor, Susan Pink. Their combined professionalism has been impressive, refreshing, and reassuring.

Among many friends in the UK, I am especially grateful to colleagues at the University of St Andrews, including in particular Robert Hoyland and Jo van Steenbergen, my Middle Eastern history comrades-in-arms, as well as Steve Murdoch, whose occasionally successful attempts to persuade me to "go for a run," proved that I was capable of giving 101 percent. Thanks are due also to Bernie and Diar for providing, among other things, the Persian nourishment necessary to recover from such excessive exertions. I am also grateful to Lorna, Elsie, Vanessa, and Elizabeth for skilfully compensating for my many lapses in memory throughout the year as I sought to juggle between teaching, administration, and the completion of this manuscript. In this respect, the patience of all my colleagues has been admirable. My thanks also to Amir and Jenny for their continued friendship and support, especially at times when mental fatigue ensured that I was a less than scintillating interlocutor.

The ideas and perspectives outlined in this book have benefited from discussions with colleagues from a wide variety of backgrounds and regions, including Iran, the United States, and Europe. Many of these individuals by necessity must remain anonymous, but I am particularly grateful to two institutions for their support: the Royal Institute for International Affairs (Chatham House)—my home in London—and the Liechtenstein Institute on Self Determination at Princeton University, under the dynamic leadership of Wolfgang Danspeckgruber, whose regular colloquia and seminars have enabled me to discover and discuss issues with American and European colleagues whom I otherwise would not have had the opportunity to meet. Michael Axworthy, Gary Sick, Dick Bulliet, and Sir Lawrence Freedman were all kind enough to read the manuscript at extremely short notice and to offer their comments. I have also benefited enormously from the various discussions, occasionally impassioned, that have taken place on the Gulf 2000 internet forum. Last but by no means least, I am grateful to the National Archives in the UK for permission to quote from selected Foreign and Cabinet Office files. The responsibility for the interpretation offered is mine alone. I hope that, living as we do in interesting times, the thesis propounded provides food for thought.

NOTES

INTRODUCTION

1. Yousef Mazandi, *Iran: Abar Ghodrat-e Qarn?* (Iran: Superpower of the Century), Alborz, Tehran, 1373 / 1994.

2. G. N. Curzon, *Persia and the Persian Question*, Vol. 1 (London: Frank Cass and Co., 1966 [first published 1892]), pp. 3–4.

CHAPTER 1

1. W. Morgan Shuster, *The Strangling of Persia: Story of the European Diplomacy and Oriental Intrigue That Resulted in the Denationalization of Twelve Million Mohammedans* (Washington: Mage Publishers, 1987 [first published 1912]), p. xiii–xiv.

2. Morgan Shuster, op. cit. pp. 37–38.

3. For details, see Gholamreza Tabatabai Majd, *Moadat va gharar dadhaye tarikhi dar doreh Qajariye* (Historical Treaties and Agreements of the Qajar Era), Tehran 1372/1993, pp. 49–72.

4. A good example of the inflation of titles is the preamble to the first commercial treaty with the US in 1856. See Y. Alexander and A. Nanes, editors, *The United States and Iran: A Documentary History* (Maryland: University Publications of America, 1980), p. 2.

5. George N. Curzon, *Persia and the Persian Question,* Vol. I (London: Frank Cass, 1966 [first published 1892]), p. 480.

6. See, for example, Edward G. Browne, *A Year among the Persians: Impressions as to the life, character and thought of the people of Persia, received during twelve*

months residence in that country in the years 1887–1888 (London: Century House, 1984 [first published 1893]), p. 99.

7. Morgan Shuster, op. cit. p. 38.

8. Morgan Shuster, op. cit. p. 35.

9. Morgan Shuster, op. cit. p. xxix.

10. Morgan Shuster, op. cit. pp. 219–20.

CHAPTER 2

1. Oliver Bast argues that the Anglo-Persian agreement of 1919 was the Iranian government's adoption of the least worst option following the failure of their mission to the Peace Conference. The Iranians had wanted a multilateral agreement but had to accept a bilateral arrangement with Britain alone. That said, the Iranian government's "good intentions" were nonetheless sullied by the later revelation that senior members of the cabinet had received bribes.

2. *Memorandum of an audience given to the American minister (Philip) by Reza Shah Pahlavi,* Y. Alexander and A. Nanes, editors, *The United States and Iran: A Documentary History* (Maryland: University Publications of America, 1980), p. 43.

3. FO 248 1410—report of the British Consul in Tabriz, December 29, 1941.

4. FO 248 1531 10105/50—*Memorandum by Pyman,* January 28, 1950.

5. N. C. Crook, "The Theatre and Ballet Arts of Iran," *The Middle East Journal,* 1949, p. 408.

6. FO 248 1427—*Persian Government and Internal Affairs,* March 15, 1943.

7. See J. A. Thorpe, "Truman's Ultimatum to Stalin on the 1946 Azerbaijan Crisis: The Making of a Myth," *Journal of Politics,* 1978, p. 188. A warning was certainly sent; see *The Secretary of State to the Charge in the Soviet Union (Kennan),* Y. Alexander and A. Nanes, editors, *The United States and Iran: A Documentary History,* pp. 162–163.

8. For an account of Qavam's negotiations, see *The Ambassador in Iran (Murray) to the Secretary of State, March 11 1946,* in Y. Alexander and A. Nanes (editors) *The United States & Iran: A Documentary History,* pp. 163–65.

9. William E. Warne, *Mission for Peace: Point 4 in Iran* (Maryland: Ibex Publishers, 1999 [first published 1956]), pp. 26–27, 81.

10. William E. Warne, op. cit. p. 121.

11. FO 371 52704—"Khalil Maliki's visit to England, 1946," File 133.

12. Even Churchill conceded that the AIOC had "fouled things up." See Donald N. Wilbur, *Overthrow of Premier Mosaddeq of Iran: November 1952–August 1953* (CIA Historical Study, March 1954), p. 82.

13. FO 371 E431/431/34—*Biographies of Leading Personalities in Persia,* January 27, 1931.

14. G. Jones, *Banking and Empire* (Cambridge: Cambridge University Press, 1986), p. 318.

15. FO 248 1514—Internal Situation, file 10101, Situation report, file no. 10101/277/51, September 4, 1951.

16. FO 248 1514, file 10101, file no. 10101/517/51, December 18, 1951.

17. FO 371 104561, file 1015, text of Mosaddeq's speech, file no. 1015/26, January 23, 1953.

18. FO 248 1493, file 101/2, file no. 101/2/211/50, October 9, 1950.

19. Quoted in F. Azimi, *Iran: the Crisis of Democracy*, p. 334. Khomeini put it far more succinctly. See also FO 248 1514, file 10101, file no. 10101/476/51, November 25, 1951.

20. Jamal Imami even complained that the decision to go to the UN had saved Mosaddeq and therefore proved British support! FO 248 1531—Internal Situation 10105/184/52, April 22, 1952.

21. William E. Warne, op. cit. pp. 24–25.

22. FO 248 1514—Internal Situation, file 10101, Situation report, file no. 10101/277/51, September 4, 1951. The Shah for his part was convinced that the US was backing Mosaddeq. See FO 248 1531—Internal Situation, 10105/54 interview with Alam, January 15, 1952; even the Fedayin-e Islam thought he had become too close to the Americans, FO 248 1540—*Fedayin i Islam*, 10141/1, March 1, 1952.

23. Anonymous source quoted in Scott Koch, op. cit. p. 10.

24. The *Times*, October 22, 1951; see also October 8, 1951, and October 23, 1951.

25. FO 248 1514—Internal Situation—10101/475/51 Musaddiq's reply to Jamal Imami, November 25, 1951.

26. FO 248 1531, file 10105, file no. 10105/124, March 24, 1952.

27. FO 248 1531—Internal Situation 10105/149/52, summarized translation of pamphlet from the Association of North East Tehran Supporters of the National Front, April 7, 1952.

28. FO 248 1531—Internal Situation 10105/153A/52, speech of Mosaddeq to 17th Majlis, April 12, 1952.

29. William E. Warne, op. cit. p. 121.

30. For details of this transition, see F. Wilkins, *Memorandum: Proposed Course of Action with respect to Iran*, August 10, 1953.

31. Scott Koch, op. cit. p. 14.

32. FO 248 1531—Internal Situation, 10105/230, June 12, 1952.

33. See, for example General Zahedi's denial as early as 1952, FO 248 1531—Internal Situation, 10105/341/52, October 20, 1952.

34. FO 371 104565, file 1015/124, April 30, 1953.

35. Kermit Roosevelt, *Countercoup: the Struggle for the Control of Iran* (New York: McGraw Hill, 1979), pp. 199–200. Published in 1979, Roosevelt's memoirs,

which owe more to Erdman than to Shuster, only seemed to justify the revolutionary cause.

36. *Arya,* Mordad 28, 1378, August 19, 1999, p. 3.

37. Donald N. Wilbur, *Overthrow of Premier Mosaddeq of Iran: November 1952–August 1953* (CIA Historical Study, March, 1954), p. 9. The reference to grey propaganda suggests statements that are partially negative. In the London draft of the plan code-named TPAJAX, part of black propaganda included the suggestion that Mosaddeq sought to foster regional separatism (TPAJAX Operational Plan London Draft), p. 16.

38. FO 371 104565—1015/126, May 1, 1953.

39. Scott A Koch, *'Zendebad, Shah!' The Central Intelligence Agency and the Fall of Iranian Prime Minister Mohammad Mosaddeq, August 1953,* History Staff, Central Intelligence Agency, Washington, DC, June 1998, p. 18. Curiously, according to Seyyid Zia Tabatabai in conversation with Sam Falle, Kashani had aspirations to be the first President of the Persian Republic, FO 248 1531—10105/325, Internal Situation, August 28, 1952.

40. See Truman's retort to US Ambassador Grady in Scott Koch, op. cit. p. 10.

41. L. P. Elwell-Sutton *Persian Oil: A Study in Power Politics* (London: Lawrence and Wishart Ltd., 1955), p. 258, quoted in Koch, op. cit. p. 4.

42. See, for example, Mosaddeq's comments to Harriman, "You do not know how crafty they [the British] are. You do not know how evil they are. You do not know how they sully everything they touch." Quoted in Scott Koch, op. cit. p. 4.

43. FO 371 110035 EP 1202/1 Annual Report on the Persian Army, December 21, 1954.

44. FO 371 157604 EP 1015/102 Internal Political Situation, May 18, 1961.

45. FO 371 120738 EP 1192/6 Defence & Military Aid, June 22, 1956.

46. FO 371 127074 EP 1015/5 Internal Political Situation, February 4, 1957.

47. FO 371 110060 EP 1534/32 Interviews with the Shah, February 25, 1954.

48. See Bostock and Jones, *Planning and Power in Iran: Ebtehaj and Economic Development under the Shah* (London: Frank Cass, 1989), p. 153.

49. FO 371 133008 EP 1017/2 Embassy Visits, February 4, 1958.

50. FO 371 140787 EP 1015/18 Internal Political Situation, Report by Professor Lambton, February 23, 1959.

51. FO 371 149762 EP 1016/6 Embassy Visits, Report by Roger McDermott, November 10, 1960.

52. FO 371 120714 EP1015/37 Internal Political Situation, October 29, 1956.

53. FO 371127075 EP 1015/45 Internal Political Situation, November 6, 1957.

54. FO 371127075 EP 1015/39 Internal Political Situation, August 28, 1957.

55. FO 371 114810 EP 1018/30 Internal Political Situation, July 18, 1955.

56. FO 371 149756 EP 1015/23 Internal Political Situation, Report by Harrison, March 8, 1960.

57. FO 371 133009 EP 1018/7 Army Plot, March 4, 1958.

58. FO 371 133009 EP 1018/4, February 28, 1958, and 1018/7, March 4, 1958. For a detailed analysis of the Qarani affair, see M. J. Gasiorowski, "The Qarani Affair and Iranian Politics," in *International Journal of Middle East Studies,* Vol. 25 (1993), pp. 625–644. See also Quarterly Political Report submitted by Sir Roger Stevens, 10116/58 Despatch no. 51, April 22, 1958, reproduced in *Iran Political Diaries 1952–1965.* Vol. 14, Archive Editions, 1997, pp. 601–602.

59. FO 371 149761 EP 1015/143 Internal Political Affairs, December 23, 1960.

60. FO 371 157610 EP 1015/229 Internal Political Situation, August 1, 1961.

61. Quoted in Bostock and Jones, ibid., pp. 160–61.

62. FO 371 133055 EP 1671 EP 1671/5 Foreign Articles, October 3, 1958.

63. The logic behind this drive is outlined in McNamara's testimony to Congress in 1964. See *Testimony of the Secretary of Defense (McNamara) before a Defense Department Subcommittee of the United States Senate Appropriations Committee,* February 3, 1964, in Y. Alexander and A. Nanes, op. cit. pp. 348–349.

64. FO 371 140856 EP 1461/2, January 15, 1959.

65. For the Shah's attitude to the aristocracy, see FO 371 133004 EP 1015/3 Internal Political Affairs, March 11, 1958. See also FO 371 133019 EP 1055/1, Talks with the Shah, May 13, 1958.

66. FO 371 149804 EP 1461/6—Land Reform, March 8, 1960; see also FO 248 1580, Land Reform, Dr. Ram in conversation with Kellas, May 30, 1960.

67. FO 248 1580 Land Reform, Comments by Webster Johnson—USOM adviser in the Agricultural Bank—1960 [undated].

68. *Message from the United States Ambassador in Tehran (Holmes) to the Secretary of State (Rusk),* May 15, 1963, in Y. Alexander and A. Nanes, op. cit. pp. 349–50.

69. See the British Ambassador Peter Ramsbotham's comments in FCO 8/1882 *Monarchy and Democracy,* November 9, 1972, point 6.

70. FO 248 1580—Record of a conversation at the Marble Palace, April 10, 1962.

71. FO 371 164186 EP 1015/128 Internal Political Situation, November 9, 1962.

72. The Iranian Foreign ministry understood that military and civilian employees of the Department of Defense and their families "forming part of their households" would be covered by the agreement. See the letter no. 299, December 18, 1963, reproduced in *Documents from the US Espionage Den (71),* p. 11.

73. The Vienna Convention was finalized on April 18, 1961, and the United States was seeking its extension in countries where it had a military presence, essentially to standardize practice. The precise legal definition was a matter of intense and prolonged debate.

74. For an excellent discussion, see Richard Pfau, "The Legal Status of American Forces in Iran," in *The Middle East Journal,* Vol. 28, no. 2 (date unclear), reprinted in *Documents from the US Espionage Den (72), The US Military Advisory Mission in Iran (3),* pp. 156–169.

75. The Under-Secretary for Foreign Affairs, Mirfendereski, later conceded that it would have been better had the bill not been submitted to the Majlis, Memorandum of Conversation, October 21, 1964, in *Documents from the US Espionage Den (71),* p. 81.

76. Letter from US Embassy Tehran to Gordon Tiger Esq, State Department, September 12, 1964, reproduced in *Documents from the US Espionage Den (71),* p. 18.

77. Telegram dated October 10, 1964, in *Documents from the US Espionage Den (71),* p. 33.

78. Memorandum for the Files dated September 17, 1964, in *Documents from the US Espionage Den (71),* p. 20.

79. Intervention of Sadegh-Ahmadi in the Official Gazette of the Majlis discussions, reproduced in *Documents from the US Espionage Den (71),* pp. 63–64; see also US attempts to offer reassurances over such hypothetical cases, Memorandum: Immunities of American Personnel, in *Documents from the US Espionage Den (72),* p. 89.

80. FO 371 175712 1015/27 Internal Political Situation, October 29, 1964; see also telegram to the State Department, October 14, 1964, in *Documents from the US Espionage Den (71),* p. 75.

81. FO 371 175712 EP 1015/29 Internal Political Situation, October 30, 1964.

82. United States Ratification of the Vienna Convention, telegram dated October 14, 1964, in *Documents from the US Espionage Den (72),* p. 84.

83. FO 371 175712 EP 1015/31 7/11/64 Internal Political Situation, November 7, 1964.

84. R. Khomeini, "The Granting of Capitulatory Rights to the US," October 27, 1964, reproduced in H. Algar (trans. and ed.), *Islam and Revolution: Writings and Declarations of Imam Khomeini* (Berkeley: Mizan Press, 1981), pp. 181–188.

85. FO 371 175712 EP 1015/28 Internal Political Situation, November 4, 1964; Vienna Convention Developments, November 7, 1964, in *Documents from the US Espionage Den (72),* pp. 5–6.

CHAPTER 3

1. *Statement of Secretary Kissinger upon the Conclusion of the United States–Iran Joint Commission* in Y. Alexander and A. Nanes (eds.), *The United States and Iran: A Documentary History* (Maryland: University Publications of America, 1980), pp. 402–404.

2. FO 371149816 EP 1671/15 The Press, November 8, 1960.

3. Toasts of the President and Mohammad Reza Pahlavi, Shah of Iran, at a State Dinner in Tehran, May 30, 1972, Nixon Library, document no. 181; Nixon's allusion to 6,000 years seems to indicate that he had bought into the mythological history of Iran as described in the national epic, the *Shahnameh*.

4. James A. Bill, *The Eagle and the Lion: The Tragedy of American-Iranian Relations* (New Haven: Yale University Press, 1988), p. 211.

5. *Inspection Report on the Conduct of Relations with Iran (NEA/IRN)*, Department of State, Office of the Inspector General, September 1978, p. 5, in *Documents from the US Espionage Den (62) US Interventions in Iran (11)*, Tehran, 1366/1987.

6. For an insight into the negotiations, see *Record of a Conversation between the Foreign and Commonwealth Secretary and the Shah of Iran, at the Iranian Embassy in Brussels on Friday 10th July, at 10.00 am* DEFE 31/40.

7. FO 371 120738 EP 1192/1 Defence and Military Aid, January 2, 1956.

8. *Inspection Report on the Conduct of Relations with Iran (NEA/IRN)*, Department of State, Office of the Inspector General, September 1978, p. 1.

9. BBC SWB ME/4485/D/1, December 28, 1973; Shah's press conference, December 23, 1973.

10. BBC SWB ME/4514/D/1, January 31 1974, interview with Peter Snow for ITV, January 29, 1974.

11. *Time* magazine, November 4, 1974, pp. 28–38. The title says it all, "Oil, Grandeur and a Challenge to the West."

12. See *Statement of State Department Under Secretary for Political Affairs (Joseph J. Sisco) before the Special Subcommittee on Investigations of the House Committee on International Relations,* in Y. Alexander and A. Nanes (eds.), p. 401.

13. BBC SWB ME/4515/D/1, February 1, 1974, interview in Al Ahram, January 30, 1974.

14. Prem 15/1684 *Meeting Shah—Rothschild, December 2, 1972.*

15. AB65/661 Iran: Introduction of Nuclear power; correspondence, 1969–1985, *Iran—Nuclear Activities*; see also *Nuclear Developments in Iran (British Nuclear Forum)*.

16. Memoirs of Dr. Etemad, www.iranian.com/Books/March98/Nuclear/Images/p1.gif, accessed September 3, 2006.

17. For details, see *Iran's Foreign Trade and current account balances worldwide and with the United States 1976 and 1977* in *Documents from the US Espionage Den (61) US Interventions in Iran (10),* Tehran, 1366/1987, pp. 117–122.

18. Quoted in James A. Bill, op. cit. pp. 209–210.

19. *A Staff Report to the Subcommittee on Foreign Assistance of the Committee on Foreign Relations, United States Senate: United States Military Sales to Iran,* in Y. Alexander and A. Nanes (eds.) pp. 407–408.

20. *Memorandum: Iranian Attitudes toward foreigners in Iran,* April 27, 1976, in *Documents from the US Espionage Den (61) US Interventions in Iran (10),* Tehran, 1366/1987, pp. 45–88.

21. See the classic statement in this regard by Alexis de Tocqueville, *The Old Regime and the Revolution,* Vol. I, F. Furet and F. Melonio (eds.), A. S. Kahan (trans.) (Chicago: University of Chicago Press, 1998), p. 95.

22. *Political Characteristics of the Iranian urban Middle Class and implications thereof for United States Policy: A Report by the Deputy Director of Greek, Turkish and Iranian Affairs (Bowling), United States Department of State to the President,* in Y. Alexander and A. Nanes (eds.), p. 322.

23. FCO 17/1516—*Sir Denis Wright's Valedictory Despatch,* April 20, 1971.

24. According to British assessments, the State Department desk officer was "struck by the level of internal discontent" he had discovered on a visit to Iran, *Wright to Melhuish,* FCO 8/1884, June 14, 1972.

25. FCO 8/2050—*Unrest in Iran,* June 17, 1972, p. 4; see also *Opposition to the Regime,* March 1, 1973.

26. FCO 8/1882—*The Survival of the Persian Monarchy,* June 8, 1972; commentary dated June 21, 1972.

27. FCO 8/1882—*Sir Patrick Wright to Sir Peter Ramsbotham,* November 9, 1972.

28. *The Conduct of Relations with Iran (NEA/IRN) Inspection Memorandum,* July 1978, p. 1, in *Documents from the US Espionage Den (62) US Interventions in Iran (11),* Tehran, 1366/1987, p. 24.

29. See J. A. Bill, op. cit. pp. 186–187.

30. Quoted in J. A. Bill, *The Eagle and the Lion,* p. 233.

31. Jalal Ale Ahmad, *Plagued by the West,* translated by Paul Sprachman (New York: Caravan Books, 1982), p. 40.

32. FCO 8/2050—*Unrest in Iran,* June 17, 1972, p. 4.

33. *Memorandum of Conversation: Tabriz Riots,* February 23, 1978; *Rioting and Civil Insurrection in Tabriz: An Initial Analysis,* in *Documents from the US Espionage Den (61) US Interventions in Iran (10),* Tehran, 1366/1987, pp. 93–99.

34. *Disturbance in Isfahan,* May 6, 1978, in *Documents from the US Espionage Den (61) US Interventions in Iran (10),* Tehran, 1366/1987, pp. 109–110.

35. *Popular Perceptions of the Amuzegar Government,* April 27, 1978, in *Documents from the US Espionage Den (61) US Interventions in Iran (10),* Tehran, 1366/1987, p. 112.

36. *General Pakravan's Desire for Greater US Advisory Role to the Shah,* April 19, 1978, in *Documents from the US Espionage Den (61) US Interventions in Iran (10),* Tehran, 1366/1987, p. 101.

37. *The Gathering Crisis in Iran,* November 2, 1978, in *Documents from the US Espionage Den (13) US Interventions in Iran (4),* Tehran, undated, p. 9.

38. *Israel & Developments in Iran* January 5, 1979, in *Documents from the US Espionage Den (63) US Interventions in Iran (12),* Tehran, 1366/1987, p. 28.

39. *Anatomy of a Revolt* in *Documents from the US Espionage Den (63) US Interventions in Iran (12),* Tehran, 1366/1987, p. 82.

40. See *Opposition to the Shah,* March 1, 1973, FCO 8/2050, p. 2.

41. *Anatomy of a Revolt* in *Documents from the US Espionage Den (63) US Interventions in Iran (12),* Tehran, 1366/1987, p. 80.

42. *The Attack on the American Consulate Tabriz,* March 19, 1979, pp. 1–10, in *Documents from the US Espionage Den (63) US Interventions in Iran (12),* Tehran, undated, pp. 43–52.

43. *Iranian Economic Trend: A Report Prepared by the American Embassy in Tehran, June 1979* in *Documents from the US Espionage Den (63) US Interventions in Iran (12),* Tehran, 1366/1987, p. 105.

44. *Monthly Status Report for August 1979,* September 2, 1979, p. 4, in *Documents from the US Espionage Den (16) US Interventions in Iran,* Tehran, undated, p. 63.

45. *Request for assistance in creating irregular military force opposed to the Islamic Movement,* August 13, 1979, in *Documents from the US Espionage Den (68) Illusion of Overthrow,* Tehran, 1366/1987, p. 154; see also *Conditions in Iran,* June 28, 1979, pp. 148–150; and *Request for Agreement for Iranian Ambassador to US,* April 15, 1979, in *Documents from the US Espionage Den (18) Diplomacy of Infiltration,* Tehran, undated, p. 80.

46. *Yazdi in New York. Where Now?,* October 12, 1979, in *Documents from the US Espionage Den (63) US Interventions in Iran (12),* Tehran, 1366/1987, p. 126.

47. *Iran Abolishes Immunity for US Military Advisers,* May 13, 1979, in *Documents from the US Espionage Den (72), The US Military Advisory Mission in Iran (3),* p. 128.

48. *Memorandum of Conversation* dated March 27–28, 1979, p. 2, in *Documents from the US Espionage Den (14) US Interventions in Iran (6),* Tehran, undated, p. 59.

CHAPTER 4

1. *Emigre Plotters,* September 6, 1979, in *Documents from the US Espionage Den (16) US Interventions in Iran,* Tehran, undated, p. 77.

2. *Memorandum of Conversation,* June 28, 1979, p. 2, in *Documents from the US Espionage Den (68) Illusion of Overthrow,* Tehran, 1368/1989, p. 149.

3. Historically, the province had been known as Khuzestan or Susistan, and Arabistan was occasionally used to describe a part of the province. The name was briefly popularized at the end of the nineteenth century and applied to the entire province, although the process by which this occurred remains unclear.

4. "Inspired Iranians Keep Iraqis out," *The Observer,* December 14, 1980; "Behind the Lines in a Mud Bogged War," *The Sunday Times,* January 4, 1981.

5. See www.pbs.org/wgbh/pages/frontline/shows/target/etc/cron.html, accessed March 4, 2006.

6. "US gave Iraq blueprint of Iranian Radar Network," *The Times,* September 25, 1980; see also *Defence and Foreign Affairs,* March 1982, for evidence of British assistance to Iraq.

7. France became a target in 1986–87 following the supply of armaments to Saddam Hussein and their use against Iranian civilian targets.

8. See James A. Bill, *The Eagle and the Lion: The Tragedy of American-Iranian Relations* (New Haven: Yale University Press, 1988), p. 306.

9. G. Roberts, *Poisonous Weapons,* www.crimesofwar.org/thebook/poisonous-weapons.html, accessed March 3, 2006; the report was leaked to the *Washington Post.*

10. James A. Bill, op. cit. p. 307.

11. Behzad Nabavi in *Nowruz,* Khordad 4, 1381/May 25, 2002, p. 9.

12. *The Other Lockerbie,* BBC Correspondent documentary, 2000.

13. Ian Mather, "Iran Digs for Victory," *The Observer,* March 8, 1987, pp. 12–13; Alan George, "Iran Claims Self Sufficiency," *Janes Defence Weekly,* January 1988, p. 17.

14. BBC SWB ME/3968 MED/17, October 11, 2000.

15. On Khomeini's propensity for consultation and delegation see, Hasan Yusefi Eshkevari's speech on "Law and the Women's Movement," delivered at the Berlin Conference, April 2000, reprinted in M. A. Zakrayi (ed), *Conference-e Berlin: Khedmat ya Khiyanat?* (The Berlin Conference: Service or Treason?) Tehran, Tar-e No, 1379/2000, p. 229.

16. See in particular M. Kadivar, *Baha-ye Azadi: defa'at Mohsen Kadivar* (The Price of Freedom: The defense of Mohsen Kadivar), Tehran, Ghazal, 1378/1999–2000, p. 200.

17. See for example Hossein Seifzadeh, *Estrateji-ye Melli va Siyasatgozari-ye khareji* (National Strategy and Foreign Policy-Making), *The Journal of Foreign Policy,* Vol. VII (Winter 1994), pp. 705–722; editorial in the *Tehran Times,* February 23, 1993; Mohammad Javad Larijani, "Islamic Society and Modernism," in *The Iranian Journal for International Affairs,* Vol. VII, No. 1, Spring 1995, p. 58.

18. See for example, "Iran annexes disputed island," *Independent,* September 2, 1992; "Tehran annexes strategic island," *Times,* September 2, 1992.

19. *Iran Times,* December 27, 1991, p. 1 and 12.

20. By some assessments, the United States and Israel, respectively, have the second and third largest communities of Persian speakers after Iran.

CHAPTER 5

1. For a small example see, *Tous,* Shahrivar 7, 1377/ August 29, 1998 p. 6; *Jame'eh,* Tir 7, 1377/June 28, 1998, p. 6; *Jame'eh,* Tir 8, 1377/June 29, 1998, p. 6; *Jame'eh* Tir, 9 1377/June 30, 1998, p. 6; see also A. K. Soroush and M. Kadivar, *Manazere dar bare-ye pluralism dini (A debate on religious pluralism),* Salam, Tehran, 1378; occasional translations of relevant foreign articles were also included, for example, *Religious Government and Democracy,* first published in the *Middle East Journal,* 52, Winter, 1998, in *Tous,* Mordad 4, 1377/July 26, 1998 p. 1.

2. See in particular discussions of the life of Martin Luther, *Jame'eh,* Tir 27, 1377/July 18, 1998, p. 6, *Jame'eh,* Tir 29, 1377/July 20, 1998, p. 6.

3. President Khatami's speech to the United Nations General Assembly, New York, September 21, 1998; for a robust defence of freedom see, Nuri A *Shokoran-e Eslah (Hemlock of Reform)* Tar-e No, Tehran, 1378, pp. 117–121.

4. BBC SWB ME/3099 S1/5, December 11, 1997, Khatami's speech to the OIC conference, December 9, 1997.

5. BBC SWB ME/3339 MED/2, September 23, 1998, *President Khatami addresses Iranian expatriates in the USA,* September 20, 1998.

6. Contrast with Khamenei's speech at the same conference BBC SWB ME/3099 S1/1, December 11, 1997.

7. BBC SWB ME/3120 MED/4, January 9, 1998, CNN interview January 8, 1998.

8. BBC SWB ME/3120 MED/5.

9. BBC SWB ME/3120 MED/2.

10. BBC SWB ME/4024 MED/7, December 15, 2000, IRNA, December 13, 2000.

11. Nuri, op. cit. pp. 141–152.

12. Nuri, op. cit. pp. 122–140; See also, *Rabeteh?! (Relations?!) Salaam,* Teheran, 1378.

13. The importance of the myth of Mosaddeq to contemporary Iranian political culture can hardly be exaggerated. See, for example, *Tous,* Mordad 28, 1377/August 19, 1998, p. 6; *Tous,* Mordad 28, 1377/August 19, 1998. p. 5; *Sobh Emrooz,* Mordad 28, 1378/August 19, 1999, p. 6; *Neshat,* Mordad 28, 1378/August 19, 1999, p. 8, which printed a half-page picture of a dejected Mossadeq with the headline "28th Mordad; sunset of the national government." For added interest see *Khordad,* Mordad 28, 1378/August 19, 1999, p. 6, in which the coup is analyzed using Marx's 18th Brumaire; *Nameh,* Mordad 25, 1382/August 2003, special issue on the fiftieth anniversary of the coup; or the previous year's issue, Mordad 1381/August 2002, special issue on national unity, in which the spectre of Mosaddeq looms large.

14. BBC SWB ME/3763 MED/8, February 14, 2000, IRNA news agency, February 11, 2000.

CHAPTER 6

1. H. Kaviani, *Dar jostejoye mohafal jenayatkaran (Investigating the murderous associations)*, Negah-ye Emruz, Tehran, 1378, p. 149–153; according to a report in *Salaam*, Emami was recruited by Fallahian during a trip to the United States. See also Ganji A *Tarik-khaneh-ye ashbah (The Cellar of phantoms)*, Tar-e No, Tehran, 1378, p. 267.

2. Conservatives were concerned that the institution of the *velayat-e faqih* was being undermined; see *Sobh Emrooz*, Shahrivar 17, 1378/September 8, 1999, p. 1.

3. See Ganji's comments published in *Sobh Emrooz*, Ganji A *Tarik-khaneh-ye ashbah (The Cellar of phantoms)* Tar-e No, Tehran, 1378, pp. 302–314; see also E Sahabi's acute analysis with the newspaper *Akhbar-e Eqtesad*, reprinted in Zekryai, op. cit. pp. 200–202.

4. BBC SWB ME/4027 MED/9, December 19, 2000, IRNA, December 16, 2000.

5. See *Iran* election special, Khordad 19, 1380/June 9, 2001.

6. BBC SWB ME/3973 MED/15, October 17, 2000, *Iran* website, October 15, 2000. A Reformist added that what was taking place was "not unlike a silent coup."

7. Abrams was initially appointed National Security Council Staff Chief for Democracy, Human Rights, and International Operations, before moving up in 2002 to become Special Assistant to the President and Senior Director on the NSC for Southwest Asia, Near East, and North African Affairs. See David Corn, "Elliot Abrams. It's Back!" *The Nation*, July 2, 2001; Terry J. Allen, *Public Serpent: Iran Contra Villain Elliot Abrams Is Back in Action in These Times*, August, 2001; *The Return of Elliot Abrams* TomPaine.com, www.tompaine.com/feature.cfm/ ID/6895, accessed December 11, 2002; see also *Iran-Contra, Amplified*, www.tom paine.com/feature2.cfm/ID/8625, accessed August 18, 2003.

8. See the interesting reflection on the attack and Iranian sympathies for Americans in M. Hajizadeh, *Aqazadeh-ha* (Aghazadeh-ha), Jameh Daran, Tehran, 1381/2002, pp. 143–146.

9. Khalilzad publicly made the claims on January 18, 2002; see Iran Press Service January 18, 2002, www.iran-press-service.com/articles_2002/Jan_2002/ afqanestan_iran_qaeda_18102.

10. The EU's rejection of Bush's comments stood in stark contrast to Blair's comments, IRNA, February 5, 2002, BBC SWB Mon MEPol. See also the French ambassador's vigoros rejection of the characterization, *Nowruz*, Khordad 20,

1381/June 10, 2002, p. 10. See also Rafsanjani's later comments that Blair was Bush's "dog," *Bonyan*, Ordibehesht 14, 1381/May 4, 2002, p. 1.

11. BBC SWB Mon ME1 MEPol, *Nowruz* website, March 18, 2002.

12. See for example, BBC SWB Mon ME1 MEPol, IRIB, July 12, 2002, *Demonstrators support Khamene'i, call for trial of 'fifth columnists';* also, *Etemad*, Mordad 29, 1381/August 20, 2002, p. 2.

13. ISNA website, February 2, 2002, BBC SWB Mon MEPol; *Nowruz*, February 2, 2002, BBC SWB Mon MEPol; Deputies proved particularly critical of the Foreign Ministry, see Elahe Koulaee's comments in *Nowruz*, Ordibehesht 24, 1381/May 14, 2002, p. 2; also *Aftab-e Yazd*, Khordad 21, 1381/June 11, 2002, p. 1.

14. Ahmad Zeydabadi quoted in ISNA website, March 16, 2002, BBC SWB Mon MEPol; see also Jala'ipour's comments in *Bonyan*, March 18, 2002, BBC SWB Mon MEPol. *Aftab-e Yazd*, Shahrivar 17, 1381/September 8, 2002, p. 5.

15. *Hayat-e No* website, June 1, 2002, BBC SWB Mon MEPol. See also *Nowruz*, Khordad 19, 1381/June 9, 2002, p. 7; *Hayat-e No*, Khordad 11, 1381/June 1, 2002, p. 1; *Nowruz*, Khordad 5, 1381/May 26, 2002, p. 1.

16. *Nowruz*, Tir 24, 1381/July 15, 2002, p. 1; *Nowruz*, Tir 23, 1381/July 14, 2002, p. 1; *Keyhan International*, July 17, 2002, p. 2, BBC SWB Mon ME1 MEPol; see also Jannati's speech, IRIB July 26, 2002, BBC SWB Mon ME1 MEPol.

17. *Entekhab*, May 23, 2002, BBC SWB Mon MEPol; *Nowruz*, May 26, 2002, BBC SWB Mon MEPol; *Mardomsalari*, Dey 18, 1381/January 8, 2003 p. 4 and 9; See Scott Peterson, *Hostile in Public, Iran Seeks Quiet Discourse with the United States, Christian Monitor*, September 25, 2003.

CHAPTER 7

1. Connie Bruck, "Exiles: How Iran's Expatriates Are Gaming the Nuclear Threat," *The New Yorker*, March 6, 2006, p. 56.

2. For the history of the MKO, see Ervand Abrahamian, *Radical Islam: the Iranian Mojahideen.*

3. Tehran Home Service, January 12, 1985, BBC Monitoring, January 22, 1985.

4. See for example, Foreign Minister Kharazi's comments at the UN in New York, AFP, September 25, 2003, and IRNA, June 2, 2003, BBC SWB Mon ME1 MEPol.

5. IRNA, June 3, 2003, BBC SWB Mon ME1 MEPol.

6. AFP, June 16, 2003.

7. In this vein, see Hasan Rowhani's summary report to President Khatami following his replacement, ISNA website, 09/05/1484/July 31, 2005.

8. *Yas-e No*, Bahman 19, 1382/February 8, 2004, p. 1; also January 19, 2004, Iranmania website. Presidential adviser Abtahi berated the return of totalitarianism, IRNA, December 11, 2003, Iranmania website. See also the analysis in *Yas-e No*, Bahman 18, 1382/February 7, 2004, p. 16. Behzad Nabavi described it as a Parliamentary coup, see *Entekhab*, Bahman 18, 1382/February 7, 2004, p. 3. Some drew direct parallels with the coup against Mosaddeq, see *Aftab-e Yazd*, Bahman 23, 1382/February 12, 2004, p. 7.

9. See for example Majid-Ansari's comments, *Aftab-e Yazd*, Bahman 27, 1382/February 16, 2004, pp. 1–2.

10. Iranian's noticed the international silence; *Aftab-e Yazd*, Esfand 10, 1382/February 29, 2004 p. 11; see *Aftab-e Yazd*, Esfand 3, 1382/February 22, 2004, p. 1.

11. For public anger and disenchantment see readers' comments, *Aftab-e Yazd*, Bahman 20, 1382/February 9, 2004, p. 11; *Aftab-e Yazd*, Bahman 23, 1382/February 12, 2004, p. 7. See Ayatollah Montazeri's comments, *Yas-e No*, Bahman 20, 1382/February 9, 2004, p. 1.

12. See, for example, Elahe Koulaie's criticism of bias, *Tehran Times* website, April 7, 2003, BBC SWB Mon ME1 MEPol. See also Rafsanjani's comments in *Rahbord*, Farvardin 16, 1382/April 5, 2003.

13. *Iran Conservatives to Ease Engagements*, AFP, February 18, 2004.

14. See in this context, Gordon Prather "Condi Kills an EU-Iranian Agreement," *Antiwar.com*, July 11, 2005, www.antiwar.com/prather/?articleid=6601, accessed December 7, 2005.

15. See Secretary Rice's comments, "Rice Outlines Next Steps in Iran Showdown," *Time*, September 20, 2005.

AFTERWORD

1. "Iran Declares Key Nuclear Advance," http://news.bbc.co.uk/1/hi/world/middle_east/4900260.stm.

2. The classic exposition of this view is William Kristol's article in the *Weekly Standard*, July 24, 2006, vol. 11, issue 42. "It's Our War: Bush should go to Jerusalem—and the US should confront Iran." The classic response was provided by Pat Buchanan "No, This is not our War" July 28, 2006, in www.chroniclemagazine.org.

3. Bernard Lewis, "August 22nd: Does Iran Have something in store?" *Wall Street Journal*, August 8, 2006.

4. "Iran's Nuclear Negotiator on failure of Western policy," Larijani's interview with Mehr news agency, October 18, 2006, BBC Monitoring.

5. Majlis Deputy, Dr. Emad Afroogh, quoted in Omid Memarian "Election Backlash against Ahmadinejad," www.worldpress.org, December 26, 2006.

6. "Khatami and Hashemi should intervene," The *Etemad* Web site, January 23, 2007, BBC Monitoring.

7. See for example Said Laylaz's column in *Ayandeh No*, January 21, 2007, BBC Monitoring.

8. This comment was made during his presentation of the budget to the Majlis on January 21, 2007.

9. Such assessments were reinforced by analyses from the Revolutionary Guards. See Rahim Safavi's comments on the *Fars News Agency* Web site dated January 31, 2007.

10. The interview was conducted on IRIB Channel 2 on January 23, BBC Monitoring; for critical reaction see, editorial in *Etemad-e Melli* dated January 25, 2007, BBC Monitoring, and the report by Hamid Reza Shokuhi, "Analysis of the President's interview broadcast by TV Channel 2: Twenty other questions for the president." The *Mardom-Salari* Web site, January 25, 2007, BBC Monitoring.

11. The man behind the conference, Mohammad Ali Ramin, was interviewed by the Persian news Web site *Baztab*. The fact that he thought it possible to open a branch of his "Holocaust Foundation" in Berlin reveals the depth of his detachment from reality. Dated 6 Dey 1385 / December 27, 2006.

12. See Mohsen Rezai's warnings of an American attack, IRIB Channel 2, January 18, 2007, BBC Monitoring.

13. Somewhat curiously, Wali Jumblatt described Hizbollah as *magus*, effectively, Zoroastrians!

14. "Bush Warns of epic battle between Shi'ites, Sunnis," *Jerusalem Post*, January 25, 2007.

GLOSSARY

Achaemenid (559 B.C.–330 B.C.)   The first imperial dynasty, founded by Cyrus the Great and overthrown by Alexander the Great.

Agha Mohammad Khan (died 1797)   The founder of the Qajar state.

Amir Kabir   A Prime Minister who attempted to reform the Iranian state in the middle of the nineteenth century. The reference point for most subsequent reformist and enlightened Iranian statesmen.

Cyrus the Great   The founder of the Achaemenid Persian Empire. He conquered Babylon in 539 B.C. and liberated the Jews, and was hence known as the Lord's Anointed in the Bible. As the first monarch to unite the Medes and the Persians (that is, the Iranians), he is increasingly characterized by modern Iranians as the Father of the Nation.

Dr. Mohammad Mosaddeq   The Nationalist Prime Minister who oversaw the nationalization of the Anglo-Iranian Oil Company. He was overthrown in a coup orchestrated by the CIA and MI6 in 1953. He casts a long shadow on the political history of modern Iran.

Fath Ali Shah (reigned 1798–1834)   The nephew of the Agha Mohammad Khan and the second Shah of the Qajar dynasty. During his reign, Iran was drawn into the network of European alliances, was defeated by the Russians, and lost its Great Power status.

Mohammad Reza Shah (reigned 1941–1979)   The second and last monarch of the Pahlavi dynasty.

Nader Shah (reigned 1736–1747)   Overthrew the Safavid dynasty and established his own short-lived Iranian empire.

Pahlavi (1925–1979)   The dynasty that succeeded the Qajars and lasted until the Islamic Revolution of 1979.

Qajar (1797–1925)   Despite a promising start, the Qajar dynasty oversaw a general decline of the imperial Iranian state.

Reza Shah (reigned 1925–1941)   The founder of the Pahlavi dynasty. His rule witnessed the foundation of the modern state.

Safavid (1501–1736)   The dynasty that established the parameters and borders of the modern Iranian state and made Shia Islam the State religion.

KEY TERMS

Ayatollah   Literally, *sign of God.* An honorific title given to the most senior Shia jurists.

Al Qaeda   An extremist Sunni Islamist movement led by Osama Bin Laden. Along with its anti-Western orientation, Al Qaeda views the Shias as heretics who should likewise be violently opposed.

Baathist   The ruling political party in Iraq from 1968–2003.

Bazaar   Persian for *market.* Also used in a political sense to denote business interests.

Fatwa   A religious judgement.

Firman   A royal decree.

Friday Prayers   Weekly public prayers institutionalized in the Islamic Republic as a political event in which leaders follow communal prayers with a political speech. The most famous are those held on the grounds of Tehran University, though similar events are held throughout the country. Friday Prayer leaders are considered prominent government figures. Attendance has declined dramatically in recent years.

Guardian Council   The supervisory body in the Islamic Republic, composed of six religious and six lay lawyers whose function is to assess the compatibility of parliamentary legislation with Islamic law. Six members are elected by the sitting Parliament and the rest are appointed by the Supreme Leader. Powers were controversially extended in the 1990s to allow the supervision of elections and the vetting of candidates.

Hardliners   The term used to define those with a dogmatic adherence to Islamic orthodoxy and authoritarianism. Hardliners are opposed to any form of democratic development.

Hizbollah   Literally, *the Party of God.* The most prominent example is Lebanese Hizbollah, established in 1982. Hizbollah is distinct and wholly separate from the vigilante group in Iran known as the Ansar-e Hizbollah (Helpers of the Party of God).

Imam   In Sunni Islam, denotes any prominent religious leader. In Shia Islam, the term is usually used with reference to the descendents of the Prophet Muhammad through his son-in-law Ali, the first Imam. Twelver Shias believe that the twelfth (hidden) Imam will return at the end of time to inaugurate a government of justice.

Imperial Calendar   The calendar imposed by Mohammad Reza Shah in 1976, which was dated from the accession of Cyrus the Great.

Iran/Persia   Iran is the name traditionally used by the inhabitants of the country. Persia was the name used by foreigners, inheriting the Greek and Roman designation for the country. This name was derived from the southern province (Pars/Fars), which provided two of the greatest ancient dynasties. In 1934, the Iranian government requested that foreigners desist from using Persia, but the term is gradually coming back into general use because for most Westerners the term Iran lacks any historical context or association.

Islamic Republic   The state established after the overthrow of the Pahlavi monarchy in 1979.

Islamic Revolution   The political and cultural revolution that overthrew the Pahlavi monarchy and established the Islamic Republic.

Jihad   Literally, *struggle*. The term has been generalized in Western usage to mean *holy war*.

Majlis   The Parliament; established following the Constitutional Revolution of 1906.

Mullah   A member of the ulema.

Reformists   The term used to define those who seek the reform of the Islamic Republic and the development of (Islamic) democracy.

Revolutionary Guard   The elite military organization of the Islamic Republic. Initially voluntary, now largely conscripted. They replaced the Imperial Guard.

Shah   The Persian term for king.

Shia   The minority branch in Islam, the state religion in Iran, and the majority in Iraq, Bahrein, and Azerbaijan. Significant minorities are in Saudi Arabia and Lebanon. Shias are themselves divided into a number of different sects; the vast majority are designated as Twelvers and believe in the succession of twelve Imams. *See also* Imam.

Taleban   From taleb, literally, *student;* the Taleban are the product of radical Sunni madrasahs (schools) mainly in Pakistan and espouse a puritanical interpretation of Islam

Ulema   A religious scholar or cleric.

SOURCES AND GUIDE TO
FURTHER READING

In earlier sections of the book, references have been made to British and American diplomatic and intelligence sources. Many of these, particularly as they relate to the 1953 coup, are accessible and available to the researcher, and a significant number can be accessed through the internet. For later periods (post 1975), publicly available, primary documentary sources have been complemented by published document collections (an increasing number are now available in Persian), Persian newspapers and journal articles, and interviews with individual participants. These individuals, which have had to remain anonymous, include senior government and diplomatic sources in both Iran and Europe, as well as other officials from nongovernmental and civil society groups. For those interested in exploring the topics raised in this book in more depth, the following texts are suggested as an introduction to the wider field.

For the reader seeking a general background history, the best single-volume introduction is David O. Morgan, *Medieval Persia 1040–1797* (Longman, 1988). For the more inquisitive, the choices are limited and one is faced with tackling the extensive if authoritative volumes of the *Cambridge History of Iran*. Of most relevance to readers of this book is the last volume (Volume 7), *From Nader Shah to the Islamic Republic*. For a history of the twentieth century, see A. M. Ansari, *Modern Iran since 1921* (Longman: 2003)

Numerous scholarly studies have been made of the Qajar period. Of particular value is Abbas Amanat's *Pivot of the Universe* (I. B. Tauris, 1997), which looks at the failed attempts of reform in the late nineteenth century and Iran's relationship with the British and Russians in particular. For the Constitutional Revolution, more choices are available. A very good start is Edward G. Browne's *The Persian Revolution* (which has been reprinted several times). Browne, a Cambridge academic, was a keen supporter of the Constitutional Revolution and held views that were mirrored by Morgan Shuster. Browne still has a street named after him in Tehran. More contemporary analyses include those by Ervand Abrahamian, *Iran Between Two Revolutions* (Princeton, 1982), which also covers most of the twentieth century, and Vanessa Martin, *Islam & Modernism: The Persian Revolution of 1906* (I. B. Tauris, 1989).

For those interested in the period of the coup, two excellent collections of articles are represented by James A. Bill and Wm. Roger Louis, *Musaddiq, Iranian Nationalism and Oil* (I. B. Tauris, 1988), and Mark Gasiorowski and Malcolm Byrne, *Mohammad Mosaddeq and the 1953 Coup in Iran* (Syracuse, 2004). Both Gasiorowski and Bill are prolific writers on Iran and Iran-US relations in particular and should be required reading for all students. Bill's *The Eagle and the Lion: The Tragedy of US-Iran Relations* (Yale, 1989) remains the standard text detailing the intimate relations between the Pahlavi and American elites. Another astute observer of Iran-US relations is William Beeman, whose most recent book, *The Great Satan versus the Mad Mullahs: How the United States and Iran Demonize Each Other* (Greenwood, 2005) is a scholarly investigation into the process of mutual antagonism. His earlier book, *Language, Status and Power in Iran* (Indiana, 1986) is also an excellent analysis of the semantics of interaction.

Relatively few surveys are available for the period of the revolution and its aftermath, though this is compensated by the relative abundance of memoirs and recollections. Although most are useful, they should nonetheless be treated with some caution, because many sought to excuse or justify their own positions during the revolution, not least of course the Shah himself. Among the most reflective of these are the memoirs of the British Ambassador Sir Anthony Parsons, *The Pride and the Fall* (now out of print). A growing number of memoirs are being published in Persian, and the Harvard Oral History Project, which collates the oral testimonies of Iranians who helped shape the twentieth century history of Iran, should gradually transform our understanding of the early revolution.

Probably the best single analysis of the revolution and its historical context is Arjomand's *The Turban for the Crown* (Oxford, 1988). Another useful text is Nikkie Keddie's *Modern Iran: Roots and Results of a Revolution* (Yale, 2003), which is an updated edition of her earlier *Roots of Revolution* (Yale, 1981). Both books situate the revolution in a broader historical context.

The standard English language biography of Ayatollah Khomeini is provided by Baqer Moin, *Khomeini: Life of the Ayatollah* (I. B. Tauris, 1999). For the period of the Iran-Iraq War, the standard text is Shahram Chubin and Charles Tripp, *Iran & Iraq at War* (I. B. Tauris, 1988). For those interested in the foreign policy of the Islamic Republic, the analyses of both Chubin and Shaul Bakhash repay attention.

For those interested in the intellectual changes within Iran during 1990s, see the writings of Abdolkarim Soroush, translated by Sadri & Sadri in *Reason, Freedom and Democracy in Islam* (Oxford, 2000). For an analysis of domestic politics and the Khatami period, see A. M. Ansari, *Iran, Islam & Democracy: The Politics of Managing Change* (Chatham House, 2006).

INDEX